Teach Yourself VISUALLY™
Excel 2003

Visual

From
maranGraphics®

&

Wiley Publishing, Inc.

Teach Yourself VISUALLY™ Excel 2003

Published by
Wiley Publishing, Inc.
909 Third Avenue
New York, NY 10022

Published simultaneously in Canada

Copyright © 2003 by maranGraphics, Inc.
    5755 Coopers Avenue
    Mississauga, Ontario, Canada
    L4Z 1R9

Library of Congress Control Number: 2003109654

ISBN: 0-7645-3996-5

Manufactured in the United States of America

10 9 8 7 6 5 4 3 2 1

1K/SW/RR/QT/MG

Trademark Acknowledgments

Important Numbers

For U.S. corporate orders, please call maranGraphics at 800-469-6616 or fax 905-890-9434.

For general information on our other products and services or to obtain technical support, please contact our Customer Care Department within the U.S. at 800-762-2974, outside the U.S. at 317-572-3993 or fax 317-572-4002.

Permissions

Wiley Publishing, Inc.   is a trademark of Wiley Publishing, Inc.

U.S. Corporate Sales	U.S. Trade Sales
Contact maranGraphics at (800) 469-6616 or fax (905) 890-9434.	Contact Wiley at (800) 762-2974 or fax (317) 572-4002.

maranGraphics is a family-run business
located near Toronto, Canada.

At **maranGraphics**, we believe in producing great computer books—one book at a time.

Each maranGraphics book uses the award-winning communication process that we have been developing over the last 25 years. Using this process, we organize screen shots, text and illustrations in a way that makes it easy for you to learn new concepts and tasks.

We spend hours deciding the best way to perform each task, so you don't have to! Our clear, easy-to-follow screen shots and instructions walk you through each task from beginning to end.

Our detailed illustrations go hand-in-hand with the text to help reinforce the information. Each illustration is a labor of love—some take up to a week to draw!

We want to thank you for purchasing what we feel are the best computer books money can buy. We hope you enjoy using this book as much as we enjoyed creating it!

Sincerely,

The Maran Family

Please visit us on the Web at:
www.maran.com

CREDITS

Author:
Ruth Maran

Excel 2003 Update Directors:
Raquel Scott
Kelleigh Johnson

Project Manager:
Judy Maran

Editing and Screen Captures:
Roderick Anatalio
Adam Giles

Layout Designer:
Steven Schaerer

Illustrator & Screen Artist:
Russ Marini

**Illustrator, Screen Artist &
Assistant Layout Designer:**
Richard Hung

**Indexing, Editing and
Screen Captures:**
Raquel Scott

**Wiley Vice President and
Executive Group Publisher:**
Richard Swadley

**Wiley Vice President
and Publisher:**
Barry Pruett

Wiley Editorial Support:
Jody Lefevere
Sandy Rodrigues
Lindsay Sandman

Post Production:
Robert Maran

ACKNOWLEDGMENTS

Thanks to the dedicated staff of maranGraphics, including
Roderick Anatalio, Adam Giles, Richard Hung,
Kelleigh Johnson, Wanda Lawrie, Jill Maran,
Judy Maran, Robert Maran, Ruth Maran,
Russ Marini, Steven Schaerer, Raquel Scott
and Roxanne Van Damme.

Finally, to Richard Maran who originated the easy-to-use graphic
format of this guide. Thank you for your inspiration and guidance.

TABLE OF CONTENTS

Chapter 1

GETTING STARTED

Introduction to Excel 2
Start Excel 4
Parts of the Excel Window..................................5
Change the Active Cell 6
Scroll Through a Worksheet 7
Enter Data 8
Select Cells 10
Complete a Series 12
Select a Command 14
Using the Task Pane 16
Getting Help 18

Chapter 2

SAVE AND OPEN YOUR WORKBOOKS

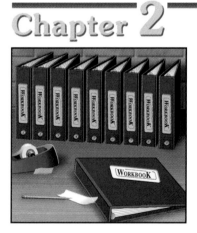

Save a Workbook..................................22
Create a New Workbook 24
Switch Between Workbooks 25
View All Open Workbooks 26
Compare Workbooks 28
Close a Workbook 29
Save Workbooks in a Workspace File..................................30
Save a Workbook With a New Name 31
Open a Workbook 32
Search for a Workbook..................................34

Chapter 3

EDIT YOUR WORKSHEETS

Edit Data 38
Delete Data 40
Undo Changes 41
Move or Copy Data 42
Check Spelling 44
Using AutoCorrect 46

Using the Research Task Pane 48
Find Data...50
Replace Data 52
Link Data 54
Name Cells 56
Add a Comment...58
Insert Symbols 60
Insert a Stock Quote 62

Chapter 4

WORK WITH ROWS AND COLUMNS

Change Column Width 66
Change Row Height 67
Insert a Row or Column................................68
Delete a Row or Column 70
Insert Cells...72
Delete Cells 73
Hide Columns 74
Freeze Rows and Columns.............................76
Split a Worksheet 78

Chapter 5

WORK WITH FORMULAS AND FUNCTIONS

Introduction to Formulas and Functions 82
Enter a Formula 84
Enter a Function 86
Perform Common Calculations 90
Copy a Formula 92
Display All Formulas 96
Check Errors in Formulas 98
Create Scenarios 100
Create a Scenario Summary Report 104

TABLE OF CONTENTS

Chapter 6

CHANGE YOUR SCREEN DISPLAY

Zoom In or Out 108
Display Full Screen 109
Display or Hide the Status Bar 110
Display or Hide a Toolbar 111
Move a Toolbar 112
Resize a Toolbar..113

Chapter 7

FORMAT YOUR WORKSHEETS

Change Font of Data.....................................116
Change Size of Data 117
Change Font for All New Workbooks 118
Bold, Italicize or Underline Data.....................120
Change Horizontal Alignment of Data 121
Change Vertical Alignment of Data.................122
Change Appearance of Data 124
Change Data Color 126
Change Cell Color 127
Indent Data 128
Center Data Across Columns 129
Wrap Text in Cells 130
Add Borders to Cells....................................132
Change Number Format 134
Copy Formatting..136
Apply an AutoFormat 138
Apply Conditional Formatting..........................140

Chapter 8

PRINT YOUR WORKSHEETS

Preview a Worksheet Before Printing................146
Print a Worksheet 148
Set a Print Area 150

Center Data on a Printed Page........................152
Change Page Orientation 153
Change Margins 154
Change Print Options 156
Insert a Page Break...................................158
Add a Header or Footer 160
Add a Custom Header or Footer 162
Change Size of Printed Data 164
Repeat Labels on Printed Pages 166

Chapter 9

WORK WITH MULTIPLE WORKSHEETS

Switch Between Worksheets...........................170
Rename a Worksheet 171
Insert a Worksheet 172
Delete a Worksheet...................................173
Move a Worksheet 174
Add Color to a Worksheet Tab.....................175
Move or Copy Data Between Worksheets 176
Enter a Formula Across Worksheets 178
Using the Watch Window Toolbar 180

Chapter 10

WORK WITH CHARTS

Introduction to Charts 184
Create a Chart...186
Move or Resize a Chart 190
Print a Chart 192
Change the Chart Type 193
Change Chart Titles 194
Rotate Chart Text 195
Format Chart Text 196
Add Data to a Chart.................................198
Add a Data Table to a Chart 200
Change the Way Data is Plotted...................201
Change the Appearance of a Data Series 202

TABLE OF CONTENTS

Chapter 11

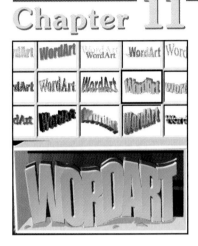

WORK WITH OBJECTS

Add WordArt 206
Add an AutoShape 208
Add a Text Box...210
Add a Picture 212
Add a Clip Art Image 214
Move or Resize an Object 218
Change the Color of an Object 220
Rotate an Object 221
Add a Shadow to an Object 222
Make an Object 3-D 223
Add a Diagram 224

Chapter 12

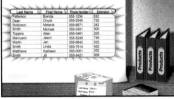

MANAGE DATA IN A LIST

Create a List...230
Add a Record 232
Delete a Record 233
Sort Data in a List 234
Display a Total Row 238
Filter a List 239

Chapter 13

PROTECT YOUR DATA

Protect a Workbook 244
Protect Workbook Elements 248
Protect a Worksheet 250

Chapter 14

TIME-SAVING FEATURES

Create a Custom Series 254
Customize a Toolbar 256
Create a New Toolbar 260
Turn on Smart Tags 262
Using Smart Tags 264
Create a Macro 266
Run a Macro 270

Chapter 15

USING SPEECH RECOGNITION

Set Up Speech Recognition 274
Using Dictation Mode 280
Using Voice Command Mode.........................282
Using Text to Speech 284

Chapter 16

EXCEL AND THE INTERNET

E-mail a Worksheet 288
Create a Hyperlink 290
Preview a Workbook as a Web Page 292
Save a Workbook as a Web Page 294

INTRODUCTION TO EXCEL

Excel is a spreadsheet program you can use to organize, analyze and attractively present data such as a budget or sales report.

Each Excel file, called a workbook, contains several worksheets that you can use to store your data and charts.

Edit and Format Data

Excel allows you to efficiently enter, edit and format data in a worksheet. You can quickly enter a series of numbers, find and replace data or check data for spelling errors. You can also make data stand out in a worksheet by adding borders or changing the font, color, style or alignment of the data.

Use Formulas and Functions

Formulas and functions allow you to perform calculations and analyze data in a worksheet. Common calculations include finding the sum, average or total number of values in a list. As you work, Excel checks your formulas for problems and can help you correct common errors in your formulas.

Print Worksheets

You can produce a paper copy of a worksheet you create. Before printing, you can see on your screen how the worksheet will look when printed. Excel also allows you to adjust the margins or change the size of printed data.

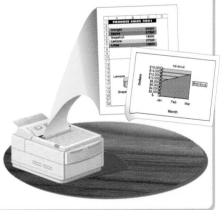

Create Charts and Objects

Excel helps you create colorful charts from worksheet data to visually display the data. You can also create objects, such as AutoShapes, WordArt and diagrams, to enhance the appearance of a worksheet and illustrate important concepts.

Manage Data in a List

Excel provides tools that help you manage and analyze a large collection of data, such as a mailing list or product list. You can sort or filter the data in a list.

Use Speech Recognition

Speech recognition allows you to use your voice to enter data into a worksheet. You can also use speech recognition to select commands from menus, toolbars and dialog boxes using your voice.

Excel and the Internet

Excel offers features that allow you to take advantage of the Internet. You can create a hyperlink in a workbook to connect the workbook to a Web page. You can also save a workbook you create as a Web page. This allows you to place the workbook on the Internet for other people to view.

START EXCEL

When you start Excel, a blank worksheet appears on your screen. You can enter data into this worksheet.

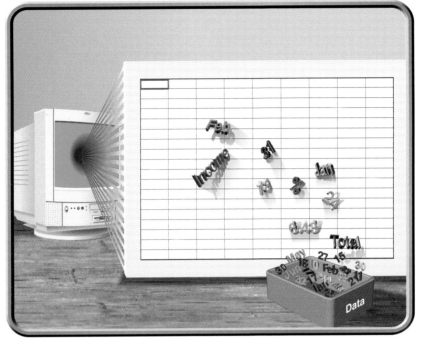

The Getting Started task pane also appears when you start Excel. You can use the task pane to quickly perform common tasks in Excel.

When you finish using Excel, you can exit the program. You should always exit all open programs before turning off your computer.

START EXCEL

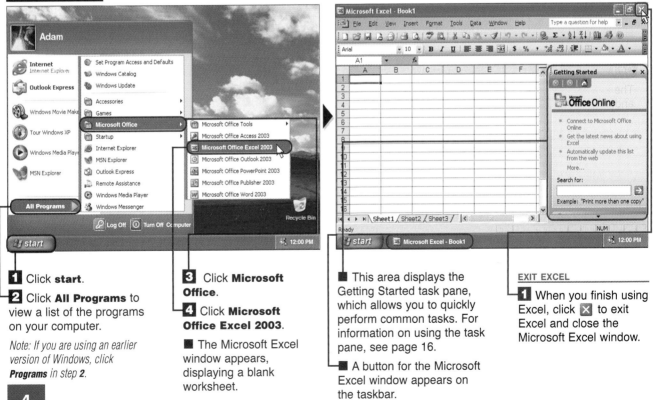

■1 Click **start**.

■2 Click **All Programs** to view a list of the programs on your computer.

Note: If you are using an earlier version of Windows, click ***Programs*** *in step* ***2***.

■3 Click **Microsoft Office**.

■4 Click **Microsoft Office Excel 2003**.

■ The Microsoft Excel window appears, displaying a blank worksheet.

■ This area displays the Getting Started task pane, which allows you to quickly perform common tasks. For information on using the task pane, see page 16.

■ A button for the Microsoft Excel window appears on the taskbar.

EXIT EXCEL

■1 When you finish using Excel, click ⊠ to exit Excel and close the Microsoft Excel window.

PARTS OF THE EXCEL WINDOW

The Excel window displays many items you can use to work with your data.

Title Bar
Shows the name of the displayed workbook.

Menu Bar
Provides access to lists of commands available in Excel and displays an area where you can type a question to get help information.

Standard Toolbar
Contains buttons you can use to select common commands, such as Save and Print.

Formatting Toolbar
Contains buttons you can use to select common formatting commands, such as Bold and Underline.

Formula Bar
Displays the cell reference and the contents of the active cell. A cell reference identifies the location of each cell in a worksheet and consists of a column letter followed by a row number, such as **A1**.

Active Cell
Displays a thick border. You enter data into the active cell.

Cell
The area where a row and column intersect.

Column
A vertical line of cells. A letter identifies each column.

Row
A horizontal line of cells. A number identifies each row.

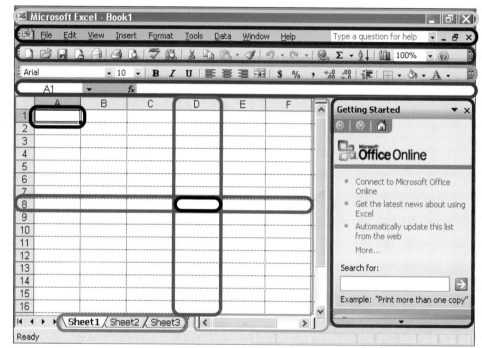

Worksheet Tabs
Each Excel file, called a workbook, is divided into several worksheets. Excel displays a tab for each worksheet.

Scroll Bars
Allow you to browse through a worksheet.

Task Pane
Contains options you can select to perform common tasks, such as creating a new workbook.

CHANGE THE ACTIVE CELL

You can use the mouse or keyboard to make any cell in your worksheet the active cell. You enter data into the active cell.

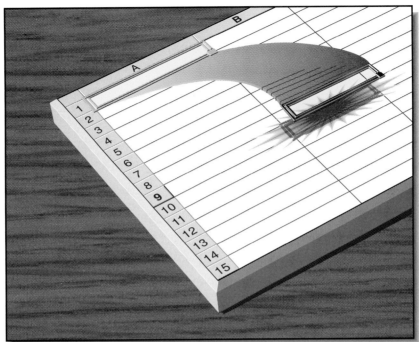

You can only make one cell in your worksheet active at a time.

CHANGE THE ACTIVE CELL

■ The active cell displays a thick border.

■ The cell reference for the active cell appears in this area. A cell reference identifies the location of each cell in a worksheet and consists of a column letter followed by a row number (example: **A1**).

1 Click the cell you want to make the active cell.

Note: You can also press the ←, →, ↑ or ↓ key to change the active cell.

■ The cell reference for the new active cell appears in this area.

6

You can scroll through your worksheet to view other areas of the worksheet. This is useful when your worksheet contains a lot of data and your computer screen cannot display all the data at once.

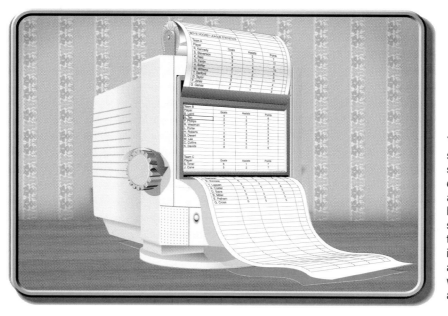

You can use a scroll bar to scroll up and down or left and right. The location of the scroll box on the scroll bar indicates which area of the worksheet you are viewing.

SCROLL THROUGH A WORKSHEET

	A	B	C	D	E	F	G
3	Pool A	Games Played	Goals Scored	Wins	Losses	Ties	Points
4	Brian's Boys	6	15	4	1	1	
5	The Good Guys	6	13	3	1	2	
6	Greg'n' Gang	6	12	4	2	0	
7	The Professionals	6	12	3	3	0	
8	All The Way	6	8	1	3	2	
9	Team Spirit	6	4	1	5	0	
10							
11	Pool B	Games Played	Goals Scored	Wins	Losses	Ties	Points
12	We Score	6	16	4	2	0	
13	The Firefighters	6	14	3	2	1	
14	Challengers	6	12	3	3	0	
15	Headers	6	9	2	2	2	
16	The Hurricanes	6	7	1	5	0	

SCROLL UP OR DOWN

1 To scroll up or down one row, click ▲ or ▼ .

■ To quickly scroll to any row in your worksheet, position the mouse over the scroll box and then drag the scroll box along the scroll bar until the row you want to view appears.

	A	B	C	D	E	F	G
3	Pool A	Games Played	Goals Scored	Wins	Losses	Ties	Points
4	Brian's Boys	6	15	4	1	1	
5	The Good Guys	6	13	3	1	2	
6	Greg'n' Gang	6	12	4	2	0	
7	The Professionals	6	12	3	3	0	
8	All The Way	6	8	1	3	2	
9	Team Spirit	6	4	1	5	0	
10							
11	Pool B	Games Played	Goals Scored	Wins	Losses	Ties	Points
12	We Score	6	16	4	2	0	
13	The Firefighters	6	14	3	2	1	
14	Challengers	6	12	3	3	0	
15	Headers	6	9	2	2	2	
16	The Hurricanes	6	7	1	5	0	

SCROLL LEFT OR RIGHT

1 To scroll left or right one column, click ◄ or ► .

■ To quickly scroll to any column in your worksheet, position the mouse over the scroll box and then drag the scroll box along the scroll bar until the column you want to view appears.

ENTER DATA

You can enter data, such as text, numbers and dates, into your worksheet quickly and easily.

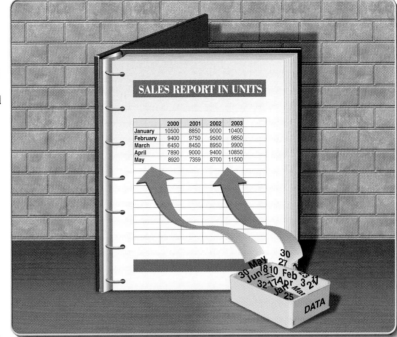

Excel automatically left aligns text and right aligns numbers and dates you enter in cells.

ENTER DATA

1 Click the cell where you want to enter data. Then type the data.

■ The data you type appears in the active cell and in the formula bar.

■ If you make a typing mistake while entering data, press the ◄Backspace key to remove the incorrect data. Then type the correct data.

2 Press the Enter key to enter the data and move down one cell.

Note: To enter the data and move one cell in any direction, press the ←, →, ↑ or ↓ key.

3 Repeat steps 1 and 2 until you finish entering all your data.

Note: In this book, the size of data was changed to 12 points to make the data easier to read. To change the size of data, see page 117.

How can I quickly enter numbers?

You can use the number keys on the right side of your keyboard to quickly enter numbers into your worksheet. To be able to use these number keys, **NUM** must be displayed at the bottom of your screen. You can press the [Num Lock] key to display **NUM** on your screen.

Why did Excel change the appearance of a date I entered?

When you enter a date into your worksheet, Excel may change the format of the date to one of the following formats: 3/14/2003, 14-Mar or 14-Mar-03. To change the format of dates, see page 134.

■ If the text is too long to fit in a cell, the text will spill into the neighboring cell. If the neighboring cell contains data, Excel will display as much of the text as the column width will allow.

■ If a number is too large to fit in a cell, Excel will display the number in scientific notation or as number signs (#).

Note: To change the width of a column to display text or a number, see page 66.

AUTOCOMPLETE

■ If the first few letters you type match the text in another cell in the same column, Excel will complete the text for you.

1 To enter the text Excel provides, press the [Enter] key.

■ To enter different text, continue typing.

SELECT CELLS

Before performing many tasks in Excel, you must select the cells you want to work with. Selected cells appear highlighted on your screen. This makes cells you select stand out from the rest of the cells in your worksheet.

INCOME STATEMENT			
REVENUE	120,000	135,000	140,000
Payroll	15,000	15,000	15,000
Rent	7,500	7,500	7,500
Supplies	4,500	6,200	7,640
INCOME			

You must select the cells containing data you want to move or copy to another location in your worksheet or change to a different font or size. To move or copy data, see page 42. To change the font or size of data, see pages 116 and 117.

To move or copy data, see page 42. To change the font or size of data, see pages 116 and 117.

SELECT CELLS

SELECT A CELL

1 Click the cell you want to select.

■ The cell becomes the active cell and displays a thick border.

SELECT A GROUP OF CELLS

1 Position the mouse ⊕ over the first cell you want to select.

2 Drag the mouse ⊕ until you highlight all the cells you want to select.

■ To select multiple groups of cells, press and hold down the **Ctrl** key as you repeat steps **1** and **2** for each group of cells you want to select.

■ To deselect cells, click any cell.

How do I select all the cells in my worksheet?

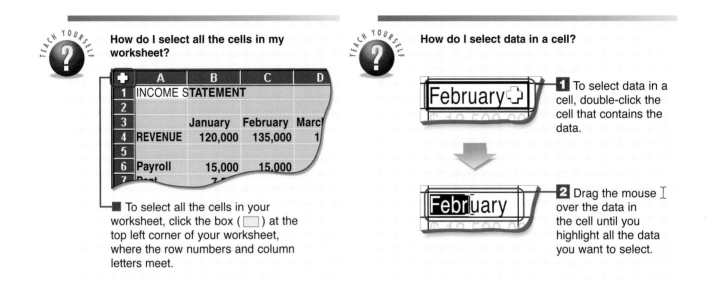

	A	B	C	D
1	INCOME STATEMENT			
2				
3		January	February	March
4	REVENUE	120,000	135,000	1
5				
6	Payroll	15,000	15,000	
7				

■ To select all the cells in your worksheet, click the box (▢) at the top left corner of your worksheet, where the row numbers and column letters meet.

How do I select data in a cell?

February

1 To select data in a cell, double-click the cell that contains the data.

Feb|uary

2 Drag the mouse I over the data in the cell until you highlight all the data you want to select.

SELECT A ROW

1 Click the number of the row you want to select.

■ To select multiple rows, position the mouse ➡ over the number of the first row you want to select. Then drag the mouse ➡ until you highlight all the rows you want to select.

SELECT A COLUMN

1 Click the letter of the column you want to select.

■ To select multiple columns, position the mouse ⬇ over the letter of the first column you want to select. Then drag the mouse ⬇ until you highlight all the columns you want to select.

COMPLETE A SERIES

Excel can save you time by completing a text or number series for you. A series is a sequence of data that changes, such as a range of consecutive numbers.

You can complete a series across a row or down a column in a worksheet. Excel completes a text series based on the text you enter in one cell. Excel completes a number series based on the numbers you enter in two cells.

COMPLETE A TEXT SERIES

1 Enter the text you want to start the series.

2 Click the cell containing the text you entered.

3 Position the mouse ⇧ over the bottom right corner of the cell (⇧ changes to +).

4 Drag the mouse + over the cells you want to include in the series.

■ The cells display the text series.

Note: If Excel cannot determine the text series you want to complete, it will copy the text in the first cell to all the cells you select.

■ To deselect cells, click any cell.

Why does the Auto Fill Options button (▦) appear when I complete a series?

You can use the Auto Fill Options button (▦) to change the way Excel completes a series. For example, you can specify that Excel should not use the formatting from the original cell. Click the Auto Fill Options button to display a list of options and then select the option you want to use. The Auto Fill Options button is available only until you perform another task.

Can I complete a series that will repeat data in several cells?

Yes. Perform steps **1** to **4** on page 12, except enter the same text or data into the first two cells in step **1**. Excel will repeat the information in all the cells you select.

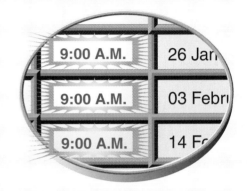

COMPLETE A NUMBER SERIES

1 Enter the first two numbers you want to start the series.

2 Select the cells containing the numbers you entered. To select cells, see page 10.

3 Position the mouse ⬚ over the bottom right corner of the selected cells (⬚ changes to +).

4 Drag the mouse + over the cells you want to include in the series.

■ The cells display the number series.

■ To deselect cells, click any cell.

SELECT A COMMAND

You can select a
command from a
menu or toolbar
to perform a
task in Excel.

File

New...		Ctrl+N
Open...		Ctrl+O
Close		
Save		Ctrl+S
Save As...		
Save as Web Page...		
File Search...		
Permission		▶
Web Page Preview		

When you first start
Excel, the most
commonly used
commands and buttons
appear on each menu and
toolbar. As you work, Excel
customizes the menus and
toolbars to display the
commands and buttons you
use most often.

Population Growth chart image shown.

SELECT A COMMAND

USING MENUS

1 Click the name of the
menu you want to display.

■ A short version of the
menu appears, displaying
the most commonly used
commands.

2 To expand the menu
and display all the
commands, position
the mouse ⌖ over ⌄.

■ The expanded menu
appears, displaying all
the commands.

3 Click the command
you want to use.

*Note: A dimmed command is
currently not available.*

■ To close a menu without
selecting a command, click
outside the menu.

How can I make a command appear on the short version of a menu?

When you select a command from an expanded menu, the command is automatically added to the short version of the menu. The next time you display the short version of the menu, the command you selected will appear.

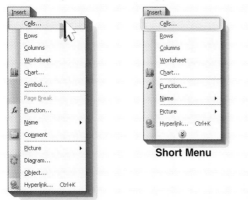

Expanded Menu

Short Menu

How can I quickly select a command?

You can use a shortcut menu to quickly select a command.

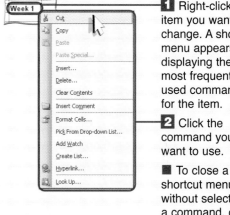

1 Right-click an item you want to change. A shortcut menu appears, displaying the most frequently used commands for the item.

2 Click the command you want to use.

■ To close a shortcut menu without selecting a command, click outside the menu.

USING TOOLBARS

1 To display the name of a toolbar button, position the mouse ⬚ over the button.

■ After a moment, the name of the button appears in a yellow box. The button name can help you determine the task the button performs.

2 A toolbar may not be able to display all its buttons. Click ⬚ to display additional buttons for the toolbar.

■ Additional buttons for the toolbar appear.

3 To use a toolbar button to select a command, click the button.

USING THE TASK PANE

You can use the task pane to perform common tasks in Excel. The Getting Started task pane appears each time you start Excel.

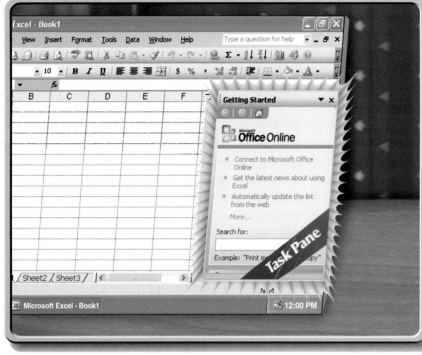

You can display or hide the task pane at any time. When you perform some tasks, such as searching for a workbook, the task pane will automatically appear.

USING THE TASK PANE

DISPLAY OR HIDE THE TASK PANE

1 Click **View**.

2 Click **Task Pane**.

Note: If Task Pane does not appear on the menu, position the mouse over the bottom of the menu to display the menu option.

■ The task pane appears or disappears.

■ You can position the mouse over ▲ or ▼ to browse through the information in the task pane.

■ To quickly hide the task pane at any time, click ☒.

16

What are some of the task panes available in Excel?

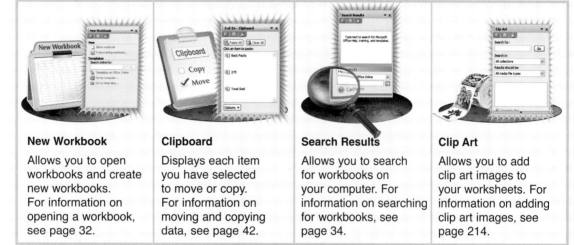

New Workbook

Allows you to open workbooks and create new workbooks. For information on opening a workbook, see page 32.

Clipboard

Displays each item you have selected to move or copy. For information on moving and copying data, see page 42.

Search Results

Allows you to search for workbooks on your computer. For information on searching for workbooks, see page 34.

Clip Art

Allows you to add clip art images to your worksheets. For information on adding clip art images, see page 214.

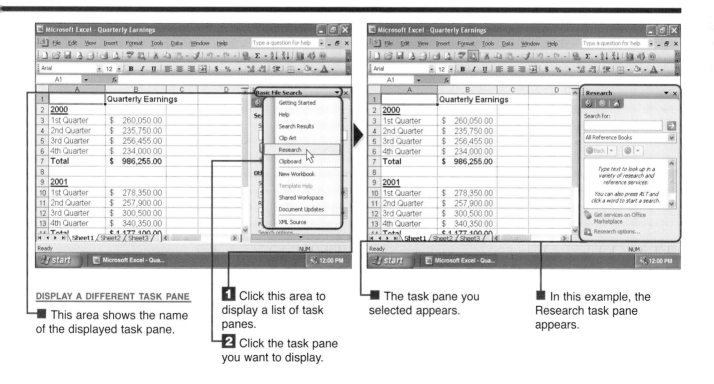

DISPLAY A DIFFERENT TASK PANE

■ This area shows the name of the displayed task pane.

1 Click this area to display a list of task panes.

2 Click the task pane you want to display.

■ The task pane you selected appears.

■ In this example, the Research task pane appears.

If you do not know
how to perform a
task in Excel, you
can search for help
information on the
task.

Some help
information is only
available on the
Internet. You must
be connected to
the Internet to
access online
help information.

GETTING HELP

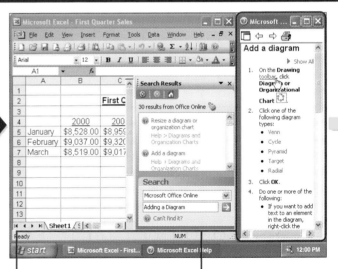

1 Click this area and type the task you want to get help information on. Then press the **Enter** key.

■ The Search Results task pane appears.

■ This area displays a list of related help topics. You can use the scroll bar to browse through the available topics.

2 Click the help topic of interest.

■ A window appears, displaying information about the help topic you selected.

3 To display additional information for a word or phrase that appears in color, click the word or phrase.

**What do the icons beside each
help topic represent?**

Here are some icons you will see
beside help topics.

	Displays a help topic.
	Opens a Web page that takes you through step-by-step training for the task.
	Displays a pre-designed template, such as an expense report.
	Opens a Web page that offers a product or service to enhance Microsoft Office.
	Opens a Web page that displays an article on a specific topic.

**How can I get help information
when working with a dialog box?**

You can click ❓ in the top right
corner of a dialog box. A window
will appear, displaying help
information for the dialog box.

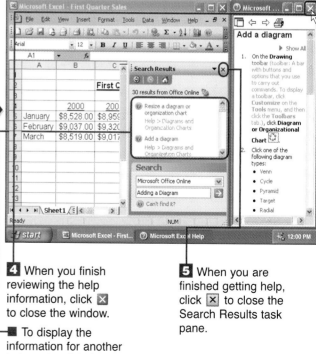

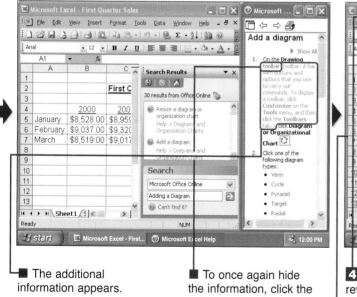

■ The additional
information appears.

*Note: Selecting a colored
word or phrase will display
information such as a definition,
tip or list of steps.*

■ To once again hide
the information, click the
colored word or phrase.

4 When you finish
reviewing the help
information, click ✕
to close the window.

■ To display the
information for another
help topic, click the
help topic.

5 When you are
finished getting help,
click ✕ to close the
Search Results task
pane.

CHAPTER 2

Save and Open Your Workbooks

Are you wondering how to save, close or open an Excel workbook? Learn how in this chapter.

Save a Workbook 22

Create a New Workbook 24

Switch Between Workbooks...............25

View All Open Workbooks 26

Compare Workbooks 28

Close a Workbook 29

Save Workbooks in a
    Workspace File 30

Save a Workbook With a
    New Name 31

Open a Workbook 32

Search for a Workbook.....................34

SAVE A WORKBOOK

You can save your workbook to store it for future use. Saving a workbook allows you to later review and edit the workbook.

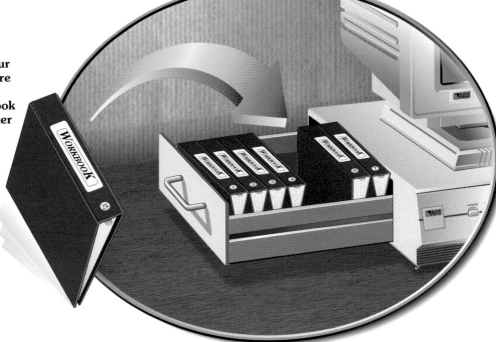

SAVE A WORKBOOK

1 Click 🖫 to save your workbook.

■ The Save As dialog box appears.

Note: If you previously saved your workbook, the Save As dialog box will not appear since you have already named the workbook.

2 Type a name for the workbook.

*Note: A workbook name cannot contain the * : ? > < | or " characters.*

What are the commonly used locations that I can access?

Provides access to folders and workbooks you recently worked with.

Allows you to store a workbook on the Windows desktop.

Provides a convenient place to store a workbook.

Allows you to store a workbook on a drive on your computer, such as a floppy or external hard drive.

Allows you to store a workbook on your network.

■ This area shows the location where Excel will store your workbook. You can click this area to change the location.

■ This area allows you to access commonly used locations. You can click a location to save your workbook in the location.

3 Click **Save** to save your workbook.

■ Excel saves your workbook and displays the name of the workbook at the top of your screen.

SAVE CHANGES

You should regularly save changes you make to a workbook to avoid losing your work.

1 Click 🖫 to save the changes you made to your workbook.

23

CREATE A NEW WORKBOOK

You can easily create a new workbook to store new data, such as a budget or sales report.

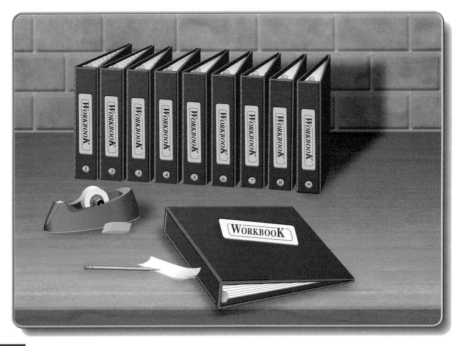

When you create a new workbook, Excel displays a blank worksheet on your screen. You do not have to close the workbook currently displayed on your screen before creating a new workbook.

CREATE A NEW WORKBOOK

1 Click 🗋 to create a new workbook.

Note: If 🗋 is not displayed, click ⁑ on the Standard toolbar to display the button.

■ A new workbook appears. The previous workbook is now hidden behind the new workbook.

■ Excel gives the new workbook a temporary name, such as Book2, until you save the workbook. To save a workbook, see page 22.

■ A button for the new workbook appears on the taskbar.

SWITCH BETWEEN WORKBOOKS

You can have several workbooks open at once. Excel allows you to easily switch from one open workbook to another.

SWITCH BETWEEN WORKBOOKS

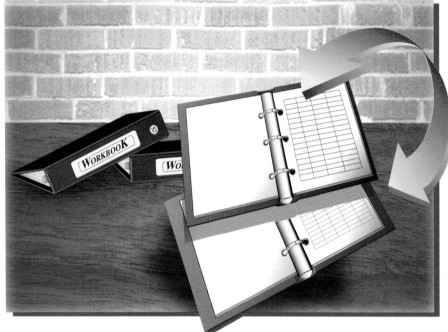

1 Click **Window** to display a list of all the workbooks you have open.

2 Click the name of the workbook you want to switch to.

■ The workbook appears.

■ This area shows the name of the displayed workbook.

■ The taskbar displays a button for each open workbook. You can also click the buttons on the taskbar to switch between the open workbooks.

VIEW ALL OPEN WORKBOOKS

If you have several workbooks open, some of them may be hidden from view. You can display the contents of all your open workbooks at once.

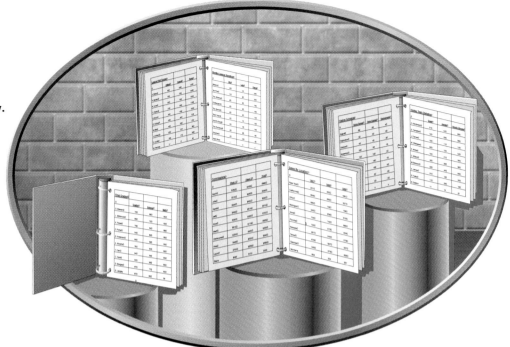

VIEW ALL OPEN WORKBOOKS

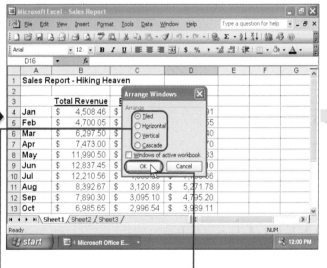

1 Click **Window**.

2 Click **Arrange**.

Note: If Arrange does not appear on the menu, position the mouse ⌖ over the bottom of the menu to display the menu option.

■ The Arrange Windows dialog box appears.

3 Click an option to select the way you want to arrange your open workbooks (○ changes to ◉).

4 Click **OK** to arrange your workbooks.

How can I arrange open workbooks on my screen?

Tiled

The workbooks appear as tiled squares, allowing you to clearly view the contents of each workbook.

Horizontal

The workbooks appear one above the other.

Vertical

The workbooks appear side by side.

Cascade

The workbooks overlap each other, allowing you to clearly view the title bar of each workbook.

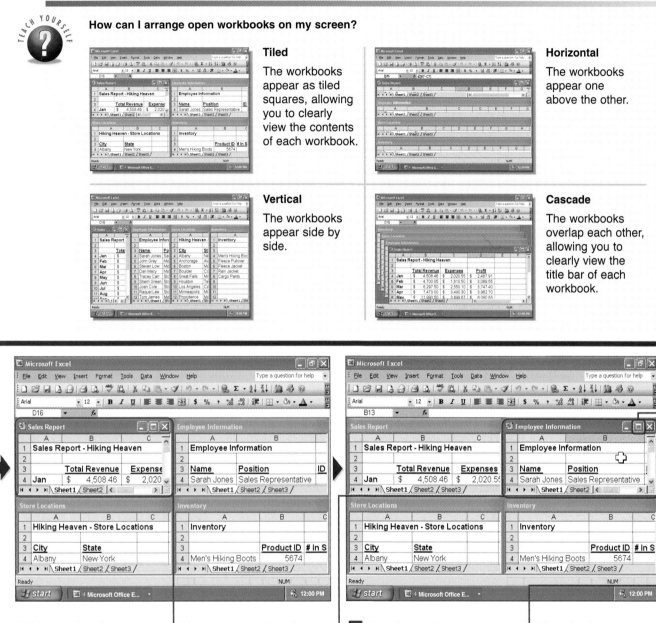

■ Your workbooks appear neatly arranged.

■ You can work with only one workbook at a time. The current workbook displays a dark title bar.

5 To make another workbook current, click anywhere in the workbook.

■ To make the current workbook fill your screen, click 🔲.

COMPARE WORKBOOKS

You can display two workbooks on your screen at once. Excel displays one workbook above the other so you can easily compare data in corresponding rows. Comparing workbooks is useful if you want to compare an edited workbook to the original version of the workbook.

Sportz Inc.

First Quarter Sales Report

	January	February	March
Jim	51,000	24,000	31,400
Mary	36,700	36,700	37,560
Arthur	30,000	78,000	38,500
Nancy	45,800	37,800	21,600
Cathy	60,500	42,500	78,300
Terry	47,800	15,800	95,200
Scott	55,200	22,200	12,300
Andrew	39,000	34,000	37,000
Krista	41,500	90,500	27,500
Randy	58,000	58,000	18,200
Michael	68,540	24,540	37,500
Jason	89,000	28,000	27,000
Robert	32,050	25,050	27,000

Sportz Inc.

First Quarter Sales Report

	January	February	March
Jim	36,000	24,000	60,400
Mary	36,300	56,700	17,560
Arthur	36,000	78,000	37,500
Nancy	37,800	69,800	21,600
Cathy	98,500	12,500	78,300
Terry	34,800	15,800	95,200
Scott	80,200	22,200	12,300
Andrew	15,000	25,000	37,000
Krista	42,500	90,500	27,5
Randy	58,000	5	
Michael	68,540	24	
Jason	89,000	28,	
Robert	32,050	25,0	

Revised

When you scroll through one workbook, Excel automatically scrolls through the other workbook for you, so you can compare the contents of the two workbooks.

COMPARE WORKBOOKS

1 Open the two workbooks you want to compare.

Note: To open a workbook, see page 32.

2 Click **Window** in the current workbook.

3 Click **Compare Side by Side with** to compare the current workbook with the other open workbook.

■ Excel displays the workbooks on your screen. One workbook appears above the other workbook.

■ The Compare Side by Side toolbar also appears.

4 To scroll through the workbooks, drag the scroll box up or down in one workbook. Excel automatically scrolls the other workbook for you.

5 When you finish comparing the workbooks on your screen, click **Close Side by Side**.

CLOSE A WORKBOOK

When you finish working with a workbook, you can close the workbook to remove it from your screen.

When you close a workbook, you do not exit the Excel program. You can continue to work with other workbooks.

CLOSE A WORKBOOK

■ Before closing a workbook, you should save any changes you made to the workbook. To save a workbook, see page 22.

1 Click **File**.

2 Click **Close** to close the workbook.

■ The workbook disappears from your screen.

■ If you had more than one workbook open, the second last workbook you worked with appears on your screen.

QUICKLY CLOSE A WORKBOOK

■ To quickly close a workbook, click ⊠.

SAVE WORKBOOKS IN A WORKSPACE FILE

You can save workbooks in a workspace file to have Excel remember the size and location of each workbook on your screen. You can later open the workspace file to open all the workbooks at once.

Before saving workbooks in a workspace file, save each workbook. To save a workbook, see page 22.

SAVE WORKBOOKS IN A WORKSPACE FILE

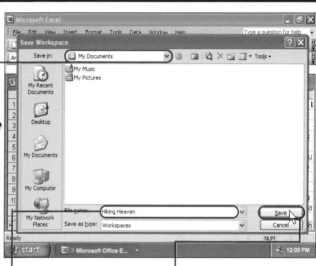

1 Display and arrange the workbooks you want to include in the workspace file. To arrange open workbooks, see page 26.

2 Click **File**.

3 Click **Save Workspace**.

Note: If Save Workspace does not appear on the menu, position the mouse ▷ over the bottom of the menu to display the menu option.

■ The Save Workspace dialog box appears.

4 Type a name for the workspace file.

■ This area shows the location where Excel will store your workspace file. You can click this area to change the location.

5 Click **Save** to save your workspace file.

■ You can later open your workspace file as you would open any workbook. To open a workbook, see page 32.

You can save a
workbook with
a different name.
This is useful
if you want to
create a copy
of the workbook.

SAVE A WORKBOOK WITH A NEW NAME

1 Click **File**.

2 Click **Save As**.

■ The Save As dialog box appears.

3 Type a new name for the workbook.

■ This area shows the location where Excel will store your workbook. You can click this area to change the location.

4 Click **Save** to save your workbook with the new name.

■ Excel saves a copy of your workbook with the new name.

OPEN A WORKBOOK

You can open a saved workbook to view the workbook on your screen. Opening a workbook allows you to review and make changes to the workbook.

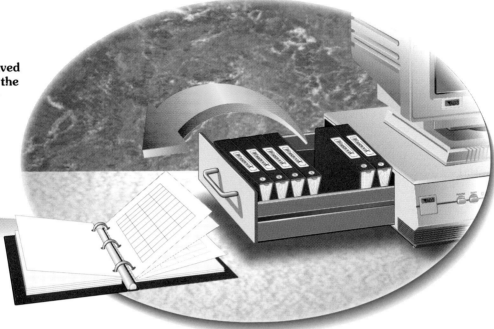

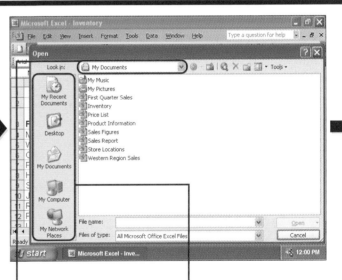

1 Click 📂 to open a workbook.

■ The Open dialog box appears.

■ This area shows the location of the displayed workbooks. You can click this area to change the location.

■ This area allows you to access workbooks in commonly used locations. You can click a location to display the workbooks stored in the location.

Note: For information on the commonly used locations, see the top of page 23.

32

How can I quickly open a workbook I recently worked with?

Excel remembers the names of the last four workbooks you worked with. You can use the Getting Started task pane or the File menu to quickly open one of these workbooks.

Note: The Getting Started task pane appears each time you start Excel. To display the Getting Started task pane, see page 16.

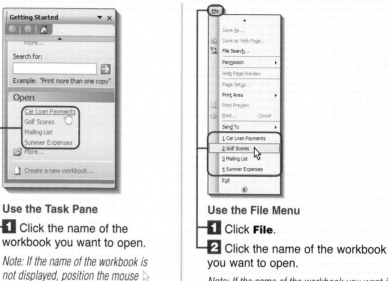

Use the Task Pane

1 Click the name of the workbook you want to open.

Note: If the name of the workbook is not displayed, position the mouse over the bottom of the task pane to display the name.

Use the File Menu

1 Click **File**.

2 Click the name of the workbook you want to open.

Note: If the name of the workbook you want is not displayed, position the mouse over the bottom of the menu to display the name.

---

2 Click the name of the workbook you want to open.

3 Click **Open** to open the workbook.

■ The workbook opens and appears on your screen. You can now review and make changes to the workbook.

■ This area displays the name of the open workbook.

■ If you already had a workbook open, the new workbook appears in a new Microsoft Excel window. You can click the buttons on the taskbar to switch between the open workbooks.

SEARCH FOR A WORKBOOK

If you cannot remember the name or location of a workbook you want to work with, you can search for the workbook.

SEARCH FOR A WORKBOOK

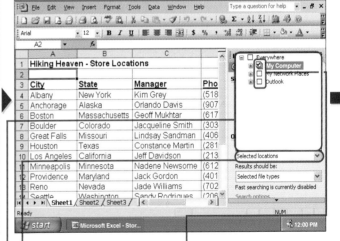

1 Click **File**.

2 Click **File Search** to search for a workbook.

■ The Basic File Search task pane appears.

3 Click this area and type one or more words you want to search for.

Note: If this area already contains text, drag the mouse I over the existing text before performing step 3.

4 Click ∨ in this area to select the locations you want to search.

■ A check mark (✔) appears beside each location that Excel will search.

Note: By default, Excel will search all the drives and folders on your computer.

5 You can click the box beside a location to add (☑) or remove (☐) a check mark.

6 Click outside the list of locations to close the list.

How will Excel use the words I specify to search for workbooks?

Excel will search the contents of workbooks and the file names of workbooks for the words you specify. When searching the contents of workbooks, Excel will search for various forms of the words. For example, searching for "run" will find "run," "running" and "ran."

Search for:
run

Finds:
• run
• running
• ran

When selecting the locations and types of files I want to search for, how can I display more items?

Each item that displays a plus sign (⊞) contains hidden items. To display the hidden items, click the plus sign (⊞) beside the item (⊞ changes to ⊟). To once again hide the items, click the minus sign (⊟) beside the item.

---

7 Click ⌄ in this area to specify the types of files you want to search for.

■ A check mark (✔) appears beside each type of file that Excel will search for.

8 You can click the box beside a file type to add (☑) or remove (☐) a check mark.

9 Click outside the list of file types to close the list.

10 Click **Go** to start the search.

■ This area lists the workbooks that contain the word(s) you specified.

■ To open a workbook in the list, click the workbook.

■ To close the task pane at any time, click ✖.

CHAPTER 3

Edit Your Worksheets

Do you want to edit the data in your worksheets or check your worksheets for spelling errors? This chapter teaches you how.

Edit Data 38

Delete Data 40

Undo Changes..................................41

Move or Copy Data 42

Check Spelling..................................44

Using AutoCorrect 46

Using the Research Task Pane 48

Find Data 50

Replace Data 52

Link Data...54

Name Cells 56

Add a Comment...............................58

Insert Symbols 60

Insert a Stock Quote 62

EDIT DATA

You can edit data in your worksheet to correct a mistake or update data.

1 Double-click the cell containing the data you want to edit.

■ A flashing insertion point appears in the cell.

2 Press the ← or → key to move the insertion point to where you want to remove or add characters.

3 To remove the character to the left of the insertion point, press the +Backspace key.

■ To remove the character to the right of the insertion point, press the Delete key.

Can I edit data in the formula bar?

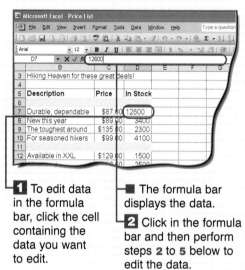

1 To edit data in the formula bar, click the cell containing the data you want to edit.

■ The formula bar displays the data.

2 Click in the formula bar and then perform steps **2** to **5** below to edit the data.

Can I edit data using only my keyboard?

If you have trouble double-clicking or prefer to use your keyboard, you can use only your keyboard to edit data. Press the ←, →, ↑ or ↓ key to select the cell you want to make the active cell and then press the **F2** key to edit the data in the active cell. The insertion point appears at the end of the data in the cell.

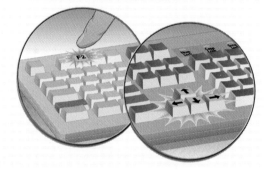

4 To add data where the insertion point flashes on your screen, type the data.

5 When you finish making changes to the data, press the **Enter** key.

REPLACE ALL DATA IN A CELL

1 Click the cell containing the data you want to replace with new data.

2 Type the new data and then press the **Enter** key.

DELETE DATA

You can remove data you no longer need from cells in your worksheet. You can delete data from a single cell or from several cells at once.

When you delete the data in a cell, Excel does not remove the formatting you applied to the cell, such as a new font or color. Any new data you enter into the cell will display the same formatting as the data you deleted. To clear the formatting from cells, see the top of page 137.

To clear the formatting from cells, see the top of page 137.

DELETE DATA

■1 Select the cells containing the data you want to delete. To select cells, see page 10.

To select cells, see page 10.

■2 Press the Delete key.

■ The data in the cells you selected disappears.

■ To deselect cells, click any cell.

UNDO CHANGES

Excel remembers the last changes you made to your worksheet. If you regret these changes, you can cancel them by using the Undo feature.

The Undo feature can cancel your last editing and formatting changes. If you do not like the results of canceling an editing or formatting change, you can easily reverse the results.

UNDO CHANGES

1 Click ↺ to undo the last change you made to your worksheet.

Note: If ↺ is not displayed, click ⁞ on the Standard toolbar to display the button.

■ Excel cancels the last change you made to your worksheet.

■ You can repeat step **1** to cancel previous changes you made.

■ To reverse the results of using the Undo feature, click ↻.

Note: If ↻ is not displayed, click ⁞ on the Standard toolbar to display the button.

MOVE OR COPY DATA

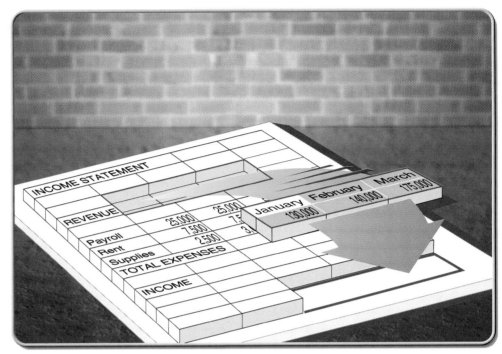

You can move or copy data to a new location in your worksheet.

Moving data allows you to reorganize data in your worksheet. When you move data, the data disappears from its original location.

Copying data allows you to repeat data in your worksheet without having to retype the data. When you copy data, the data appears in both the original and new locations.

MOVE OR COPY DATA

USING DRAG AND DROP

1 Select the cells containing the data you want to move. To select cells, see page 10.

2 Position the mouse ⊹ over a border of the selected cells (⊹ changes to ✛).

3 To move the data, drag the mouse ⇖ to where you want to place the data.

Note: A gray box indicates where the data will appear.

■ The data moves to the new location.

■ To copy data, perform steps **1** to **3**, except press and hold down the `Ctrl` key as you perform step **3**.

How can I use the Clipboard task pane to move or copy data?

The Clipboard task pane displays the last 24 items you have selected to move or copy using the toolbar buttons. To display the Clipboard task pane, see page 16. To place a clipboard item into your worksheet, click the cell where you want to place the item and then click the item in the task pane.

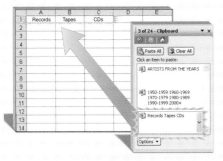

Why does the Paste Options button (📋) appear when I copy data?

You can use the Paste Options button (📋) to change the way Excel copies data when you use the Copy button (📋). For example, you can specify that you want to copy only the formatting of the original cells to the new location. Click the Paste Options button to display a list of options and then select the option you want to use. The Paste Options button is available only until you perform another task.

USING THE TOOLBAR BUTTONS

1 Select the cells containing the data you want to move or copy. To select cells, see page 10.

2 Click one of the following buttons.

✂ Move data

📋 Copy data

3 Click the cell where you want to place the data. This cell will become the top left cell of the new location.

4 Click 📋 to place the data in the new location.

■ The data appears in the new location.

Note: A moving, dotted border may appear around the cells you selected to move or copy. To remove the border, press the **Esc** *key.*

CHECK SPELLING

You can find and correct all the spelling errors in your worksheet.

Spelling Error: wether

Suggestions: weather wetter whether wither

Excel compares every word in your worksheet to words in its dictionary. If a word in your worksheet does not exist in the dictionary, the word is considered misspelled.

CHECK SPELLING

1 Click cell **A1** to start the spell check at the beginning of your worksheet.

2 Click ![abc icon] to start the spell check.

■ The Spelling dialog box appears if Excel finds a misspelled word.

■ This area displays the misspelled word.

■ This area displays suggestions for correcting the word.

What parts of a worksheet does Excel check for spelling errors?

In addition to text in cells, Excel spell checks text in items such as comments, charts, AutoShapes, text boxes, diagrams and headers and footers.

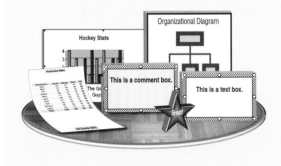

Can Excel automatically correct my typing mistakes?

Yes. Excel automatically corrects common spelling errors as you type. Here are a few examples.

adn	➡	and
alot	➡	a lot
comittee	➡	committee
don;t	➡	don't
nwe	➡	new
occurence	➡	occurrence
recieve	➡	receive
seperate	➡	separate
teh	➡	the

To view a complete list of the spelling errors that Excel will automatically correct, perform the steps on page 46.

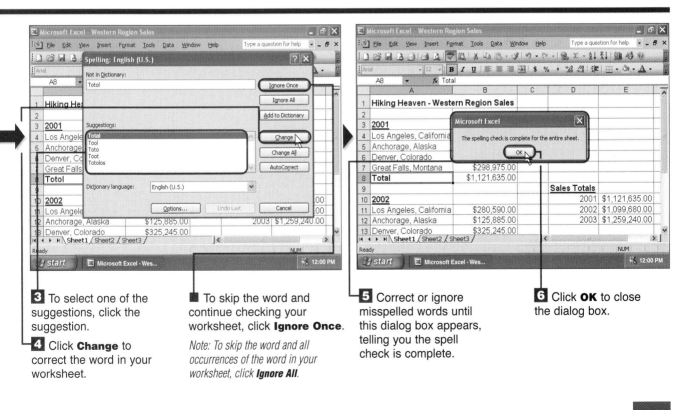

3 To select one of the suggestions, click the suggestion.

4 Click **Change** to correct the word in your worksheet.

■ To skip the word and continue checking your worksheet, click **Ignore Once**.

*Note: To skip the word and all occurrences of the word in your worksheet, click **Ignore All**.*

5 Correct or ignore misspelled words until this dialog box appears, telling you the spell check is complete.

6 Click **OK** to close the dialog box.

USING AUTOCORRECT

Excel automatically corrects hundreds of common typing and spelling errors as you type. You can create an AutoCorrect entry to add your own words and phrases to the list of errors that Excel corrects.

(c)	©
(tm)	TM
accordingto	according to
ahve	have
can;t	can't
chnage	change
may of been	may have been
recieve	receive
seperate	separate
teh	the

USING AUTOCORRECT

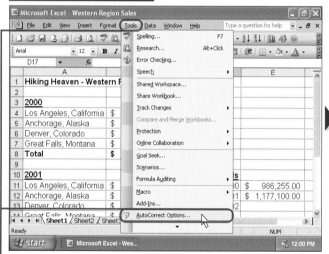

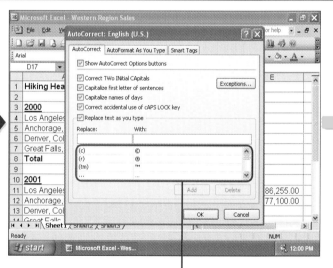

1 Click **Tools**.

2 Click **AutoCorrect Options**.

Note: If AutoCorrect Options does not appear on the menu, position the mouse ⏵ over the bottom of the menu to display the menu option.

■ The AutoCorrect dialog box appears.

■ This area displays the list of AutoCorrect entries included with Excel.

What other types of errors does Excel automatically correct?

When you type two consecutive uppercase letters, Excel automatically converts the second letter to lowercase. When you type a lowercase letter as the first letter of a sentence or the name of a day, Excel automatically converts the letter to uppercase.

How can I delete an AutoCorrect entry?

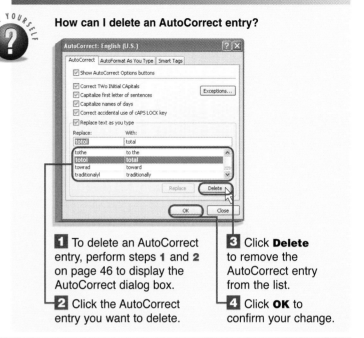

1 To delete an AutoCorrect entry, perform steps **1** and **2** on page 46 to display the AutoCorrect dialog box.

2 Click the AutoCorrect entry you want to delete.

3 Click **Delete** to remove the AutoCorrect entry from the list.

4 Click **OK** to confirm your change.

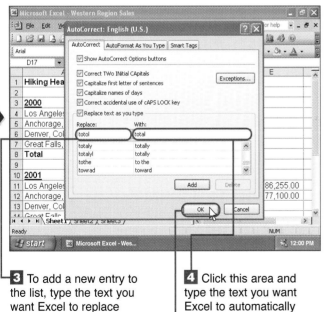

3 To add a new entry to the list, type the text you want Excel to replace automatically.

4 Click this area and type the text you want Excel to automatically insert into your worksheets.

5 Click **OK** to confirm your change.

INSERT AN
AUTOCORRECT ENTRY

■ After you create an AutoCorrect entry, Excel will automatically insert the entry each time you type the corresponding text.

1 Type the text Excel will automatically replace and then press the **Spacebar** or Enter key.

■ Excel automatically replaces the text with the AutoCorrect entry.

USING THE RESEARCH TASK PANE

You can use the Research task pane to gather reference material without ever having to leave your Excel worksheet. For example, you can look up a word in a dictionary or search through an encyclopedia on the Web.

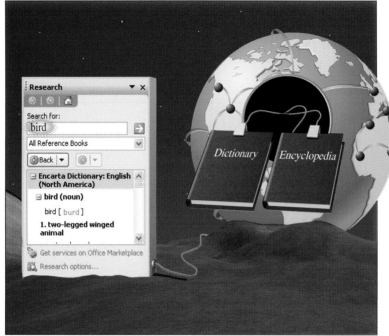

To use some of the resources offered in the Research task pane, your computer must be connected to the Internet.

Links to Web sites in the Research task pane that are preceded by a money icon (💹) require you to register and pay before you can view the information.

USING THE RESEARCH TASK PANE

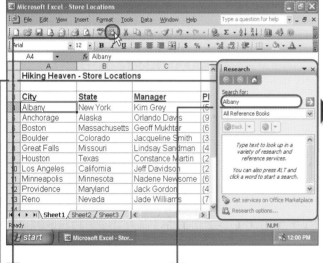

1 Click 🔍 to display the Research task pane.

■ The Research task pane appears.

2 Click this area and type a word you want to research.

Note: If this area contains text, drag the mouse I over the text to select the text before performing step 2.

3 Click this area to display a list of the resources you can use for your research.

4 Click the resource you want to use to find information.

Note: In this example, we select Encarta Encyclopedia. The following screens depend on the resource you select.

What types of resources can I search using the Research task pane?

Reference Books

You can choose to look up terms in reference books, such as the Encarta Dictionary or a thesaurus.

Research Sites

You can research information online using eLibrary, Encarta Encyclopedia, Factiva News Search or MSN Search.

Business and Financial Sites

You can access company and stock market information through Gale Company Profiles or MSN Money Stock Quotes. For information on inserting stock quotes, see page 62.

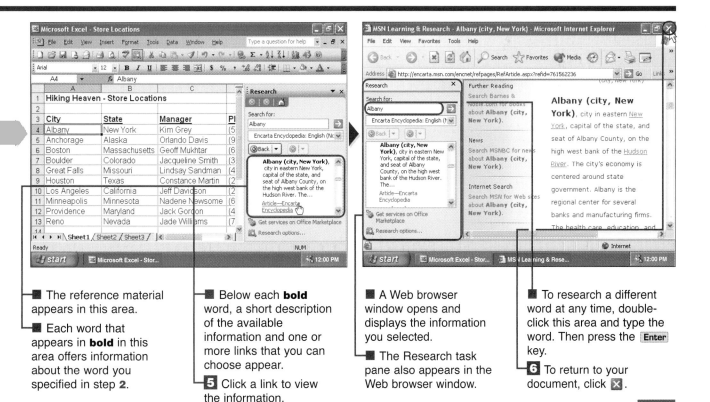

■ The reference material appears in this area.

■ Each word that appears in **bold** in this area offers information about the word you specified in step **2**.

■ Below each **bold** word, a short description of the available information and one or more links that you can choose appear.

5 Click a link to view the information.

■ A Web browser window opens and displays the information you selected.

■ The Research task pane also appears in the Web browser window.

■ To research a different word at any time, double-click this area and type the word. Then press the `Enter` key.

6 To return to your document, click ☒.

49

FIND DATA

You can use the Find feature to quickly locate every occurrence of a word or number in your worksheet.

FIND DATA

1 Click **Edit**.

2 Click **Find**.

■ The Find and Replace dialog box appears.

3 Type the word or number you want to find.

4 Click **Find Next** to start the search.

Note: A dialog box appears if Excel cannot find the word or number you specified. Click OK to close the dialog box and then skip to step 6.

How will Excel search for the word or number I specify?

When you search for data in your worksheet, Excel will search for every instance of the data, even if the data appears in a formula or is part of a larger word or number. For example, if you search for the number 105, Excel will also find the numbers **105**.35, 2**105** and **105**6.

Can I search only a specific section of my worksheet?

Yes. To search only a specific section of your worksheet, select the cells you want to search before starting the search. To select cells, see page 10.

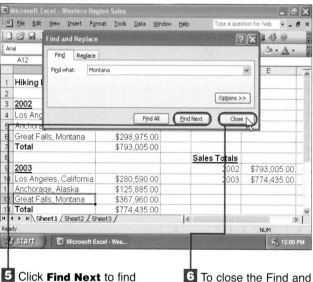

	A	B	C	D	E
1		1998	1999	2000	2001
2	January	10500	7890	11700	8850
3	February	9400	8940	4400	4900
4	March	6450	8260	5650	6450
5	April	7890	8940	8790	9780
6	May	8920	4520	9820	7790
7	June	8850	8360	8850	6450
8	July	9100	7090	12090	4900
9	August	8850	8247	2570	5750
10	September	8940	6800	7450	6360
11	October	8820	2893	5280	9390
12	November	7577	2240	6970	710
	December	4695	7788	2745	

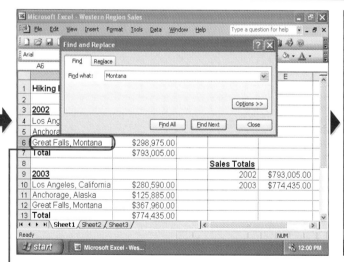

■ Excel highlights the first cell containing the word or number.

Note: If the Find and Replace dialog box covers a cell containing the word or number you want to find, Excel will automatically move the dialog box to a new location.

5 Click **Find Next** to find the next matching word or number. Repeat this step until you find the word or number you are searching for.

6 To close the Find and Replace dialog box at any time, click **Close**.

REPLACE DATA

You can find and replace every occurrence of a word or number in your worksheet. This is useful if you have incorrectly entered data throughout your worksheet.

REPLACE DATA

1 Click **Edit**.

2 Click **Replace**.

Note: If Replace does not appear on the menu, position the mouse over the bottom of the menu to display the menu option.

■ The Find and Replace dialog box appears.

3 Type the word or number you want to replace with new data.

4 Click this area and type the word or number you want to replace the data you typed in step **3**.

Note: If the areas already contain data, drag the mouse I over the existing data and then type the word or number.

5 Click **Find Next** to start the search.

Can Excel find and replace a number used in my formulas?

Yes. Excel automatically searches the formulas in your worksheet for the number you specified. This is useful if you want to change a number used in several formulas. For example, if sales tax increases from 7% to 8%, you can search for all occurrences of **.07** in your formulas and replace them with **.08**.

Can I use wildcard characters to find the data I want to replace?

Yes. You can use an asterisk (*) or a question mark (?) to find the data you want to replace. The asterisk (*) represents one or more characters. The question mark (?) represents a single character. For example, type **Wend?** to find Wendi and Wendy.

■ Excel highlights the first cell containing the word or number you specified.

6 Click one of these options.

Replace All - Replace all occurrences of the word or number in the worksheet.

Replace - Replace the word or number.

Find Next - Ignore the word or number.

Note: To cancel the search at any time, press the Esc *key.*

■ In this example, Excel replaces the word or number and searches for the next match.

Note: If you selected Replace All in step 6, a dialog box appears, stating that the data was replaced. Click OK to close the dialog box and then skip to step 8.

7 Replace or ignore matching data until you find all the occurrences of the data you want to replace.

8 Click **Close** to close the Find and Replace dialog box.

LINK DATA

You can link data in one cell to another cell. When the data in the original cell changes, the linked data also changes.

Linking data is useful when you want cells to always display the same information. For example, you can link a formula in one cell to another cell in your worksheet. If the result of the formula changes, the linked cell will display the new result. For information on formulas, see pages 82 to 85.

LINK DATA

1 Click the cell containing the data you want to link to another cell.

2 Click ▣.

3 Click the cell where you want to place the linked data.

4 Click ▣.

Can I link data to a cell in another worksheet?

Yes. You can link data to a cell in a different worksheet in the same workbook or a worksheet in another workbook. Perform steps **1** to **6** below, except switch to the worksheet you want to link the data to before performing step **3**. To switch between worksheets, see page 170. To switch between workbooks, see page 25.

Can I move or delete the data in the original cell without affecting the link?

When you move the data in the original cell, the link is not affected if the linked cell is in the same workbook. When you delete the data in the original cell, the linked cell displays a zero (0).

■ The Paste Options button appears in your worksheet.

5 Click the Paste Options button to display a list of options.

6 Click **Link Cells**.

Note: The cell you are linking may not display the same data as the original cell until you perform step 6.

■ The linked data appears in the cell.

■ The formula bar displays the location of the original cell.

■ To remove the moving border around the original cell, press the Esc key.

■ When the data in the original cell changes, the linked data also changes.

You can give cells in your worksheet a meaningful name. Using named cells can save you time when selecting cells or entering formulas and functions.

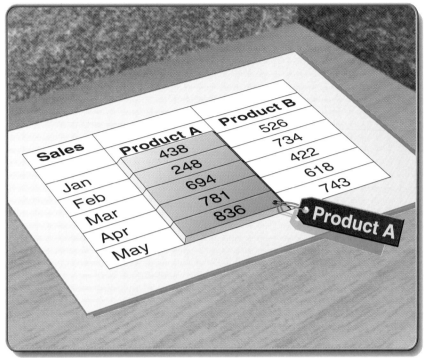

You can name a single cell or a range of cells in your worksheet.

NAME CELLS

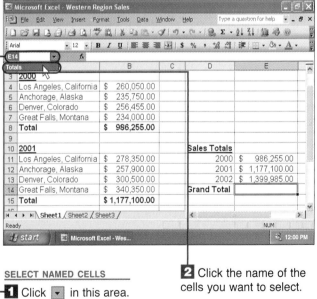

1 Select the cells you want to name. To select cells, see page 10.

2 Click this area to highlight the existing information.

3 Type the name you want to use for the cells and then press the Enter key.

■ To deselect cells, click any cell.

SELECT NAMED CELLS

1 Click ▼ in this area.

2 Click the name of the cells you want to select.

What should I consider when naming cells?

You should consider the following guidelines when naming cells:

➤ Cell names can be up to 255 characters in length.

➤ Cell names must begin with either a letter or an underscore character (_). The remaining characters can be any combination of letters, numbers, underscore characters or periods.

➤ Cell names cannot include spaces.

➤ Cell names cannot be a cell reference, such as **D4**.

➤ Cell names can contain both uppercase and lowercase letters.

■ Excel highlights the cells in your worksheet.

USING NAMED CELLS IN
FORMULAS AND FUNCTIONS

Naming cells can make formulas and functions easier to enter and understand.

■ In this example, we use cells named "Totals" in a function.

■ This cell contains the function **=SUM(Totals)** instead of the function **=SUM(E11:E13)**.

Note: For information on formulas and functions, see pages 82 to 89.

ADD A COMMENT

You can add a comment to a cell in your worksheet. A comment can be a note, explanation or reminder about data you need to verify later.

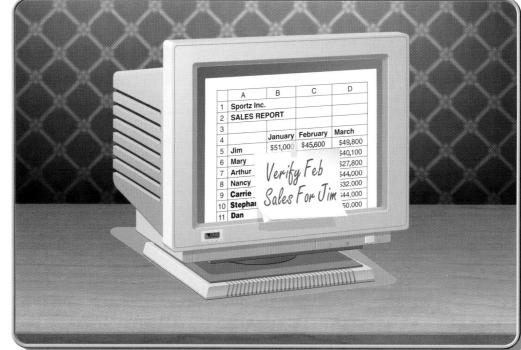

1 Click the cell you want to add a comment to.

2 Click **Insert**.

3 Click **Comment**.

Note: If Comment does not appear on the menu, position the mouse ⍾ over the bottom of the menu to display the menu option.

■ A yellow comment box appears, displaying your name.

4 Type the comment you want to add.

5 When you finish typing your comment, click outside the comment box.

How can I display all the comments in my worksheet at once?

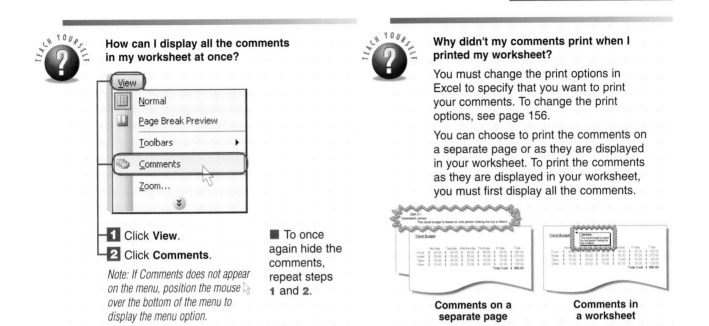

1 Click **View**.

2 Click **Comments**.

Note: If Comments does not appear on the menu, position the mouse over the bottom of the menu to display the menu option.

■ To once again hide the comments, repeat steps **1** and **2**.

Why didn't my comments print when I printed my worksheet?

You must change the print options in Excel to specify that you want to print your comments. To change the print options, see page 156.

You can choose to print the comments on a separate page or as they are displayed in your worksheet. To print the comments as they are displayed in your worksheet, you must first display all the comments.

Comments on a separate page

Comments in a worksheet

DISPLAY A COMMENT

■ A red triangle (◥) appears in a cell that contains a comment.

1 Position the mouse ⊹ over the cell containing the comment you want to view.

■ The comment box appears, displaying the comment.

2 To hide the comment box, move the mouse ⊹ outside the cell.

DELETE A COMMENT

1 Click the cell containing the comment you want to delete.

2 Click **Edit**.

3 Click **Clear**.

4 Click **Comments**.

■ The red triangle (◥) disappears from the cell.

INSERT SYMBOLS

You can insert symbols that do not appear on your keyboard into your worksheet.

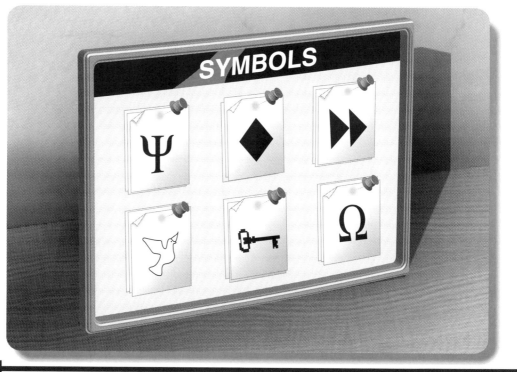

INSERT SYMBOLS

1 Click a cell in your worksheet where you want a symbol to appear.

2 Click **Insert**.

3 Click **Symbol**.

Note: If Symbol does not appear on the menu, position the mouse ⬦ over the bottom of the menu to display the menu option.

■ The Symbol dialog box appears, displaying the symbols for the current font.

4 To display the symbols for another font, click 🔽 in this area.

5 Click the font that provides the symbols you want to display.

How can I quickly insert a symbol I recently used?

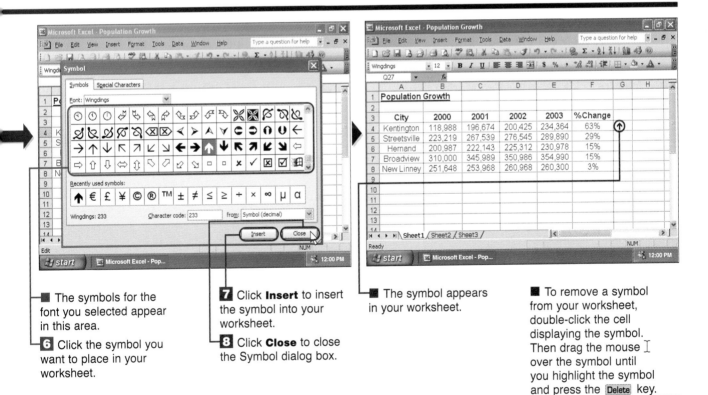

1 Perform steps **1** to **3** below to display the Symbol dialog box.

■ This area displays the most recently used symbols.

2 Double-click the symbol you want to place in your worksheet.

3 Click **Close** to close the Symbol dialog box.

■ The symbols for the font you selected appear in this area.

6 Click the symbol you want to place in your worksheet.

7 Click **Insert** to insert the symbol into your worksheet.

8 Click **Close** to close the Symbol dialog box.

■ The symbol appears in your worksheet.

■ To remove a symbol from your worksheet, double-click the cell displaying the symbol. Then drag the mouse ⟂ over the symbol until you highlight the symbol and press the Delete key.

INSERT A STOCK QUOTE

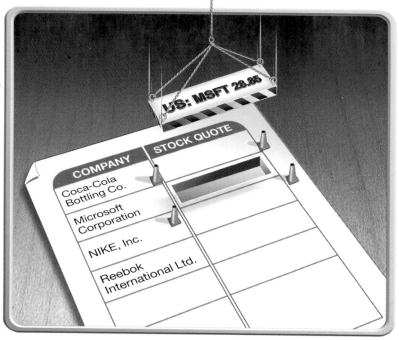

You can use Excel's Research task pane to insert stock quotes into your worksheet.

Excel allows you to access stock quotes through MSN Money Stock Quotes.

INSERT A STOCK QUOTE

1 Click 🔍 to display the Research task pane.

■ The Research task pane appears.

2 Click this area and type the financial symbol for the stock quote you want to find.

Note: If this area contains text, drag the mouse ⊥ over the text to select the text before performing step 2.

3 Click this area to display a list of resources you can use to search for information.

4 Click **MSN Money Stock Quotes**.

How can I find the financial symbol of a company I want to insert a stock quote for?

You can find financial symbols by using the stock symbol lookup tool available at the finance.yahoo.com/l Web site. The following is a list of financial symbols for some common companies.

Company Name	Symbol
eBay Inc.	EBAY
FedEx Corporation	FDX
Goodyear Tire & Rubber	GT
Wal-Mart Stores Inc.	WMT
Wells Fargo & Company	WFC

Can I access detailed information about a company of interest using the Research task pane?

Yes. You can use Gale Company Profiles to find detailed company information. Perform steps **1** to **4** below, except select **Gale Company Profiles** in step **4**. Information such as the company's address, phone and fax numbers, number of employees and fiscal year end date appear in the Research task pane.

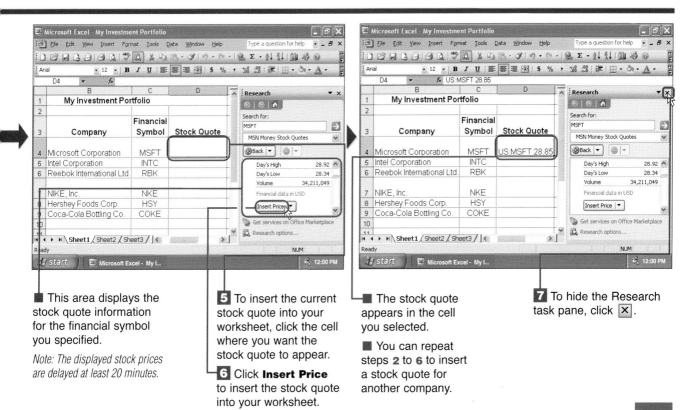

■ This area displays the stock quote information for the financial symbol you specified.

Note: The displayed stock prices are delayed at least 20 minutes.

5 To insert the current stock quote into your worksheet, click the cell where you want the stock quote to appear.

6 Click **Insert Price** to insert the stock quote into your worksheet.

■ The stock quote appears in the cell you selected.

■ You can repeat steps **2** to **6** to insert a stock quote for another company.

7 To hide the Research task pane, click ✕.

CHAPTER 4

Work With Rows and Columns

Are you wondering how to adjust, insert, delete or hide rows and columns in a worksheet? Read this chapter to find out how.

Change Column Width 66

Change Row Height 67

Insert a Row or Column....................68

Delete a Row or Column 70

Insert Cells.....................................72

Delete Cells 73

Hide Columns 74

Freeze Rows and Columns 76

Split a Worksheet............................78

Name	Address	C			
Sue Jones	65 Apple Tree Lane	Aus			
Matt Andrews	4 Steven Drive	Mi			
Jim Smith	8910 Colt Rd.	Los Ang	PA	19104	21
Karen Taylor	21 Kirk Drive	Philadelphia	AR	72231	501-5
Mandy Roberts	44 Sunset St.	Little Rock	NY	10199	212-
Sam Hunter	689 Walker Ave.	New York	OR	97208	503
Phillip Morgan	779 Pine St.	Portland			

CHANGE COLUMN WIDTH

You can change the width of columns to improve the appearance of your worksheet and display any hidden data.

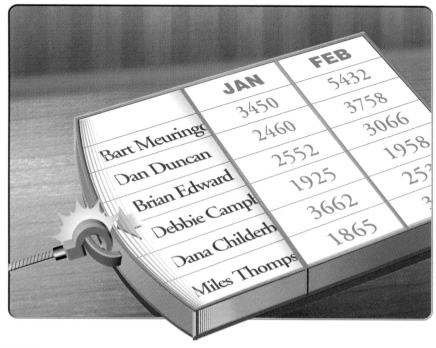

Data in a cell may be hidden if the cell is not wide enough to display the data and the neighboring cell also contains data. You can increase the column width to display all the data in the cell.

CHANGE COLUMN WIDTH

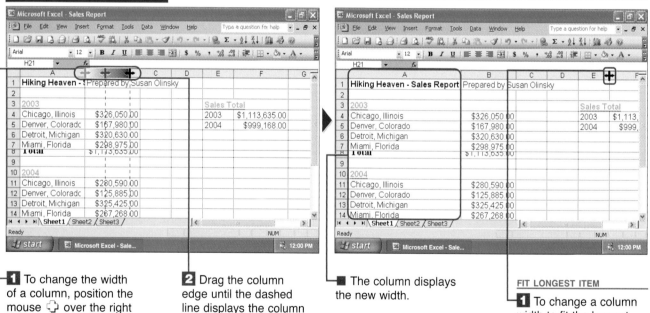

1 To change the width of a column, position the mouse ⇩ over the right edge of the column heading (⇩ changes to ✛).

2 Drag the column edge until the dashed line displays the column width you want.

■ The column displays the new width.

FIT LONGEST ITEM

1 To change a column width to fit the longest item in the column, double-click the right edge of the column heading.

CHANGE ROW HEIGHT

You can change the height of rows to add space between the rows of data in your worksheet.

CHANGE ROW HEIGHT

1 To change the height of a row, position the mouse ⊕ over the bottom edge of the row heading (⊕ changes to ✛).

2 Drag the row edge until the dashed line displays the row height you want.

■ The row displays the new height.

FIT TALLEST ITEM

1 To change a row height to fit the tallest item in the row, double-click the bottom edge of the row heading.

INSERT A ROW OR COLUMN

You can add a row or column to your worksheet to insert additional data.

EMPLOYEE HOURS

	Week 1	Week 2	Week 3
Deb Shuter	45	32	37
Jen Wright	35	33	37
Dave Bibby	20	38	35
Jeff Evans	30	35	36
Sue Thomas	35	36	39
Julie Simak	37	38	41
Kevin Cooper	38	42	42

When you add a row or column, Excel automatically adjusts the row numbers and column letters in your worksheet for you.

INSERT A ROW

Excel will insert a row above the row you select.

1 To select a row, click the row number.

2 Click **Insert**.

3 Click **Rows**.

■ The new row appears and all the rows that follow shift downward.

■ To deselect a row, click any cell.

68

Do I need to adjust my formulas when I insert a row or column?

No. When you insert a row or column, Excel automatically updates any formulas affected by the insertion. For information on formulas, see pages 82 to 85.

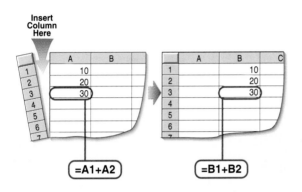

Insert Column Here

=A1+A2   =B1+B2

How do I insert several rows or columns at once?

You can use one of the methods shown below to insert several rows or columns at once, but you must first select the number of rows or columns you want to insert. For example, to insert two columns, select two columns and then perform steps **2** and **3** below. To select multiple rows or columns, see page 11.

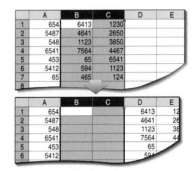

INSERT A COLUMN

Excel will insert a column to the left of the column you select.

1 To select a column, click the column letter.

2 Click **Insert**.

3 Click **Columns**.

■ The new column appears and all the columns that follow shift to the right.

■ To deselect a column, click any cell.

DELETE A ROW OR COLUMN

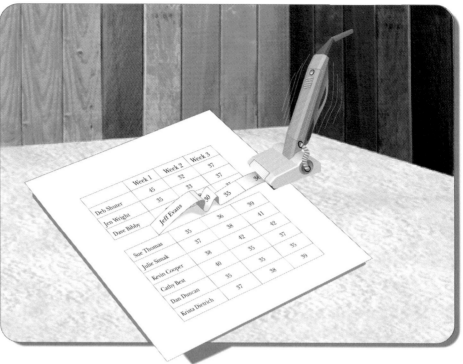

You can delete a row or column to remove data you no longer want to display in your worksheet.

When you delete a row, the remaining rows in your worksheet shift upward. When you delete a column, the remaining columns shift to the left. Excel automatically adjusts the row numbers and column letters in your worksheet for you.

DELETE A ROW

1 To select the row you want to delete, click the row number.

2 Click **Edit**.

3 Click **Delete** to delete the row.

■ The row disappears and all the rows that follow shift upward.

■ To deselect a row, click any cell.

Why did #REF! appear in a cell after I deleted a row or column?

If #REF! appears in a cell in your worksheet, you may have deleted data needed to calculate a formula. Before you delete a row or column, make sure the row or column does not contain data that is used in a formula. For information on formulas, see pages 82 to 85.

How do I delete several rows or columns at once?

You can use one of the methods shown below to delete several rows or columns at once, but you must first select the rows or columns you want to delete. For example, to delete three columns, select the columns and then perform steps **2** and **3** below. To select multiple rows or columns, see page 11.

DELETE A COLUMN

1 To select the column you want to delete, click the column letter.

2 Click **Edit**.

3 Click **Delete** to delete the column.

■ The column disappears and all the columns that follow shift to the left.

■ To deselect a column, click any cell.

INSERT CELLS

If you want to add new data to the middle of existing data in your worksheet, you can insert cells. The surrounding cells move to make room for the new cells.

Car Expenses			
	Janua... $ 102.00		
Car Loan	$ 451.00	$ 451.00	
Fuel		$ 89.00	
Insurance	$ 177.00	$ 177.00	
Parking	$ 75.00	$ 68.00	
Maintenance	$ 356.12	$ 32.89	
Miscellaneous	$ 12.50	$ 42.39	

INSERT CELLS

1 Select the cells where you want to insert new cells. To select cells, see page 10.

Note: Excel will insert the same number of cells as you select.

2 Click **Insert**.

3 Click **Cells**.

Note: If Cells does not appear on the menu, position the mouse over the bottom of the menu to display the menu option.

■ The Insert dialog box appears.

4 Click an option to shift the surrounding cells to the right or down to make room for the new cells (○ changes to ◉).

5 Click **OK** to insert the cells.

■ Excel inserts the new cells and shifts the surrounding cells in the direction you specified.

■ To deselect cells, click any cell.

You can remove cells you no longer need from your worksheet. The surrounding cells move to fill the empty space.

	Income	Expenses	Profit
January	$ 245,000	$ 203,345	$ 41,655
February	$ 245,995	$ 199,900	$ 75,990
March	$ 250,000	$ 210,700	$ 28,400
April	$ 275,890	$ 210,445	$ 10,540
May	$ 239,100	$ 207,600	$ 6,190
June	$ 220,985	$ 209,200	$ 26,470
July	$ 213,790		
August	$ 235,670		

$ 209,560 $ 36,435
00,480 $ 49,520

DELETE CELLS

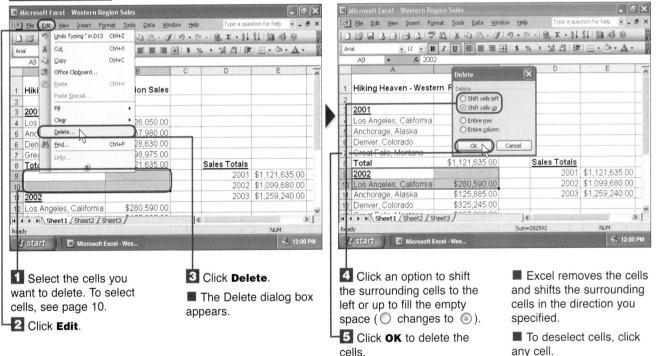

1 Select the cells you want to delete. To select cells, see page 10.

2 Click **Edit**.

3 Click **Delete**.

■ The Delete dialog box appears.

4 Click an option to shift the surrounding cells to the left or up to fill the empty space (○ changes to ◉).

5 Click **OK** to delete the cells.

■ Excel removes the cells and shifts the surrounding cells in the direction you specified.

■ To deselect cells, click any cell.

HIDE COLUMNS

You can hide columns in your worksheet to reduce the amount of data displayed on your screen or temporarily remove confidential data.

You can hide a single column or multiple columns in your worksheet.

Hidden columns will not appear when you print your worksheet. This allows you to produce a printed copy of your worksheet that does not include unneeded or confidential data.

HIDE COLUMNS

1 Select the columns you want to hide. To select columns, see page 11.

2 Click **Format**.

3 Click **Column**.

4 Click **Hide** to hide the columns.

■ The columns you selected disappear from your worksheet.

■ To deselect cells, click any cell.

**Will hiding columns affect the formulas
and functions in my worksheet?**

Hiding columns will not affect the results of
formulas and functions in your worksheet.
Excel will use data in the hidden columns
to perform calculations even though the
data is hidden from view. For information
on formulas and functions, see pages 82
to 89.

Can I hide rows in my worksheet?

Yes. Select the rows you want to hide. To
select rows, see page 11. Then perform
steps **2** to **4** on page 74, selecting **Row** in
step **3**. To display the hidden rows, select
the rows directly above and below the
hidden rows. Then perform steps **2**
to **4** on page 75, selecting **Row** in step **3**.

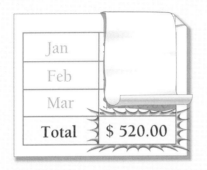

DISPLAY HIDDEN COLUMNS

1 Select the columns on
each side of the hidden
columns. To select columns,
see page 11.

■ If the hidden column is the
first column in the worksheet,
click this area to select all the
columns in the worksheet.

2 Click **Format**.

3 Click **Column**.

4 Click **Unhide** to display
the hidden columns.

■ The hidden columns
reappear in your worksheet.

■ To deselect cells,
click any cell.

FREEZE ROWS AND COLUMNS

You can freeze rows and columns in your worksheet so they will not move. This allows you to keep row and column labels displayed on your screen as you move through a large worksheet.

FREEZE ROWS AND COLUMNS

Excel will freeze the rows above and the columns to the left of the cell you select.

1 To select a cell, click the cell.

2 Click **Window**.

3 Click **Freeze Panes**.

Can I freeze only rows or only columns in my worksheet?

Yes. To freeze only rows, select the row below the rows you want to freeze. To freeze only columns, select the column to the right of the columns you want to freeze. Then perform steps **2** and **3** below. To select a row or column, see page 11.

	A	B	C	D	E	F
1						
2						
3						
4						
5						
6						
7						

	A	B	C	D	E	F
1						
2						
3						
4						
5						
6						
7						

Freeze Only Rows   **Freeze Only Columns**

How do I unfreeze rows and columns in my worksheet?

When you no longer want to keep rows and columns frozen on your screen, perform steps **2** and **3** below, selecting **Unfreeze Panes** in step **3**.

■ A horizontal line appears in your worksheet.

■ The rows above the horizontal line are frozen. These rows will remain on your screen as you move through your worksheet.

■ To move through the rows below the horizontal line, click ⬆ or ⬇.

■ A vertical line appears in your worksheet.

■ The columns to the left of the vertical line are frozen. These columns will remain on your screen as you move through your worksheet.

■ To move through the columns to the right of the vertical line, click ◀ or ▶.

77

SPLIT A WORKSHEET

You can split your worksheet into separate sections. This allows you to display different areas of a large worksheet at the same time.

Each section of a split worksheet contains a copy of the entire worksheet.

SPLIT A WORKSHEET VERTICALLY

1 Position the mouse over this area (changes to ↔).

2 Drag the mouse ↔ to where you want to split your worksheet.

■ The worksheet splits vertically into two sections.

■ To move through the columns to the left of the dividing line, click ◄ or ►.

■ To move through the columns to the right of the dividing line, click ◄ or ►.

When I print a worksheet that is split into separate sections, will Excel print multiple copies of the worksheet?

No. Excel will print the worksheet only once. The dividing line that splits your worksheet will not appear when you print the worksheet.

How do I remove a split from my worksheet?

Position the mouse ⌐ over the dividing line in your worksheet (⌐ changes to ◄╫► or ╪). Then double-click the dividing line to remove the split.

SPLIT A WORKSHEET HORIZONTALLY

1 Position the mouse ⌐ over this area (⌐ changes to ╪).

2 Drag the mouse ╪ to where you want to split your worksheet.

■ The worksheet splits horizontally into two sections.

■ To move through the rows above the dividing line, click ▲ or ▼.

■ To move through the rows below the dividing line, click ▲ or ▼.

CHAPTER 5

Work With Formulas and Functions

Would you like to perform calculations on the data in your worksheet? Learn how in this chapter.

Introduction to Formulas and Functions 82

Enter a Formula 84

Enter a Function 86

Perform Common Calculations 90

Copy a Formula 92

Display All Formulas 96

Check Errors in Formulas....................98

Create Scenarios 100

Create a Scenario Summary Report...104

INTRODUCTION TO FORMULAS AND FUNCTIONS

A formula allows you to calculate and analyze data in your worksheet.

A formula always begins with an equal sign (=).

OPERATORS

A formula can contain one or more operators. An operator specifies the type of calculation you want to perform.

Arithmetic Operators

You can use arithmetic operators to perform mathematical calculations.

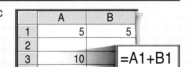

Operator	Description
+	Addition (A1+B1)
-	Subtraction (A1-B1)
*	Multiplication (A1*B1)
/	Division (A1/B1)
%	Percent (A1%)
^	Exponentiation (A1^B1)

Comparison Operators

You can use comparison operators to compare two values. Comparison operators return a value of TRUE or FALSE.

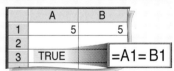

Operator	Description
=	Equal to (A1=B1)
>	Greater than (A1>B1)
<	Less than (A1<B1)
>=	Greater than or equal to (A1>=B1)
<=	Less than or equal to (A1<=B1)
<>	Not equal to (A1<>B1)

ORDER OF CALCULATIONS

When a formula contains more than one operator, Excel performs the calculations in a specific order.

	Order of Calculations
1	Percent (%)
2	Exponentiation (^)
3	Multiplication (*) and Division (/)
4	Addition (+) and Subtraction (-)
5	Comparison operators

	A	
1	2	=A1+A2+A3*A4 =2+4+6*8=54
2	4	=A1+(A2+A3)*A4 =2+(4+6)*8=82
3	6	
4	8	=A1*(A3-A2)+A4 =2*(6-4)+8=12
5		
6		=A2^A1+A3 =4^2+6=22

You can use parentheses ( ) to change the order in which Excel performs calculations. Excel will perform the calculations inside the parentheses first.

CELL REFERENCES

When entering formulas, use cell references instead of actual data whenever possible. For example, enter the formula =A1+A2 instead of =10+20.

When you use cell references and you change a number used in a formula, Excel will automatically redo the calculation for you.

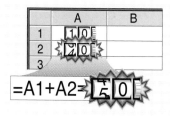

FUNCTIONS

A function is a ready-to-use formula that you can use to perform a calculation on the data in your worksheet. Examples of commonly used functions include AVERAGE, COUNT, MAX and SUM.

	A	
1	10	
2	20	=AVERAGE(A1:A4) =(10+20+30+40)/4 = 25
3	30	
4	40	=COUNT(A1:A4) = 4
5		=MAX(A1:A4) = 40
6		=SUM(A1:A4) =10+20+30+40 = 100

■ A function always begins with an equal sign (=).

■ The data Excel will use to calculate a function is enclosed in parentheses ( ).

Specify Individual Cells

When a comma (,) separates cell references in a function, Excel uses each cell to perform the calculation. For example, =SUM(A1,A2,A3) is the same as the formula =A1+A2+A3.

Specify a Group of Cells

When a colon (:) separates cell references in a function, Excel uses the specified cells and all cells between them to perform the calculation. For example, =SUM(A1:A3) is the same as the formula =A1+A2+A3.

ENTER A FORMULA

You can enter a formula into any cell in your worksheet. A formula helps you calculate and analyze data in your worksheet.

When entering formulas, you should use cell references instead of actual data whenever possible.

A formula always begins with an equal sign (=).

ENTER A FORMULA

1 Click the cell where you want to enter a formula.

2 Type an equal sign (=) to begin the formula.

3 Type the formula and then press the Enter key.

Note: As you enter the formula, Excel adds a colored outline to each cell you refer to in the formula.

■ The result of the calculation appears in the cell.

4 To view the formula you entered, click the cell containing the formula.

■ The formula bar displays the formula for the cell.

What happens if I change a number used in a formula?

When you use cell references and you change a number used in a formula, Excel will automatically redo the calculation for you.

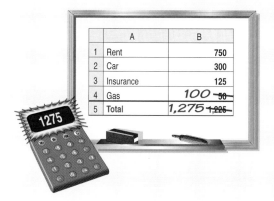

How can I quickly enter cell references into a formula?

To quickly enter cell references, perform steps 1 and 2 on page 84 and then click the first cell you want to use in the formula. Type the operator you want to use to perform the calculation and then click the next cell you want to use in the formula. When you finish entering cell references and operators, press the Enter key to perform the calculation.

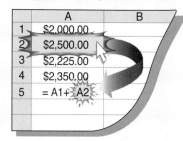

EDIT A FORMULA

1 Double-click the cell containing the formula you want to change.

■ The formula appears in the cell.

■ Excel outlines each cell used in the formula with a different color.

2 Press the ← or → key to move the flashing insertion point to where you want to remove or add characters.

■ To remove the character to the left of the insertion point, press the Backspace key.

3 To add data where the insertion point flashes on your screen, type the data.

4 When you finish making changes to the formula, press the Enter key.

85

ENTER A FUNCTION

Excel helps you enter functions into your worksheet. Functions allow you to perform calculations without having to type long, complex formulas.

=SUM(A1:A4)
=AVERAGE(A1:A4)
=ROUND(E4,2)
=COUNT(B1:B6)
=MAX(E1:E4)

Excel offers over 200 functions to help you analyze data in your worksheet. There are financial functions, math and trigonometry functions, date and time functions, statistical functions and many more.

ENTER A FUNCTION

1 Click the cell where you want to enter a function.

2 Click 𝑓𝑥 to enter a function.

■ The Insert Function dialog box appears.

3 Click this area to display the categories of available functions.

4 Click the category containing the function you want to use.

*Note: If you do not know which category contains the function you want to use, select **All** to display a list of all the functions.*

Can Excel help me find the function I should use to perform a calculation?

If you do not know which function to use to perform a calculation, you can have Excel recommend a function.

1 Perform steps **1** and **2** below to display the Insert Function dialog box.

2 Type a brief description of the calculation you want to perform and then press the **Enter** key.

■ This area displays a list of recommended functions you can use to perform the calculation. You can perform steps **5** to **11** below to use a function Excel recommends.

■ This area displays the functions in the category you selected.

5 Click the function you want to use.

■ This area describes the function you selected.

6 Click **OK** to continue.

■ The Function Arguments dialog box appears. If the dialog box covers data you want to use in the function, you can move the dialog box to a new location.

7 To move the dialog box, position the mouse over the title bar and then drag the dialog box to a new location.

CONTINUED

ENTER A FUNCTION

When entering
a function, you
must specify
which numbers
you want to use
in the calculation.
You may need to
specify several
numbers or only
one number,
depending on
the function
you are using.

ENTER A FUNCTION (CONTINUED)

■ This area displays
boxes where you enter
the numbers you want
to use in the function.

■ This area describes
the numbers you need
to enter.

8 To enter the first
number for the function,
click the cell that
contains the number.

*Note: If the number you want
to use does not appear in your
worksheet, type the number.*

■ The cell reference for
the number appears in
this area.

Can I enter a function by myself?

If you know the name of the function you want to use, you can type the function and cell references directly into a cell in your worksheet. You must start the function with an equal sign (=), enclose the cell references in parentheses ( ) and separate each cell reference with a comma (,). You can also separate cell references with a colon (:) to indicate that Excel should include the specified cells and all the cells between them in the function.

■ When you type a function directly into a cell, a yellow box appears, displaying the name of the function. You can click the name of the function to display help information about the function.

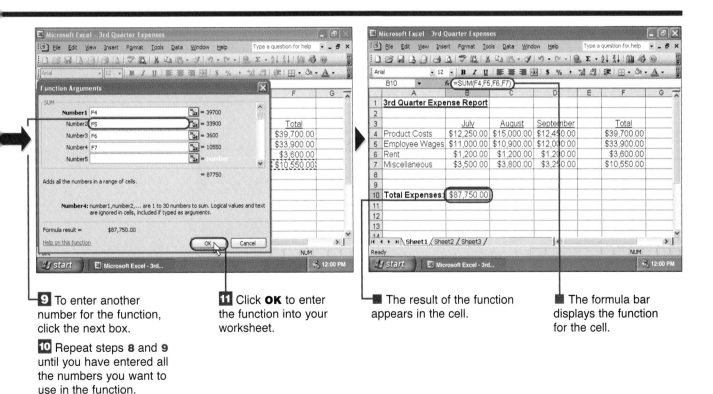

■9 To enter another number for the function, click the next box.

■10 Repeat steps **8** and **9** until you have entered all the numbers you want to use in the function.

■11 Click **OK** to enter the function into your worksheet.

■ The result of the function appears in the cell.

■ The formula bar displays the function for the cell.

PERFORM COMMON CALCULATIONS

You can quickly perform common calculations on numbers in your worksheet. For example, you can calculate the sum of a list of numbers.

PERFORM COMMON CALCULATIONS

1 Click the cell below or to the right of the cells containing the numbers you want to include in the calculation.

2 Click ⬝ in this area to display a list of common calculations.

Note: If Σ ▾ is not displayed, click ⬝ on the Standard toolbar to display the button.

3 Click the calculation you want to perform.

Note: If you want to quickly add the numbers, you can click Σ instead of performing steps 2 and 3.

■ A moving outline appears around the cells that Excel will include in the calculation.

■ If Excel outlines the wrong cells, you can select the cells that contain the numbers you want to include in the calculation. To select cells, see page 10.

■ The cell you selected in step **1** displays the function Excel will use to perform the calculation.

What common calculations can I perform?

Sum	Adds a list of numbers.
Average	Calculates the average value of a list of numbers.
Count	Calculates the number of values in a list.
Max	Finds the largest value in a list of numbers.
Min	Finds the smallest value in a list of numbers.

Can I perform calculations on several columns or rows of data at the same time?

Yes. Select the cells below or to the right of the cells that contain the numbers you want to include in the calculation. To select cells, see page 10. Then perform steps **2** and **3** below.

	Product A	Product B	Month Totals
January	10	5	
February	20	6	
March	30	3	

	Product A	Product B	Month Totals
January	10	5	15
February	20	6	26
March	30	3	33

4 Press the Enter key to perform the calculation.

■ The result of the calculation appears.

QUICKLY ADD NUMBERS

You can quickly display the sum of a list of numbers without entering a formula into your worksheet.

1 Select the cells containing the numbers you want to add. To select cells, see page 10.

■ This area displays the sum of the cells you selected.

COPY A FORMULA

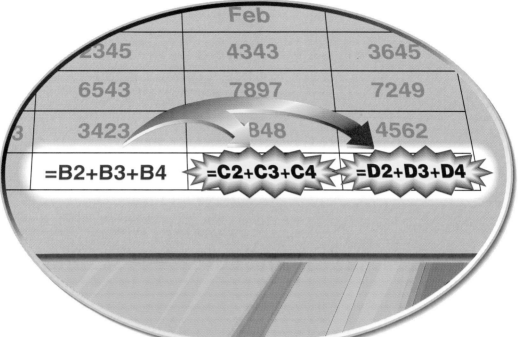

If you want to use the same formula several times in your worksheet, you can save time by copying the formula.

=B2+B3+B4 =C2+C3+C4 =D2+D3+D4

COPY A FORMULA—USING RELATIVE REFERENCES

1 Enter the formula you want to copy to other cells. To enter a formula, see page 84.

2 Click the cell containing the formula you want to copy.

■ The formula bar displays the formula for the cell.

3 Position the mouse ⬚ over the bottom right corner of the cell (⬚ changes to +).

4 Drag the mouse + over the cells you want to receive a copy of the formula.

What is a relative reference?

A relative reference is a cell reference that changes when you copy a formula.

	A	B	C
1	10	20	5
2	20	30	10
3	30	40	20
4	60	90	35
5			

=A1+A2+A3   ➡   =B1+B2+B3   =C1+C2+C3

This cell contains the formula **=A1+A2+A3**.

When you copy the formula to other cells in your worksheet, Excel automatically changes the cell references in the new formulas.

■ The results of the formulas appear.

■ The Auto Fill Options button also appears. You can click the button and then select an option to change the way Excel copies the formula. For example, you can specify that Excel should not use the formatting from the original cell.

5 To view one of the new formulas, click a cell that received a copy of the formula.

■ The formula bar displays the formula with the new cell references.

CONTINUED

COPY A FORMULA

You can copy a formula to other cells in your worksheet to save time. If you do not want Excel to change a cell reference when you copy a formula, you can use an absolute reference.

	A	B	C	D
1		R. Brown	J. Smith	K. Turner
2	Sales	100	200	300
3				
4	Commission	=$A$7*B2	=$A$7*C2	=$A$7*D2
5				
6	Commission Rate			
7	0.2			

COPY A FORMULA—USING ABSOLUTE REFERENCES

1 Enter the data you want to use in all the formulas.

2 Enter the formula you want to copy to other cells. To enter a formula, see page 84.

3 Click the cell containing the formula you want to copy.

■ The formula bar displays the formula for the cell.

4 Position the mouse ⊕ over the bottom right corner of the cell (⊕ changes to +).

5 Drag the mouse + over the cells you want to receive a copy of the formula.

94

What is an absolute reference?

An absolute reference is a cell reference that does not change when you copy a formula. To make a cell reference absolute, type a dollar sign ($) before both the column letter and row number, such as **$A$7**.

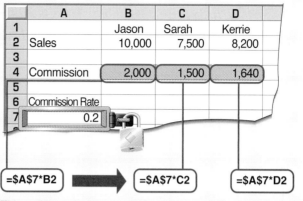

	A	B	C	D
1		Jason	Sarah	Kerrie
2	Sales	10,000	7,500	8,200
3				
4	Commission	2,000	1,500	1,640
5				
6	Commission Rate			
7	0.2			

=$A$7*B2   =$A$7*C2   =$A$7*D2

This cell contains the formula **=$A$7*B2**.

When you copy the formula to other cells in your worksheet, Excel does not change the absolute reference in the new formulas.

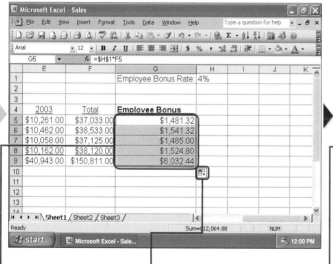

■ The results of the formulas appear.

■ The Auto Fill Options button also appears. You can click the button and then select an option to change the way Excel copies the formula. For example, you can specify that Excel should not use the formatting from the original cell.

6 To view one of the new formulas, click a cell that received a copy of the formula.

■ The formula bar displays the formula with the absolute reference and the new cell reference.

DISPLAY ALL FORMULAS

You can display the formulas in your worksheet instead of the results of the calculations.

	A	B	C	D
		Week 1	Week 2	Total
1			$ 2,200	=B2+C2
2	Tim	$ 2,000	$ 1,750	=B3+C3
3	Michael	$ 1,500	$ 1,500	=B4+C4
4	Monica	$ 1,750	$ 2,000	=B5+C5
5	Jerry	$ 2,100	$ 1,600	=B6+C6
6	Laurie	$ 1,800	$ 1,500	=B7+C7
7	Roger	$ 1,250	$ 2,300	=B8+C8
8	Mike	$ 2,100	$ 2,150	=B9+C9
9	Lisa	$ 1,950	$ 1,650	=B10+C10
10	Pat	$ 1,350	$ 1,6	=B11+C11
11	June	$ 1,250		

This is useful when you want to review or edit all the formulas in your worksheet.

DISPLAY ALL FORMULAS

■ These cells contain formulas. By default, Excel displays formula results in your worksheet.

■ The formula bar displays the formula for the active cell.

1 To display the formulas in your worksheet, click **Tools**.

2 Click **Options**.

■ The Options dialog box appears.

Why does the Formula Auditing toolbar appear when I display the formulas in my worksheet?

The Formula Auditing toolbar contains buttons that you can use to work with the formulas in your worksheet. For example, you can click one of the following buttons to work with your formulas.

Checks errors in formulas and displays a dialog box that allows you to correct errors. For information on errors in formulas, see page 98.

Add a comment to a cell that contains a formula. For information on adding comments, see page 58.

Is there another way to display the formulas in my worksheet?

You can use the keyboard to switch between the display of formulas and formula results in your worksheet. To change the display at any time, press and hold down the Ctrl key and then press the ~ key.

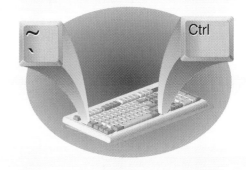

3 Click the **View** tab.

4 Click **Formulas** (☐ changes to ☑).

5 Click **OK** to confirm your change.

■ The formulas appear in your worksheet.

■ Excel automatically adjusts the column widths to clearly display the formulas.

■ To once again show the formula results in your worksheet, repeat steps **1** to **5** (☑ changes to ☐ in step **4**).

CHECK ERRORS IN FORMULAS

Excel can help you determine the cause of an error in a formula.

Excel checks your formulas for errors as you work and marks cells that display certain error messages. For information on common error messages, see page 99.

Errors in formulas are often the result of typing mistakes. Once you determine the cause of an error, you can edit the formula to correct the error. To edit a formula, see page 85.

CHECK ERRORS IN FORMULAS

■ An error message appears in a cell when Excel cannot properly calculate the result of a formula.

■ A triangle appears in the top left corner of a cell that contains an error when Excel can help you determine the cause of the error.

1 To determine the cause of an error, click a cell displaying a triangle.

■ The Error Checking button (◈) appears.

2 Click the Error Checking button to display options you can use to determine the cause of the error.

■ This area displays the name of the error.

3 You can click **Help on this error** to view help information for the error.

■ You can click **Show Calculation Steps** to have Excel help you evaluate the cause of the error.

COMMON ERRORS IN FORMULAS

An error message appears when
Excel cannot properly calculate
or display the result of a formula.

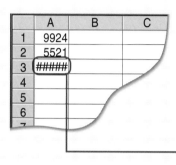

#####

The column is too
narrow to display the
result of the calculation.
You can change the
column width to display
the result. To change
the column width, see
page 66.

■ This cell contains
the formula =A1*A2

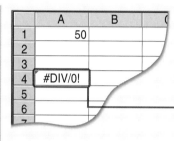

#DIV/0!

The formula divides a
number by zero (0).
Excel considers a
blank cell to have a
value of zero.

■ This cell contains
the formula =A1/A2
=50/0

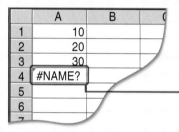

#NAME?

The formula contains a
function name or cell
reference Excel does
not recognize.

■ This cell contains the
formula =AQ+A2+A3

In this example, the cell
reference A1 was typed
incorrectly.

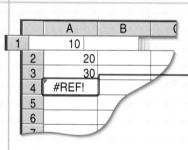

#REF!

The formula refers to a
cell that is not valid.

■ This cell contains the
formula =A1+A2+A3

In this example, a row
containing a cell used in
the formula was deleted.

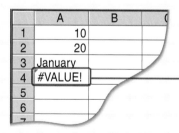

#VALUE!

The formula refers to a
cell that Excel cannot
use in a calculation.

■ This cell contains the
formula =A1+A2+A3

In this example, a cell
used in the formula
contains text.

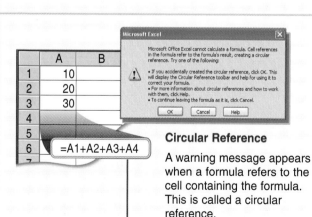

Circular Reference

A warning message appears
when a formula refers to the
cell containing the formula.
This is called a circular
reference.

■ This cell contains the
formula =A1+A2+A3+A4

CREATE SCENARIOS

A scenario is a set of alternate values for data in your worksheet. You can create multiple scenarios to see how different values affect your worksheet data.

CAR LOAN

Interest Rate	7%
# of Payments	60
Loan Amount	$ 20,000.00
Monthly Payment	$ 396.02

6%
36

Scenarios

Creating scenarios allows you to consider various outcomes. For example, you can create scenarios to see how changing interest rates will affect your car payments.

CREATE SCENARIOS

1 Select the cells containing the data you want to change in the scenarios. To select cells, see page 10.

2 Click **Tools**.

3 Click **Scenarios**.

Note: If Scenarios does not appear on the menu, position the mouse ⮞ over the bottom of the menu to display the menu option.

■ The Scenario Manager dialog box appears.

4 Click **Add** to create a new scenario.

Should I save the original data as a scenario?

Yes. Excel will only keep the original data if you save the data as a scenario. You can use the scenario you create for the original data to redisplay the data at any time.

What should I consider when entering a description for a scenario?

The description you enter for a scenario should clearly explain the purpose of the scenario. This will help you easily distinguish the scenario from other scenarios you create.

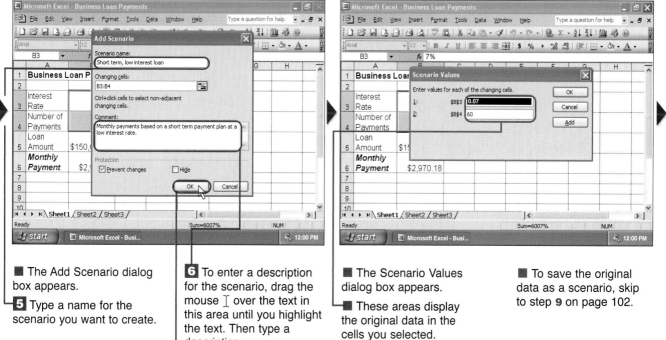

■ The Add Scenario dialog box appears.

5 Type a name for the scenario you want to create.

6 To enter a description for the scenario, drag the mouse I over the text in this area until you highlight the text. Then type a description.

7 Click **OK** to continue.

■ The Scenario Values dialog box appears.

■ These areas display the original data in the cells you selected.

■ To save the original data as a scenario, skip to step **9** on page 102.

CONTINUED

CREATE SCENARIOS

Excel saves your scenarios with your worksheet. You can display a different scenario at any time.

CAR LOAN			
		6%	
		36	
Interest Rate	7%		
# of Payments	60		
Loan Amount	$ 20,000.00		
Monthly Payment	$ 396.02		

CREATE SCENARIOS (CONTINUED)

8 To change the values for the scenario, double-click a value and then type a new value. Repeat this step for each value you want to change.

9 Click **OK** to confirm the values.

■ The Scenario Manager dialog box reappears.

■ The name of the scenario appears in this area.

10 To create another scenario, repeat steps **4** to **9** starting on page 100.

11 When you finish creating scenarios, click **Close** to close the dialog box.

How can I move the Scenario Manager dialog box so it is not covering the data in my worksheet?

To move the Scenario Manager dialog box, position the mouse ↖ over the title bar and then drag the dialog box to a new location.

How do I delete a scenario I no longer need?

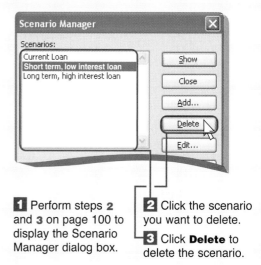

1 Perform steps **2** and **3** on page 100 to display the Scenario Manager dialog box.

2 Click the scenario you want to delete.

3 Click **Delete** to delete the scenario.

DISPLAY A SCENARIO

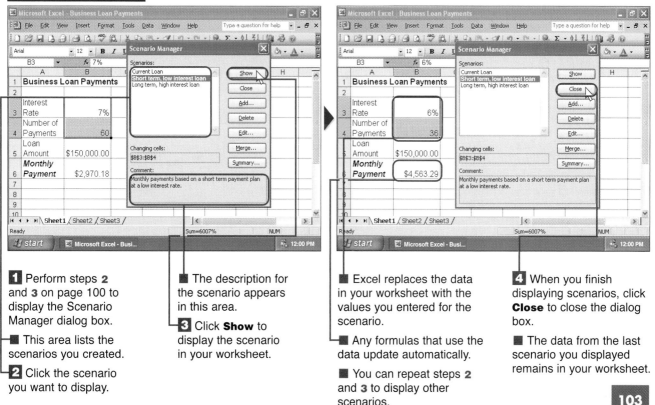

1 Perform steps **2** and **3** on page 100 to display the Scenario Manager dialog box.

■ This area lists the scenarios you created.

2 Click the scenario you want to display.

■ The description for the scenario appears in this area.

3 Click **Show** to display the scenario in your worksheet.

■ Excel replaces the data in your worksheet with the values you entered for the scenario.

■ Any formulas that use the data update automatically.

■ You can repeat steps **2** and **3** to display other scenarios.

4 When you finish displaying scenarios, click **Close** to close the dialog box.

■ The data from the last scenario you displayed remains in your worksheet.

CREATE A SCENARIO SUMMARY REPORT

You can create a summary report to display the values for each scenario and the effects of the scenarios on the calculations in your worksheet.

Summary reports are useful when you want to quickly review or print the results of all the scenarios you created.

CREATE A SCENARIO SUMMARY REPORT

1 Click **Tools**.

2 Click **Scenarios**.

Note: If Scenarios does not appear on the menu, position the mouse ⌖ over the bottom of the menu to display the menu option.

■ The Scenario Manager dialog box appears.

3 Click **Summary** to create a summary report.

■ The Scenario Summary dialog box appears.

Why does the Scenario Summary worksheet display plus (+) and minus (-) signs?

Excel groups data together in the Scenario Summary worksheet to make the data easier to work with. You can use the plus and minus signs to hide or display details in each group of data.

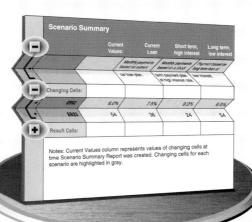

■ Click a plus sign (+) to display hidden data.

■ Click a minus sign (-) to hide data.

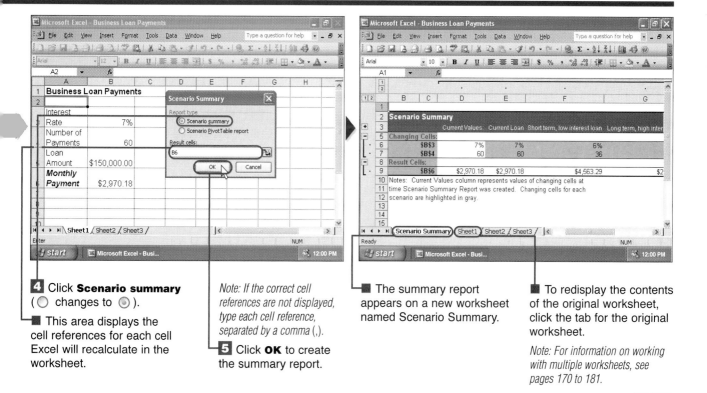

4 Click **Scenario summary** (○ changes to ◉).

■ This area displays the cell references for each cell Excel will recalculate in the worksheet.

Note: If the correct cell references are not displayed, type each cell reference, separated by a comma (,).

5 Click **OK** to create the summary report.

■ The summary report appears on a new worksheet named Scenario Summary.

■ To redisplay the contents of the original worksheet, click the tab for the original worksheet.

Note: For information on working with multiple worksheets, see pages 170 to 181.

Central Division Standings

Pool A	Games	Goals	Wins	Losses	Ties	Points
Walt's Winners	6	15	4	1	1	9
The Chargers	6	13	3	2	1	7
Terry's Tigers	6	12	3	3	0	6
The Breakaways	6	10	1	3	2	4
The GO Team	6	9	1	4	1	3

Pool B	Games	Goals	Wins	Losses	Ties	Points
		15	4	1	1	9
		13	3	1	2	8
			4	2	0	8
			3	3	0	6
			1	3	2	4
			1	5	0	2

CHAPTER 6

Change Your Screen Display

Are you interested in changing the way your worksheet appears on your screen? In this chapter, you will learn how to zoom in and out, move toolbars and more.

Zoom In or Out 108

Display Full Screen 109

Display or Hide the Status Bar 110

Display or Hide a Toolbar 111

Move a Toolbar 112

Resize a Toolbar 113

ZOOM IN OR OUT

You can enlarge or reduce the display of data on your screen.

Changing the zoom setting allows you to see data in more detail or display more data on your screen at once. Changing the zoom setting will not affect the way data appears on a printed page.

1 Click ⬝ in this area to display a list of zoom settings.

Note: If the Zoom area is not displayed, click ⬝ on the Standard toolbar to display the area.

2 Click the zoom setting you want to use.

*Note: If you select cells before performing step 1, the **Selection** setting enlarges the selected cells to fill the window. To select cells, see page 10.*

■ The worksheet appears in the new zoom setting. You can edit the worksheet as usual.

■ To return to the normal zoom setting, repeat steps **1** and **2**, selecting **100%** in step **2**.

You can display a
larger working area
by hiding parts of
the Excel screen.

Using the full
screen to view
a worksheet is
useful if you want
to display as many
cells as possible
while you review
and edit a large
worksheet.

DISPLAY FULL SCREEN

1 Click **View**.

2 Click **Full Screen**.

*Note: If Full Screen does not
appear on the menu, position
the mouse ⬚ over the bottom
of the menu to display the
menu option.*

■ Excel hides parts of the
screen to display a larger
working area.

■ To once again display the
hidden parts of the screen,
click **Close Full Screen**.

*Note: You can also repeat
steps 1 and 2 to once again
display the hidden parts of
the screen.*

DISPLAY OR HIDE THE STATUS BAR

You can display or hide the status bar at any time. The status bar displays information about the tasks you perform in Excel.

DISPLAY OR HIDE THE STATUS BAR

1 Click **View**.

■ A check mark (✔) appears beside Status Bar if the bar is currently displayed.

2 Click **Status Bar** to display or hide the bar.

Note: If Status Bar does not appear on the menu, position the mouse ⌖ *over the bottom of the menu to display the menu option.*

■ Excel displays or hides the status bar.

Note: Hiding the status bar provides a larger and less cluttered working area.

Excel offers several toolbars that you can display or hide to suit your needs. Toolbars contain buttons that you can select to quickly perform common tasks.

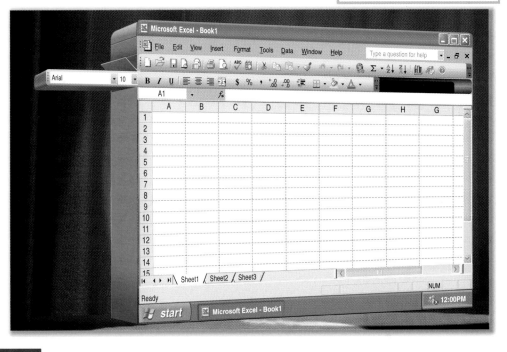

When you first start Excel, the Standard and Formatting toolbars appear on your screen.

DISPLAY OR HIDE A TOOLBAR

1 Click **View**.

2 Click **Toolbars**.

■ A list of toolbars appears. A check mark (✔) appears beside the name of each toolbar that is currently displayed.

3 Click the name of the toolbar you want to display or hide.

■ Excel displays or hides the toolbar you selected.

Note: A screen displaying fewer toolbars provides a larger and less cluttered working area.

MOVE A TOOLBAR

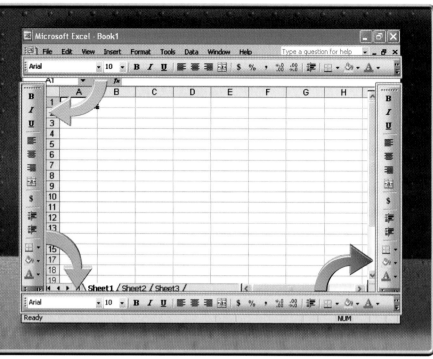

You can move a toolbar to the top, bottom, right or left edge of your screen.

You can move a toolbar to the same row as another toolbar or to its own row.

MOVE A TOOLBAR

1 Position the mouse over the left edge of the toolbar you want to move (changes to ✛).

2 Drag the toolbar to a new location.

■ The toolbar appears in the new location.

RESIZE A TOOLBAR

You can increase the size of a toolbar to display more buttons on the toolbar. This is useful when a toolbar appears on the same row as another toolbar and cannot display all of its buttons.

You cannot resize a toolbar that appears on its own row.

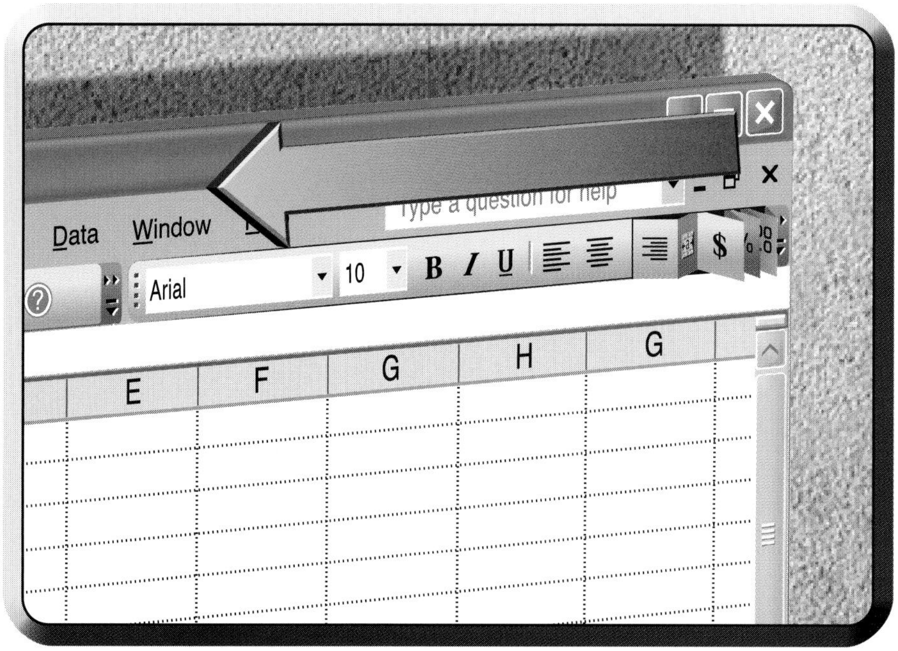

RESIZE A TOOLBAR

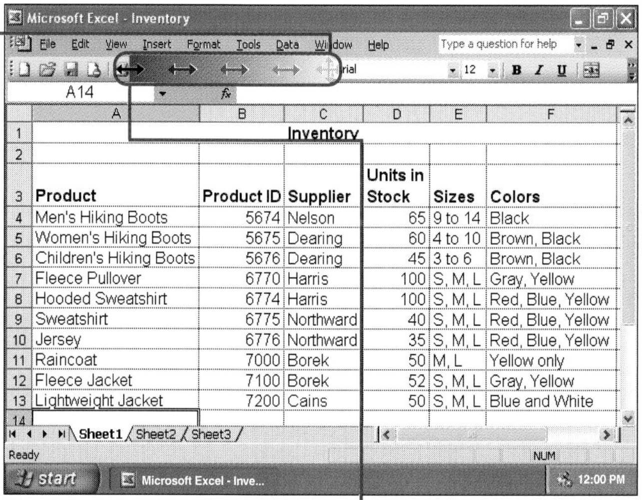

1 Position the mouse ⇖ over the left edge of the toolbar you want to resize (⇖ changes to ✥).

2 Drag the mouse ↔ until the toolbar is the size you want.

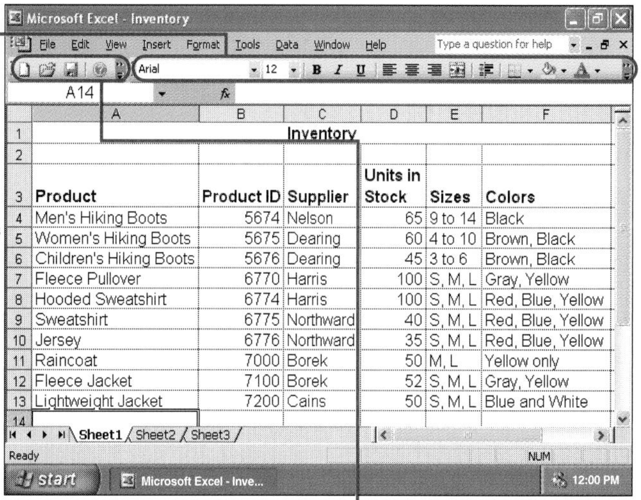

■ The toolbar displays the new size.

■ The new toolbar size affects the size of other toolbars on the same row.

	Jan	Feb	Mar	Total
East	7	7	5	19
West	6	4	7	17
South	8	7	9	24
Total	21	18	21	60

Bold *Italic* <u>Underline</u>

CHAPTER 7

Format Your Worksheets

Would you like to improve the appearance of your worksheet? This chapter shows you how to change the color of data, add borders to cells and much more.

Change Font of Data 116

Change Size of Data 117

Change Font for All New
    Workbooks 118

Bold, Italicize or Underline Data 120

Change Horizontal Alignment
    of Data 121

Change Vertical Alignment of Data ..122

Change Appearance of Data............124

Change Data Color 126

Change Cell Color 127

Indent Data 128

Center Data Across Columns 129

Wrap Text in Cells 130

Add Borders to Cells........................132

Change Number Format 134

Copy Formatting 136

Apply an AutoFormat 138

Apply Conditional Formatting 140

CHANGE FONT OF DATA

You can change the font of data to enhance the appearance of your worksheet.

By default, Excel uses the Arial font. You can use another font to draw attention to headings or emphasize important data in your worksheet.

CHANGE FONT OF DATA

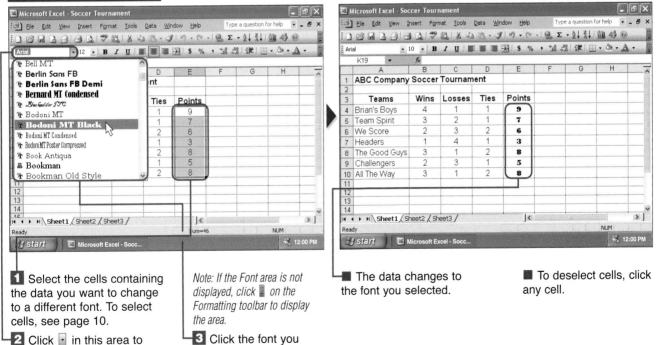

1 Select the cells containing the data you want to change to a different font. To select cells, see page 10.

2 Click ▾ in this area to display a list of the available fonts.

Note: If the Font area is not displayed, click ⁝ on the Formatting toolbar to display the area.

3 Click the font you want to use.

■ The data changes to the font you selected.

■ To deselect cells, click any cell.

CHANGE SIZE OF DATA

**You can increase
or decrease the
size of data in
your worksheet.**

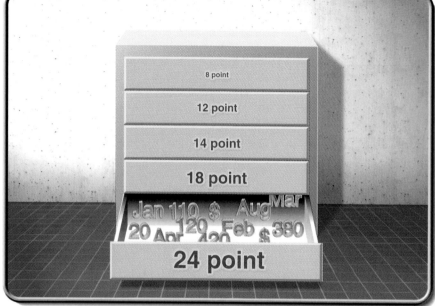

Larger data is
easier to read,
but smaller data
allows you to fit
more information
on a page.

Excel measures
the size of data in
points. There are
approximately 72
points in one inch.

CHANGE SIZE OF DATA

1 Select the cells
containing the data you
want to change to a
new size. To select
cells, see page 10.

2 Click ⋅ in this area
to display a list of the
available sizes.

*Note: If the Font Size area is
not displayed, click ⋅ on the
Formatting toolbar to display
the area.*

3 Click the size you
want to use.

■ The data changes to
the size you selected.

■ To deselect cells, click
any cell.

CHANGE FONT FOR ALL NEW WORKBOOKS

You can change the font that Excel uses for all new workbooks you create. This is useful when you want all your future workbooks to appear in a specific font.

CHANGE FONT FOR ALL NEW WORKBOOKS

1 Click **Tools**.

2 Click **Options**.

■ The Options dialog box appears.

3 Click the **General** tab.

4 To select the font you want to use for all your new workbooks, click ⌄ in this area.

5 Click the font you want to use.

Will changing the font for all new workbooks affect the data in the workbooks I have already created?

No. Excel will not change the font or size of data in the workbooks you have already created. To change the font or size of data in existing workbooks, see page 116 or 117.

What parts of my workbooks will be affected when I change the font for all new workbooks?

In addition to the data in your workbooks, the row numbers, column letters and data displayed in the formula bar will appear in the new font and size.

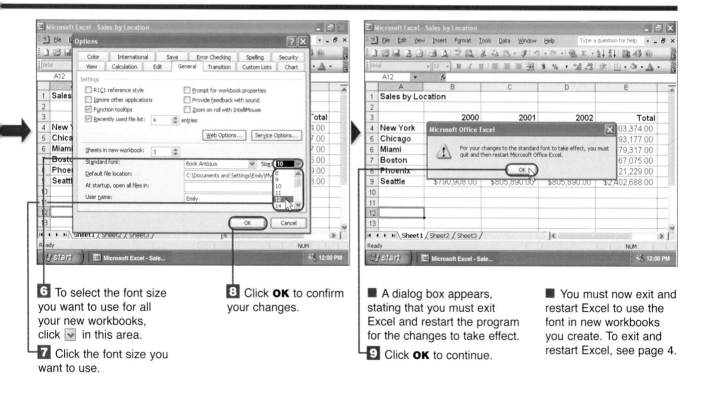

6 To select the font size you want to use for all your new workbooks, click ⌄ in this area.

7 Click the font size you want to use.

8 Click **OK** to confirm your changes.

■ A dialog box appears, stating that you must exit Excel and restart the program for the changes to take effect.

9 Click **OK** to continue.

■ You must now exit and restart Excel to use the font in new workbooks you create. To exit and restart Excel, see page 4.

BOLD, ITALICIZE OR UNDERLINE DATA

You can bold, italicize or underline data to emphasize data and enhance the appearance of your worksheet.

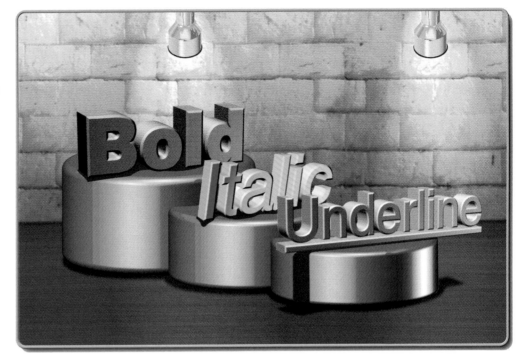

BOLD, ITALICIZE OR UNDERLINE DATA

1 Select the cells containing the data you want to bold, italicize or underline. To select cells, see page 10.

2 Click one of the following buttons.

B Bold

I Italic

U Underline

Note: If the button you want is not displayed, click 🔽 on the Formatting toolbar to display the button.

■ The data appears in the style you selected.

■ To deselect cells, click any cell.

■ To remove a bold, italic or underline style, repeat steps **1** and **2**.

CHANGE HORIZONTAL ALIGNMENT OF DATA

You can align data in different ways to enhance the appearance of your worksheet.

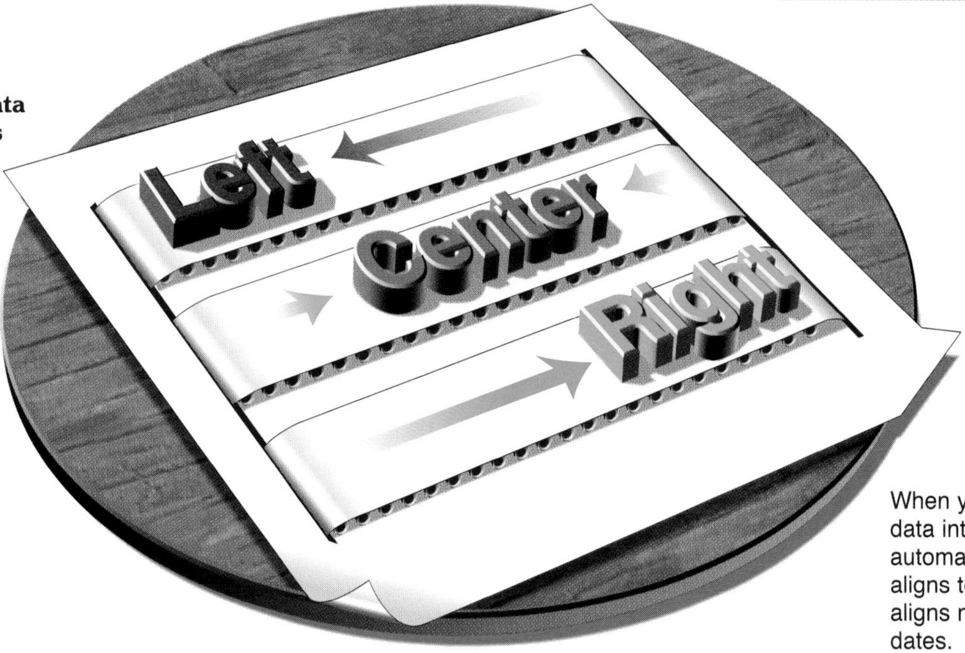

When you enter data into cells, Excel automatically left aligns text and right aligns numbers and dates.

CHANGE HORIZONTAL ALIGNMENT OF DATA

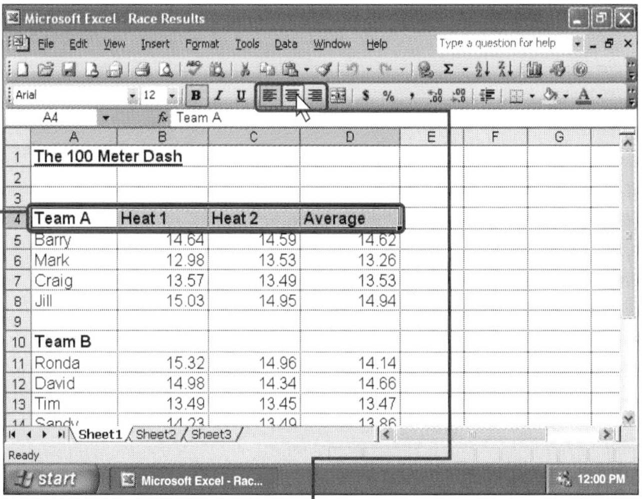

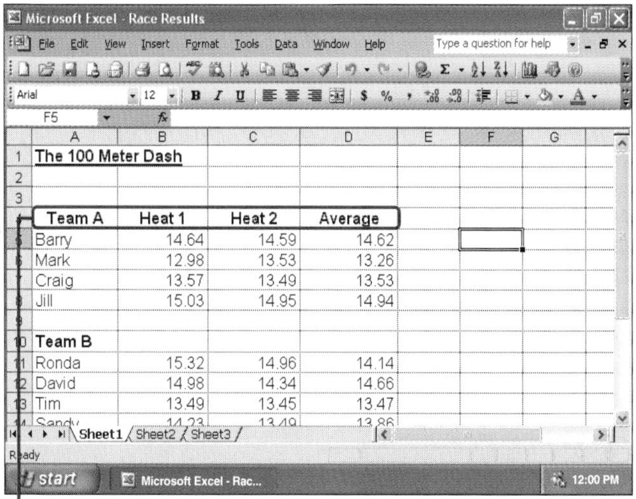

1 Select the cells containing the data you want to align differently. To select cells, see page 10.

2 Click one of the following buttons.

- Left align
- Center
- Right align

Note: If the button you want is not displayed, click on the Formatting toolbar to display the button.

■ The data appears in the new alignment.

■ To deselect cells, click any cell.

CHANGE VERTICAL ALIGNMENT OF DATA

You can change the way Excel positions data between the top and bottom edges of a cell in your worksheet. This is useful for emphasizing row and column labels.

When you enter data into a cell, Excel automatically aligns the data at the bottom of the cell.

The most commonly used vertical alignment options are top, center, and bottom.

CHANGE VERTICAL ALIGNMENT OF DATA

1 Select the cells containing the data you want to align differently. To select cells, see page 10.

2 Click **Format**.

3 Click **Cells**.

■ The Format Cells dialog box appears.

Is there another way I can emphasize row and column labels?

Yes. You can rotate data to emphasize row and column labels.

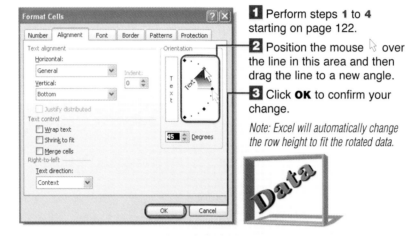

1 Perform steps **1** to **4** starting on page 122.

2 Position the mouse ⬉ over the line in this area and then drag the line to a new angle.

3 Click **OK** to confirm your change.

Note: Excel will automatically change the row height to fit the rotated data.

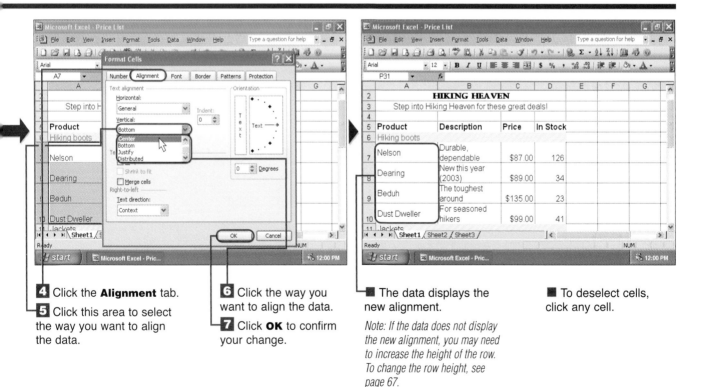

4 Click the **Alignment** tab.

5 Click this area to select the way you want to align the data.

6 Click the way you want to align the data.

7 Click **OK** to confirm your change.

■ The data displays the new alignment.

Note: If the data does not display the new alignment, you may need to increase the height of the row. To change the row height, see page 67.

■ To deselect cells, click any cell.

CHANGE APPEARANCE OF DATA

You can make data in your worksheet look more attractive by using various fonts, styles, sizes, effects and underlines.

CHANGE APPEARANCE OF DATA

1 Select the cells containing the data you want to change. To select cells, see page 10.

2 Click **Format**.

3 Click **Cells**.

■ The Format Cells dialog box appears.

4 Click the **Font** tab.

5 To select a font for the data, click the font you want to use.

6 To select a style for the data, click the style you want to use.

7 To select a size for the data, click the size you want to use.

What determines which fonts are available on my computer?

The fonts available on your computer depend on the programs installed on your computer. You can obtain additional fonts at computer stores and on the Internet.

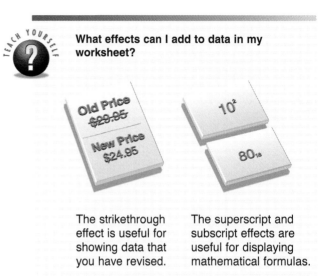

What effects can I add to data in my worksheet?

The strikethrough effect is useful for showing data that you have revised.

The superscript and subscript effects are useful for displaying mathematical formulas.

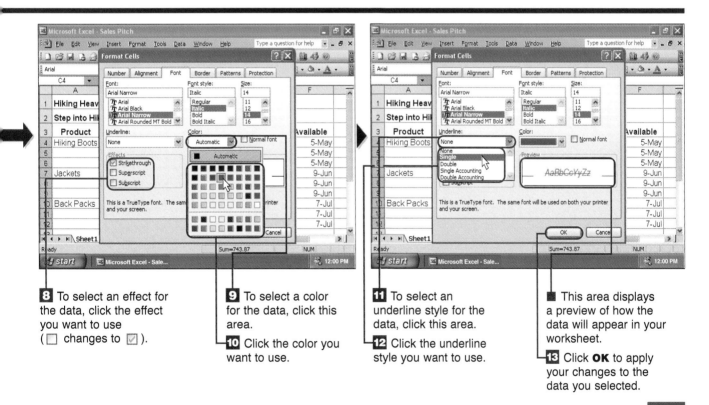

8 To select an effect for the data, click the effect you want to use (☐ changes to ☑).

9 To select a color for the data, click this area.

10 Click the color you want to use.

11 To select an underline style for the data, click this area.

12 Click the underline style you want to use.

■ This area displays a preview of how the data will appear in your worksheet.

13 Click **OK** to apply your changes to the data you selected.

CHANGE DATA COLOR

You can change the color of data in your worksheet to draw attention to headings or important information.

Adding color to data is also useful for marking data you want to review or verify later.

CHANGE DATA COLOR

1 Select the cells containing the data you want to change to a different color. To select cells, see page 10.

2 Click ⬝ in this area to display the available colors.

Note: If ![A] *is not displayed, click* ⬝ *on the Formatting toolbar to display the button.*

3 Click the color you want to use.

■ The data appears in the color you selected.

■ To deselect cells, click any cell.

■ To return data to its original color, repeat steps **1** to **3**, selecting **Automatic** in step **3**.

CHANGE CELL COLOR

You can add color to cells to make the cells stand out in your worksheet.

Changing the color of cells is useful when you want to distinguish between different areas in your worksheet. For example, in a worksheet that contains monthly sales figures, you can use a different cell color for each month.

CHANGE CELL COLOR

1 Select the cells you want to change to a different color. To select cells, see page 10.

2 Click ▾ in this area to display the available colors.

Note: If ◇▾ is not displayed, click ▸ on the Formatting toolbar to display the button.

3 Click the color you want to use.

■ The cells appear in the color you selected.

■ To deselect cells, click any cell.

■ To remove color from cells, repeat steps **1** to **3**, selecting **No Fill** in step **3**.

INDENT DATA

You can indent data to move the data away from the left edge of a cell.

INDENT DATA

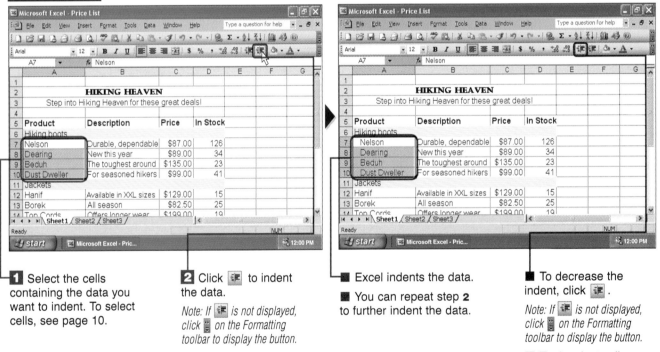

1 Select the cells containing the data you want to indent. To select cells, see page 10.

2 Click 📊 to indent the data.

Note: If 📊 is not displayed, click 📊 on the Formatting toolbar to display the button.

■ Excel indents the data.

■ You can repeat step **2** to further indent the data.

■ To decrease the indent, click 📊 .

Note: If 📊 is not displayed, click 📊 on the Formatting toolbar to display the button.

■ To deselect cells, click any cell.

128

CENTER DATA ACROSS COLUMNS

You can center data across columns in your worksheet. This is useful for centering titles over your data.

CENTER DATA ACROSS COLUMNS

1 Select the cells you want to center the data across. To select cells, see page 10.

Note: The first cell you select should contain the data you want to center.

2 Click to center the data across the columns.

Note: If is not displayed, click on the Formatting toolbar to display the button.

■ Excel centers the data across the columns.

■ If you no longer want to center the data across the columns, click the cell that contains the data and then repeat step **2**.

WRAP TEXT IN CELLS

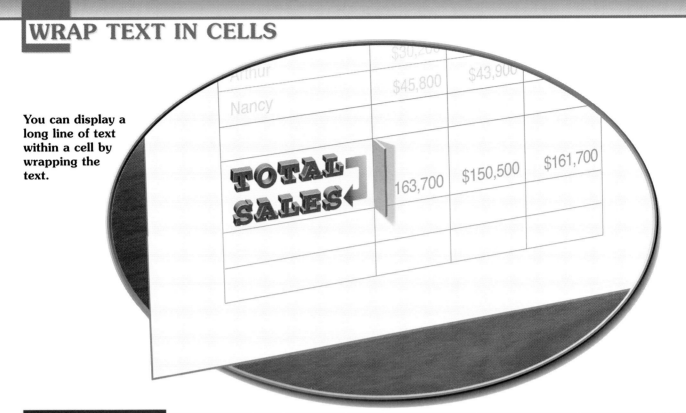

You can display a
long line of text
within a cell by
wrapping the
text.

WRAP TEXT IN CELLS

1 Select the cells containing
the text you want to wrap.
To select cells, see page 10.

2 Click **Format**.

3 Click **Cells**.

■ The Format Cells
dialog box appears.

Can I display all the text in a cell without wrapping the text?

You can have Excel reduce the size of text to fit within a cell. Perform steps **1** to **6** below, selecting **Shrink to fit** in step **5** (☐ changes to ☑).

If you later change the width of the column, Excel will automatically adjust the size of the text to fit the new width.

Can I wrap text when entering text into a cell?

Yes. Type the text you want to display on the first line of the cell. Then press and hold down the Alt key as you press the Enter key to wrap to the next line. You can then type the text for the next line. You may need to increase the column width to properly see where the text wraps. To change the column width, see page 66.

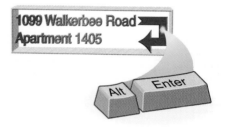

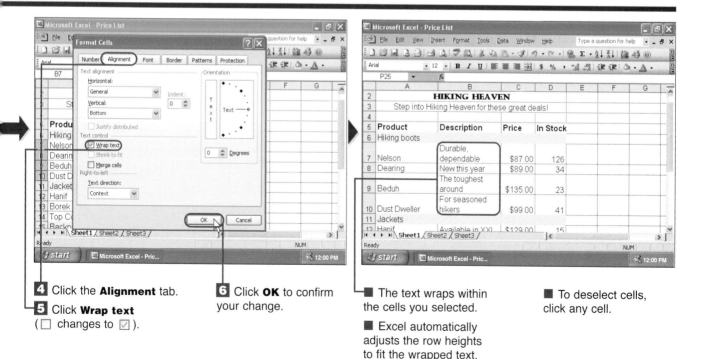

4 Click the **Alignment** tab.

5 Click **Wrap text** (☐ changes to ☑).

6 Click **OK** to confirm your change.

■ The text wraps within the cells you selected.

■ Excel automatically adjusts the row heights to fit the wrapped text.

■ To deselect cells, click any cell.

ADD BORDERS TO CELLS

You can add borders to cells to enhance the appearance of your worksheet.

Adding borders to cells is also useful if you want to divide your worksheet into sections.

ADD BORDERS TO CELLS

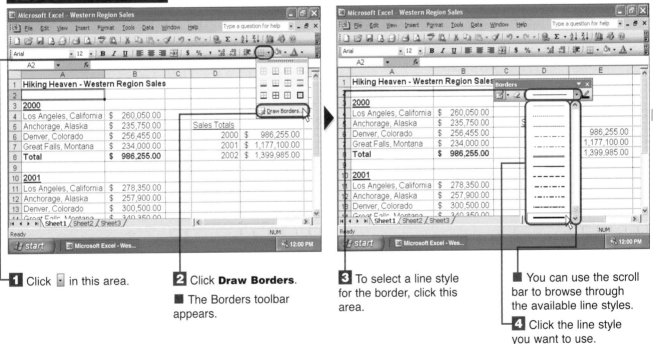

1 Click ⬝ in this area.

2 Click **Draw Borders**.

■ The Borders toolbar appears.

3 To select a line style for the border, click this area.

■ You can use the scroll bar to browse through the available line styles.

4 Click the line style you want to use.

How can I quickly add borders to cells in my worksheet?

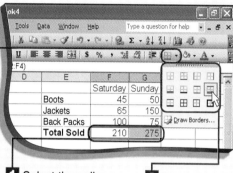

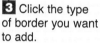

1 Select the cells you want to add borders to. To select cells, see page 10.

2 Click ▾ in this area to display commonly used types of borders.

3 Click the type of border you want to add.

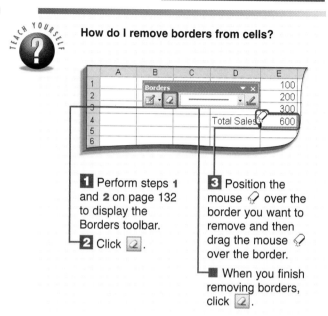

How do I remove borders from cells?

1 Perform steps **1** and **2** on page 132 to display the Borders toolbar.

2 Click ⬚.

3 Position the mouse ✐ over the border you want to remove and then drag the mouse ✐ over the border.

■ When you finish removing borders, click ⬚.

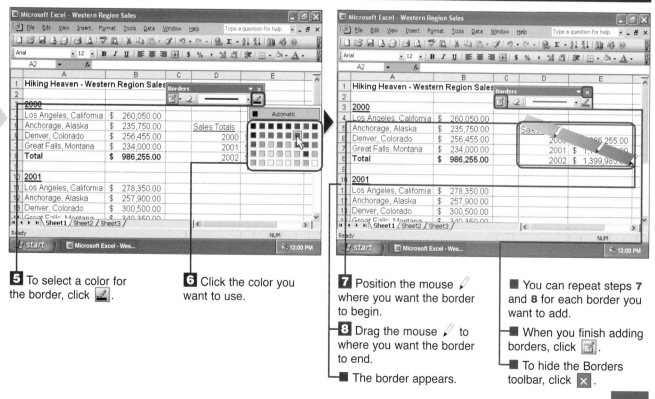

5 To select a color for the border, click ⬚.

6 Click the color you want to use.

7 Position the mouse ✐ where you want the border to begin.

8 Drag the mouse ✐ to where you want the border to end.

■ The border appears.

■ You can repeat steps **7** and **8** for each border you want to add.

■ When you finish adding borders, click ⬚.

■ To hide the Borders toolbar, click ✕.

133

CHANGE NUMBER FORMAT

You can change the appearance of numbers in your worksheet without retyping the numbers.

When you change the format of numbers, you do not change the value of the numbers.

CHANGE NUMBER FORMAT

1 Select the cells containing the numbers you want to format. To select cells, see page 10.

2 Click **Format**.

3 Click **Cells**.

■ The Format Cells dialog box appears.

4 Click the **Number** tab.

5 Click the category that describes the numbers in the cells you selected.

■ This area displays the options for the category you selected. The available options depend on the category you selected.

What categories are available for formatting numbers?

Category:	Description:	Example:
General	Applies no specific number format.	100
Number	Used to format numbers for general display.	100.00
Currency	Used to format monetary values.	$100.00
Accounting	Aligns the currency symbols and decimal points in a column of monetary values.	$ 100.00 $ 1200.00
Date	Used to format dates.	23-Apr-03
Time	Used to format times.	12:00 PM
Percentage	Used to format percentages.	25.00%
Fraction	Used to format fractions.	1/4
Scientific	Used to format numbers in scientific notation.	1.00E+02
Text	Treats numbers as text.	135 Hillcrest Street
Special	Used to format special numbers, such as Zip codes.	90210
Custom	Allows you to apply your own number format.	3-45-678

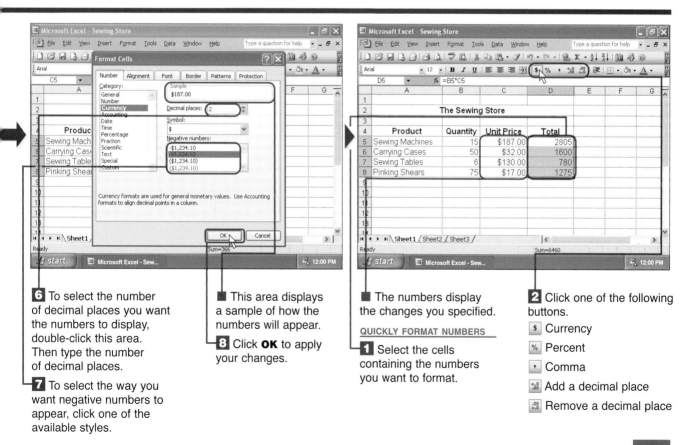

6 To select the number of decimal places you want the numbers to display, double-click this area. Then type the number of decimal places.

7 To select the way you want negative numbers to appear, click one of the available styles.

■ This area displays a sample of how the numbers will appear.

8 Click **OK** to apply your changes.

■ The numbers display the changes you specified.

QUICKLY FORMAT NUMBERS

1 Select the cells containing the numbers you want to format.

2 Click one of the following buttons.

$ Currency

% Percent

, Comma

.00 Add a decimal place

.00 Remove a decimal place

COPY FORMATTING

You can copy the formatting of a cell to make other cells in your worksheet look exactly the same.

You may want to copy the formatting of cells to make all the titles in your worksheet look the same. This will give the information in your worksheet a consistent appearance.

COPY FORMATTING

1 Click a cell that displays the formatting you want to copy to other cells.

2 Click 🖌 to copy the formatting of the cell.

■ The mouse ⬦ changes to ⬦⬚ when over your worksheet.

3 Select the cells you want to display the formatting. To select cells, see page 10.

What types of formatting can I copy?

Number Formatting

Number formatting can include currency, percentage and date formats.

Data Formatting

Data formatting can include the font, size, color and alignment of data.

Cell Formatting

Cell formatting can include borders and colors.

$6,000,000.00

How can I remove the formatting from cells?

1 Select the cells you want to remove the formatting from. To select cells, see page 10.

2 Click **Edit**.

3 Click **Clear**.

4 Click **Formats**.

Note: If you remove the formatting from cells containing dates, the dates change to numbers. To once again display the dates, you must change the format of the cells to the Date format. For more information, see page 134.

■ The cells you selected display the formatting.

■ To deselect cells, click any cell.

COPY FORMATTING TO SEVERAL AREAS

1 Click a cell that displays the formatting you want to copy to other cells.

2 Double-click 🖌 to copy the formatting of the cell.

3 Select each group of cells you want to display the formatting.

4 When you finish copying the formatting, press the **Esc** key.

APPLY AN AUTOFORMAT

Excel offers many ready-to-use designs that you can choose from to give your worksheet a professional appearance.

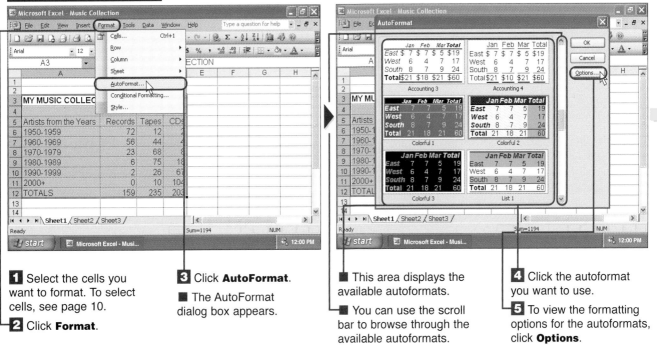

1 Select the cells you want to format. To select cells, see page 10.

2 Click **Format**.

3 Click **AutoFormat**.

■ The AutoFormat dialog box appears.

■ This area displays the available autoformats.

■ You can use the scroll bar to browse through the available autoformats.

4 Click the autoformat you want to use.

5 To view the formatting options for the autoformats, click **Options**.

What formatting will Excel apply to the cells in my worksheet?

Each autoformat includes a combination of formats, such as fonts, colors, borders, alignments and number styles. When you apply an autoformat, Excel may also adjust the column width and row height of the cells to best fit the data in the cells.

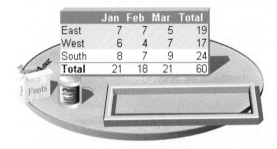

	Jan	Feb	Mar	Total
East	7	7	5	19
West	6	4	7	17
South	8	7	9	24
Total	21	18	21	60

What happens if I add data to my worksheet after applying an autoformat?

If you enter data directly to the right or below the cells you applied an autoformat to, Excel may automatically format the new data. If Excel does not automatically format the new data, you can select all the cells you want to display the autoformat and then perform steps **2** to **7** below.

■ The formatting options appear in this area. A check mark (✔) beside an option indicates that Excel will apply the option to the cells.

6 You can click an option to add (☑) or remove (☐) a check mark.

7 Click **OK** to apply the autoformat to the cells you selected.

■ The cells display the autoformat you selected.

■ To deselect cells, click any cell.

■ To remove an autoformat, repeat steps **1** to **4**, selecting **None** in step **4**. Then perform step **7**.

APPLY CONDITIONAL FORMATTING

You can have Excel apply formatting to data when the data meets a condition you specify. This can help you quickly locate important data on a large worksheet.

For example, when the number of units in stock falls below 10, you can have Excel display the number in red.

INVENTORY

Product	In Stock		Product	In Stock
Life Jackets	19		Sleeping Bags	108
Canoe Paddles	135		Tents	7
Boat Cushions	23		Compasses	54
Bailing Buckets	8		Emergency Whistles	3
Fishing Rods	120		Portable Stoves	33

APPLY CONDITIONAL FORMATTING

1 Select the cells containing the data you want Excel to format when the data meets a condition. To select cells, see page 10.

2 Click **Format**.

3 Click **Conditional Formatting**.

■ The Conditional Formatting dialog box appears.

4 Click this area to select an operator for the condition.

5 Click the operator you want to use.

What is an operator?

An operator tells Excel how to compare the data in a cell to the value you specify for a condition. For example, you can use the **greater than** operator when you want Excel to determine whether the data in a cell has a value of more than 100.

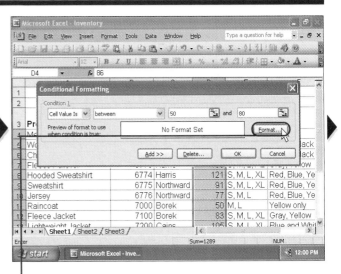

6 Click this area and type the value you want to use for the condition.

7 If you selected **between** or **not between** in step **5**, click this area and type the second value.

8 Click **Format** to specify how you want to format the data when the data meets the condition.

■ The Format Cells dialog box appears.

CONTINUED

APPLY CONDITIONAL FORMATTING

You can specify
a color and
style for data
that meets the
condition you
specified.

APPLY CONDITIONAL FORMATTING (CONTINUED)

9 To select a color for the data, click this area to display the available colors.

10 Click the color you want to use.

11 To select a style for the data, click the style you want to use.

■ This area displays a preview of the options you selected.

12 Click **OK** to confirm your changes.

142

What happens if data no longer meets the condition I specified?

If data no longer meets the condition, Excel will remove the conditional formatting from the data, but will not remove the condition from the cell. If data in the cell meets the condition in the future, Excel will apply the conditional formatting to the data.

Can I copy conditional formatting?

Yes. Copying conditional formatting is useful when you want other cells in your worksheet to display the same formatting under the same conditions. You can copy conditional formatting as you would copy any formatting in your worksheet. To copy formatting, see page 136.

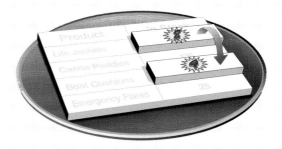

■ This area displays how data that meets the condition will appear in your worksheet.

13 Click **OK** to apply the condition to the cells you selected.

■ The data in the cells you selected displays the formatting if the data meets the condition you specified.

■ To deselect cells, click any cell.

REMOVE CONDITIONAL FORMATTING

1 To remove conditional formatting from cells, perform steps **1** to **4** on the top of page 137 to clear the formatting.

Quarterly Earnings

2000	
1st Quarter	$ 260,050.00
2nd Quarter	$ 235,750.00
3rd Quarter	$ 256,455.00
4th Quarter	$ 234,000.00
Total	$ 986,255.00
2001	
1st Quarter	$ 278,350.00
2nd Quarter	$ 257,900.00
3rd Quarter	$ 300,500.00
4th Quarter	$ 340,350.00
Total	$1,177,100.00

Apples   Oranges

Ja
Feb
Fe

4
3
2
1
0

CHAPTER 8

Print Your Worksheets

Are you ready to print your worksheet? In this chapter, you will learn how to preview your worksheet before printing and change the way your worksheet appears on a printed page.

Preview a Worksheet Before
    Printing 146

Print a Worksheet 148

Set a Print Area 150

Center Data on a Printed Page 152

Change Page Orientation 153

Change Margins 154

Change Print Options 156

Insert a Page Break 158

Add a Header or Footer 160

Add a Custom Header or Footer 162

Change Size of Printed Data 164

Repeat Labels on Printed Pages 166

PREVIEW A WORKSHEET BEFORE PRINTING

You can use the Print Preview feature to see how your worksheet will look when printed. This allows you to confirm that the worksheet will print the way you expect.

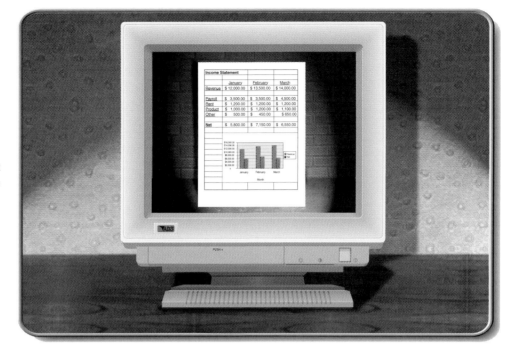

PREVIEW A WORKSHEET BEFORE PRINTING

1 Click 🔍 to preview your worksheet before printing.

Note: If 🔍 is not displayed, click ⏷ on the Standard toolbar to display the button.

■ The Print Preview window appears.

■ This area displays a page from your worksheet.

■ This area indicates which page is displayed and the total number of pages in your worksheet.

2 If your worksheet contains more than one page, you can click **Next** or **Previous** to view the next or previous page.

■ You can also use the scroll bar to view other pages.

Why does my worksheet appear in black and white in the Print Preview window?

If you are using a black-and-white printer, your worksheet appears in black and white in the Print Preview window. If you are using a color printer, your worksheet will appear in color.

Why don't the gridlines appear on my worksheet in the Print Preview window?

By default, Excel will not print the gridlines that appear around each cell in your worksheet. To print gridlines and change other print options, see page 156.

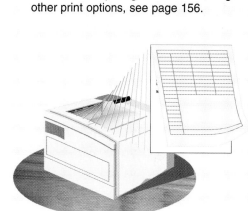

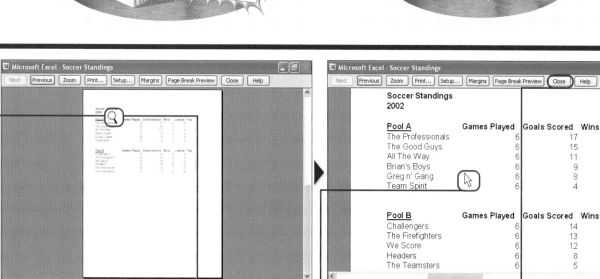

3 To magnify an area of the page, position the mouse ⬚ over the area you want to magnify (⬚ changes to ⬚).

4 Click the area to magnify the area.

■ A magnified view of the area appears.

5 To once again display the entire page, click anywhere on the page.

6 When you finish previewing your worksheet, click **Close** to close the Print Preview window.

PRINT A WORKSHEET

You can produce a paper copy of the worksheet displayed on your screen. Printing a worksheet is useful when you want to be able to refer to the worksheet without using your computer.

Before printing your worksheet, make sure your printer is turned on and contains paper.

PRINT A WORKSHEET

1 Click any cell in the worksheet you want to print.

■ To print only specific cells in your worksheet, select the cells you want to print. To select cells, see page 10.

2 Click **File**.

3 Click **Print**.

■ The Print dialog box appears.

4 Click the part of the workbook you want to print (○ changes to ◉).

Note: For information on the parts of the workbook that you can print, see the top of page 149.

5 If the part of the workbook you selected to print contains more than one page, click an option to specify which pages you want to print (○ changes to ◉).

All - Prints every page

Page(s) - Prints the pages you specify

148

What parts of a workbook can I print?

Excel allows you to specify which part of a workbook you want to print. Each workbook is divided into several worksheets.

For information on using multiple worksheets in a workbook, see pages 170 to 181.

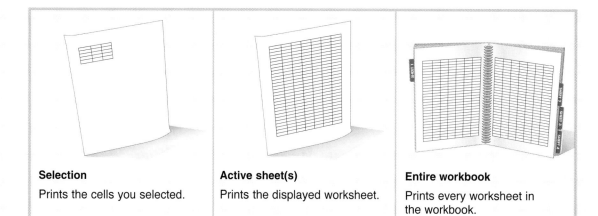

Selection

Prints the cells you selected.

Active sheet(s)

Prints the displayed worksheet.

Entire workbook

Prints every worksheet in the workbook.

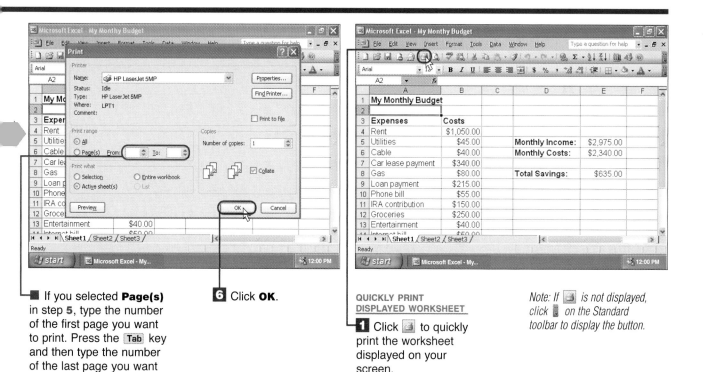

■ If you selected **Page(s)** in step **5**, type the number of the first page you want to print. Press the Tab key and then type the number of the last page you want to print.

6 Click **OK**.

QUICKLY PRINT
DISPLAYED WORKSHEET

1 Click 🖨 to quickly print the worksheet displayed on your screen.

Note: If 🖨 is not displayed, click ⁞ on the Standard toolbar to display the button.

SET A PRINT AREA

If you always print the same area of your worksheet, you can set a print area to quickly print the data. Excel will print only the data in the print area.

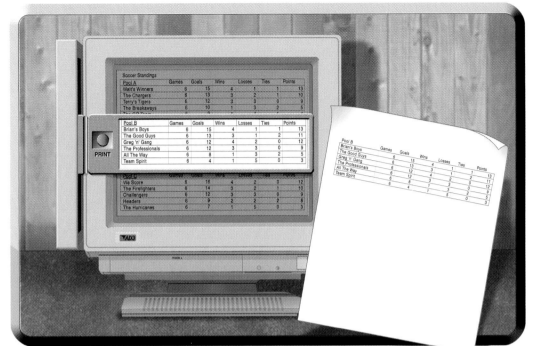

If you have not set a print area for your worksheet, Excel will print the entire worksheet.

1 Select the cells containing the data you want to include in the print area. To select cells, see page 10.

2 Click **File**.

3 Click **Print Area**.

4 Click **Set Print Area**.

■ A dashed line appears around the cells you selected.

■ To deselect cells, click any cell.

PRINT A PRINT AREA

1 Click 🖨 to print the data in the print area at any time.

150

Can I include multiple groups of cells in a print area?

Yes. Including multiple groups of cells in a print area is useful when you want to print data from several sections of a large worksheet. When you set a print area that includes multiple groups of cells, Excel prints each group of cells on a different page. To select multiple groups of cells, see page 10.

How do I print other data in my worksheet after I set a print area?

You can temporarily override a print area you have set and print other data in your worksheet. Select the cells containing the data you want to print and then perform steps **2** to **6** starting on page 148, choosing **Selection** in step **4** (○ changes to ◉).

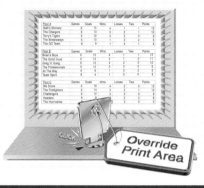

CLEAR A PRINT AREA

1 Click **File**.

2 Click **Print Area**.

3 Click **Clear Print Area** to clear the print area from your worksheet.

■ The dashed line disappears from your worksheet.

CENTER DATA ON A PRINTED PAGE

You can center data horizontally and vertically on a printed page.

Centering data on a printed page will not affect the way your worksheet appears on your screen.

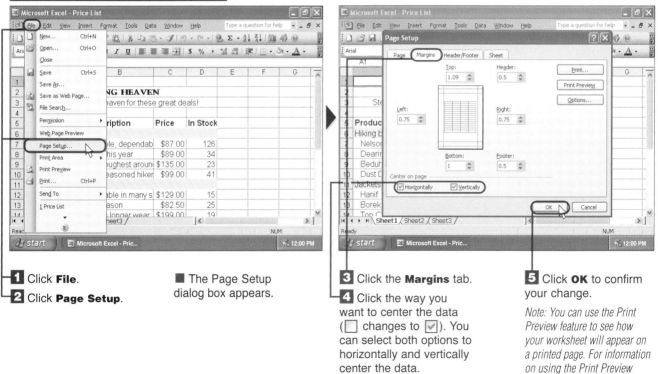

1 Click **File**.

2 Click **Page Setup**.

■ The Page Setup dialog box appears.

3 Click the **Margins** tab.

4 Click the way you want to center the data (☐ changes to ☑). You can select both options to horizontally and vertically center the data.

5 Click **OK** to confirm your change.

Note: You can use the Print Preview feature to see how your worksheet will appear on a printed page. For information on using the Print Preview feature, see page 146.

You can change the page orientation to change the way your worksheet appears on a printed page.

Excel automatically prints your worksheets in the portrait orientation. The landscape orientation is useful when you want a wide worksheet to fit on one printed page.

Changing the page orientation will not affect the way your worksheet appears on your screen.

CHANGE PAGE ORIENTATION

1 Click **File**.

2 Click **Page Setup**.

■ The Page Setup dialog box appears.

3 Click the **Page** tab.

4 Click the page orientation you want to use (○ changes to ⊙).

5 Click **OK** to confirm your change.

Note: You can use the Print Preview feature to see how your worksheet will appear on a printed page. For information on using the Print Preview feature, see page 146.

CHANGE MARGINS

You can change the margins in your worksheet. A margin is the amount of space between the data on a page and the edge of your paper.

Changing the margins allows you to adjust the amount of information that can fit on a page. You may want to change the margins to accommodate letterhead or other specialty paper.

Changing the margins will not affect the way your worksheet appears on your screen.

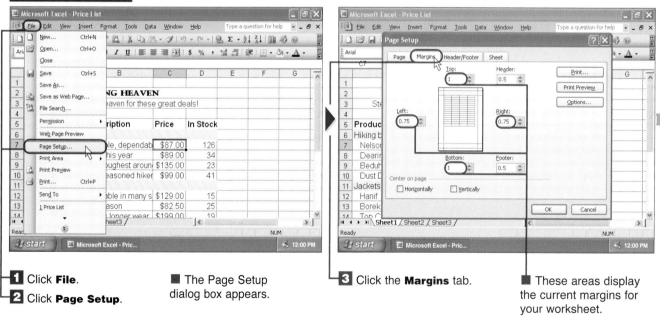

CHANGE MARGINS

1 Click **File**.

2 Click **Page Setup**.

■ The Page Setup dialog box appears.

3 Click the **Margins** tab.

■ These areas display the current margins for your worksheet.

Note: By default, Excel sets the top and bottom margins to 1 inch and the left and right margins to 0.75 inches.

Is there another way to change the margins in my worksheet?

Yes. You can use the Print Preview feature to change the margins in your worksheet.

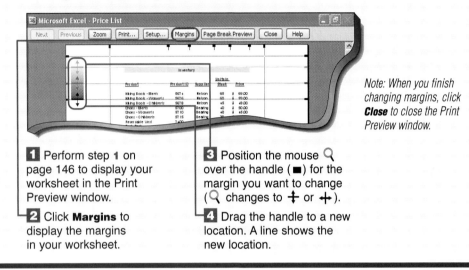

*Note: When you finish changing margins, click **Close** to close the Print Preview window.*

1 Perform step **1** on page 146 to display your worksheet in the Print Preview window.

2 Click **Margins** to display the margins in your worksheet.

3 Position the mouse Q over the handle (■) for the margin you want to change (Q changes to ╬ or ╫).

4 Drag the handle to a new location. A line shows the new location.

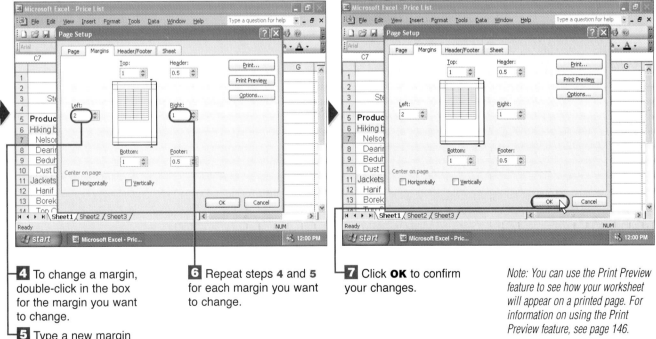

4 To change a margin, double-click in the box for the margin you want to change.

5 Type a new margin in inches.

6 Repeat steps **4** and **5** for each margin you want to change.

7 Click **OK** to confirm your changes.

Note: You can use the Print Preview feature to see how your worksheet will appear on a printed page. For information on using the Print Preview feature, see page 146.

CHANGE PRINT OPTIONS

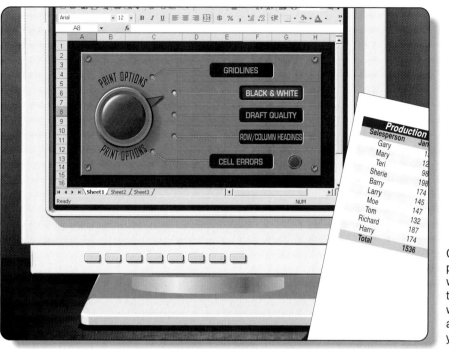

You can use the print options that Excel offers to change the way your worksheet appears on a printed page.

Changing the print options will not affect the way your worksheet appears on your screen.

CHANGE PRINT OPTIONS

1 Click **File**.

2 Click **Page Setup**.

■ The Page Setup dialog box appears.

3 Click the **Sheet** tab.

4 Click each print option you want to use (☐ changes to ☑).

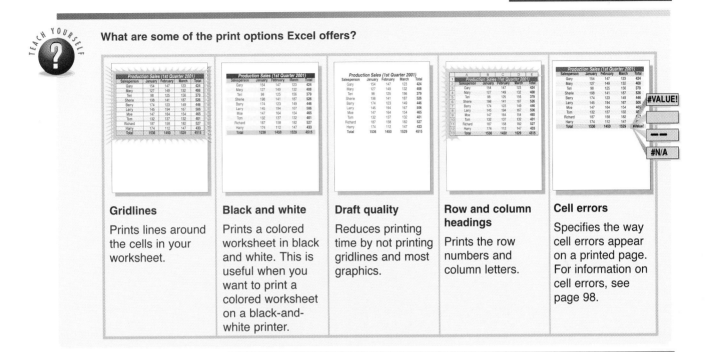

What are some of the print options Excel offers?

Gridlines

Prints lines around the cells in your worksheet.

Black and white

Prints a colored worksheet in black and white. This is useful when you want to print a colored worksheet on a black-and-white printer.

Draft quality

Reduces printing time by not printing gridlines and most graphics.

Row and column headings

Prints the row numbers and column letters.

Cell errors

Specifies the way cell errors appear on a printed page. For information on cell errors, see page 98.

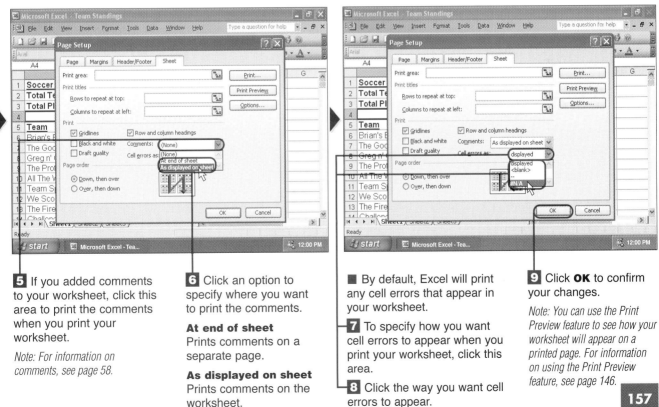

5 If you added comments to your worksheet, click this area to print the comments when you print your worksheet.

Note: For information on comments, see page 58.

6 Click an option to specify where you want to print the comments.

At end of sheet
Prints comments on a separate page.

As displayed on sheet
Prints comments on the worksheet.

■ By default, Excel will print any cell errors that appear in your worksheet.

7 To specify how you want cell errors to appear when you print your worksheet, click this area.

8 Click the way you want cell errors to appear.

9 Click **OK** to confirm your changes.

Note: You can use the Print Preview feature to see how your worksheet will appear on a printed page. For information on using the Print Preview feature, see page 146.

INSERT A PAGE BREAK

You can insert a
page break to start
a new page at a
specific location
in your worksheet.
A page break
indicates where
one page ends and
another begins.

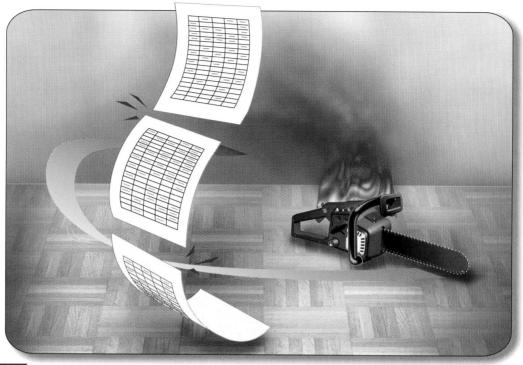

1 To select the row or
column you want to appear
at the beginning of the new
page, click the heading of
the row or column.

2 Click **Insert**.

3 Click **Page Break**.

*Note: If Page Break does not
appear on the menu, position
the mouse ⌕ over the bottom
of the menu to display the
menu option.*

■ A dashed line appears
on your screen. This line
indicates where one
page ends and another
begins.

■ The dashed line will
not appear when you
print your worksheet.

■ To deselect a row or
column, click any cell.

Will Excel ever insert page breaks automatically?

When you fill a page with data, Excel automatically inserts a page break to start a new page.

How do I delete a page break I inserted into my worksheet?

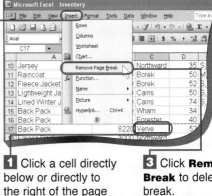

1 Click a cell directly below or directly to the right of the page break line you want to delete.

2 Click **Insert**.

3 Click **Remove Page Break** to delete the page break.

Note: If Remove Page Break does not appear on the menu, position the mouse ⋏ over the bottom of the menu to display the menu option.

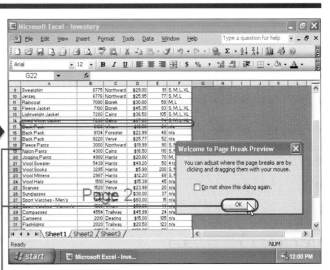

VIEW ALL PAGE BREAKS

1 Click **View**.

2 Click **Page Break Preview** to display all the page breaks in your worksheet.

■ A dialog box appears.

3 Click **OK** to close the dialog box.

■ A solid blue line shows the location of a page break you inserted into your worksheet.

Note: A dashed blue line shows the location of a page break Excel inserted for you.

■ To return to the normal view at any time, repeat steps **1** and **2**, selecting **Normal** in step **2**.

ADD A HEADER OR FOOTER

You can add a header or footer to display additional information on each page of your worksheet. A header or footer can contain information such as your name, the page number and the current date.

Product Orders

Company	Product	Unit Price	Order	Total
Sportz Unlimited	A	$ 66.75	432	$ 28,836.00
Sportz Unlimited	B	$ 59.99	591	$ 35,454.09
Sportz Unlimited	C	$ 105.97	900	$ 95,373.00
DRG Ltd.	A	$ 66.75	545	$ 36,378.75
DRG Ltd.	B	$ 59.99	387	$ 23,216.13
DRG Ltd.	C	$ 105.97	400	$ 42,388.00
Fast Track Inc.	A	$ 66.75	605	$ 40,383.75
Fast Track Inc.	B	$ 59.99	500	$ 29,995.00
Fast Track Inc.	C	$ 105.97	890	$ 94,313.30
Risky Wheelz	A	$ 66.75	1050	$ 70,087.50
Risky Wheelz	B	$ 59.99	567	$ 34,014.33
Risky Wheelz	C	$ 105.97	390	$ 41,328.30
Indoor Sports	A	$ 66.75	755	$ 50,396.25
Indoor Sports	B	$ 59.99	561	$ 33,654.39
Indoor Sports	C	$ 105.97	350	$ 37,089.50
Big Leaguers	A	$ 66.75	456	$ 30,438.00
Big Leaguers	B	$ 59.99	588	$ 35,274.12
Big Leaguers	C	$ 105.97	200	$ 21,194.00
Waveriders Inc.	A	$ 66.75	345	$ 23,028.75
Waveriders Inc.	B	$ 59.99	553	$ 33,174.47
Waveriders Inc.	C	$ 105.97	466	$ 49,382.02

Page 1

■ A **header** appears at the top of each printed page.

■ A **footer** appears at the bottom of each printed page.

ADD A HEADER OR FOOTER

1 Click **View**.

2 Click **Header and Footer**.

Note: If Header and Footer does not appear on the menu, position the mouse ♙ over the bottom of the menu to display the menu option.

■ The Page Setup dialog box appears.

3 To view a list of available headers, click this area.

4 Click the header you want to use.

Can I see how a header or footer will look before I print my worksheet?

Yes. You can use the Print Preview feature to see how a header or footer will look before you print your worksheet. For information on using the Print Preview feature, see page 146.

■ This area displays how the header will appear at the top of a page.

5 To view a list of available footers, click this area.

6 Click the footer you want to use.

■ This area displays how the footer will appear at the bottom of a page.

7 Click **OK** to add the header or footer to your worksheet.

■ To remove a header or footer from your worksheet, repeat steps **1** to **7**, selecting **(none)** in step **4** or step **6**.

ADD A CUSTOM HEADER OR FOOTER

You can add a custom header or footer to every page of your worksheet. Adding a custom header or footer allows you to specify the information the header or footer displays.

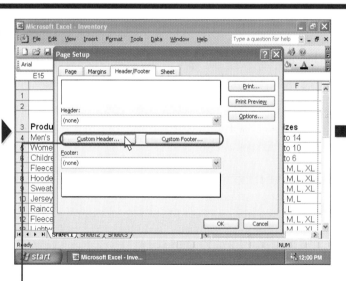

A custom header or footer can contain information such as your e-mail address.

ADD A CUSTOM HEADER OR FOOTER

1 Click **View**.

2 Click **Header and Footer**.

Note: If Header and Footer does not appear on the menu, position the mouse over the bottom of the menu to display the menu option.

■ The Page Setup dialog box appears.

3 Click the appropriate button to create a custom header or footer.

■ A dialog box appears, displaying areas for the left, center and right sections of the page.

How can Excel help me create a custom header or footer?

You can click one of the following buttons to enter or format information in a custom header or footer.

A	Format header or footer text		Insert workbook path and name
	Insert page number		Insert workbook name
	Insert total number of pages		Insert worksheet name
	Insert current date		Insert picture
	Insert current time		Format picture

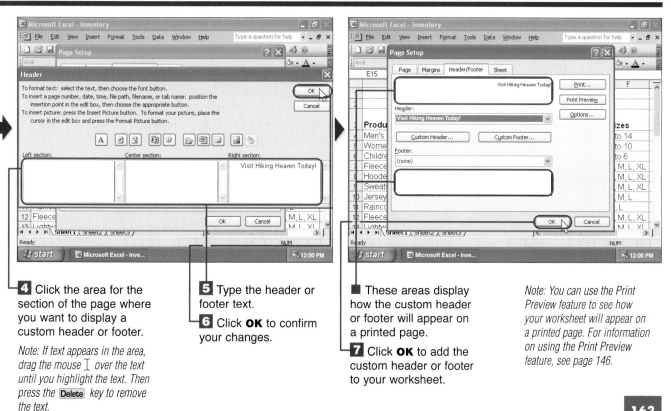

4 Click the area for the section of the page where you want to display a custom header or footer.

Note: If text appears in the area, drag the mouse I *over the text until you highlight the text. Then press the* Delete *key to remove the text.*

5 Type the header or footer text.

6 Click **OK** to confirm your changes.

■ These areas display how the custom header or footer will appear on a printed page.

7 Click **OK** to add the custom header or footer to your worksheet.

Note: You can use the Print Preview feature to see how your worksheet will appear on a printed page. For information on using the Print Preview feature, see page 146.

CHANGE SIZE OF PRINTED DATA

You can reduce the size of printed data to print your worksheet on a specific number of pages.

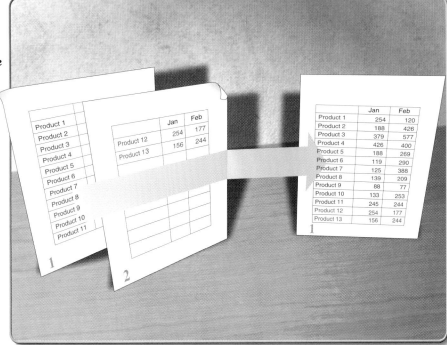

Changing the size of printed data is useful when the last page of your worksheet contains a small amount of data that you want to fit on the previous page.

CHANGE SIZE OF PRINTED DATA

1 Click **File**.

2 Click **Page Setup**.

■ The Page Setup dialog box appears.

3 Click the **Page** tab.

4 Click **Fit to** to fit the worksheet on a specific number of pages (○ changes to ◉).

What should I consider when changing the size of printed data?

When specifying the number of pages you want to print data across and down, you must consider the amount of data you need to print. If you try to fit the data on too few pages, the data may become too small to read.

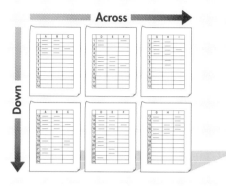

Why did the page breaks in my worksheet disappear when I changed the size of printed data?

When you change the size of printed data, Excel ignores any page breaks you have inserted into your worksheet. This allows Excel to fit the worksheet data on the number of pages you specify. For information on inserting page breaks, see page 158.

5 Type the number of pages you want the data to print across.

6 Press the `Tab` key and then type the number of pages you want the data to print down.

7 Click **OK** to confirm your changes.

■ Excel will change the size of the printed data to fit on the number of pages you specified.

Note: You can use the Print Preview feature to see how your worksheet will appear on a printed page. For information on the Print Preview feature, see page 146.

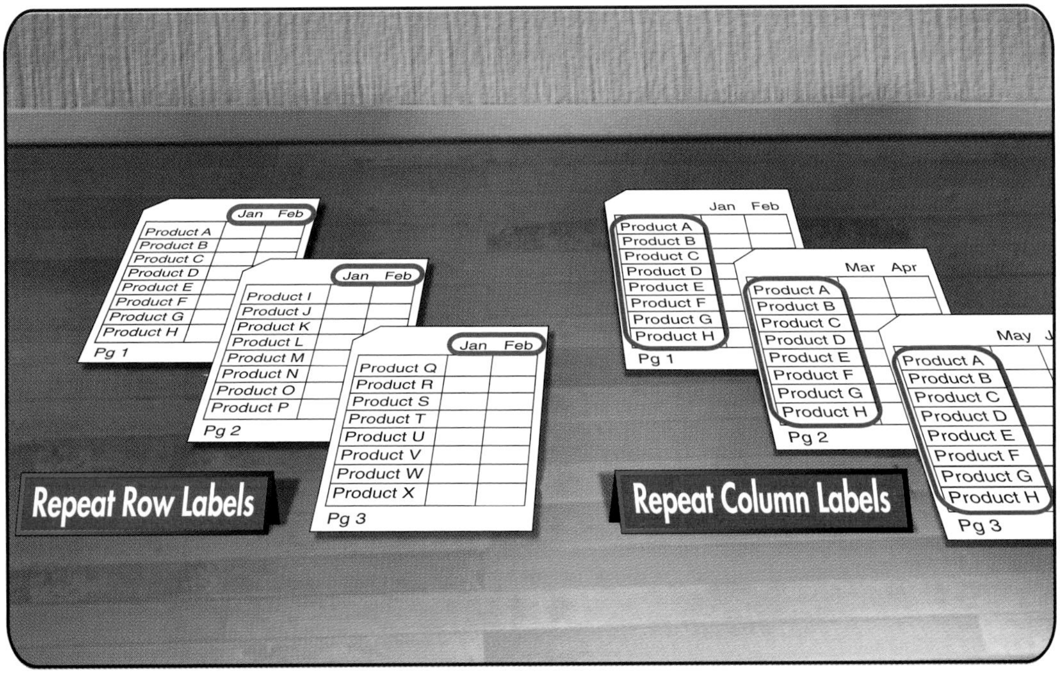

REPEAT LABELS ON PRINTED PAGES

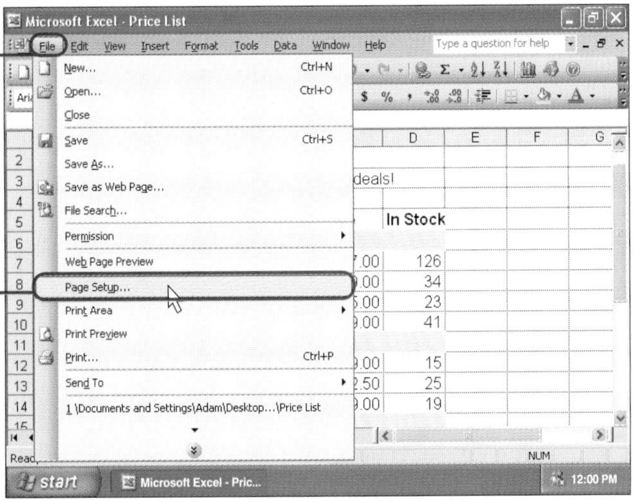

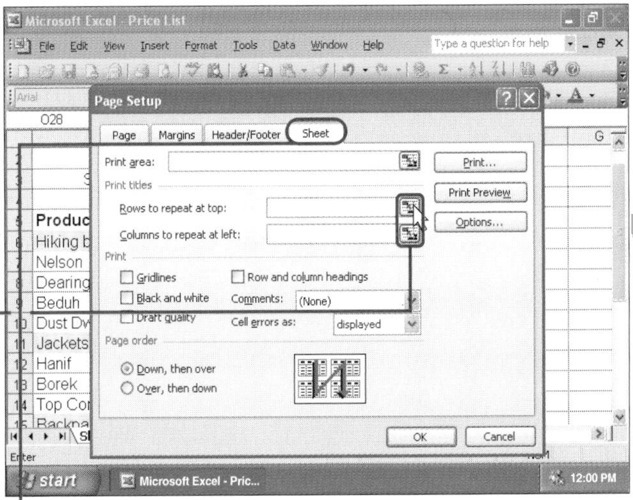

You can display the same row or column labels on every printed page of a worksheet. This can help you review worksheets that print on several pages.

Repeat Row Labels

Repeat Column Labels

1 Click **File**.

2 Click **Page Setup**.

■ The Page Setup dialog box appears.

3 Click the **Sheet** tab.

4 Click 🔲 beside one of the following options.

Rows to repeat at top
Repeat labels across the top of each page.

Columns to repeat at left
Repeat labels down the left side of each page.

Can I see how the repeated labels will look before I print my worksheet?

You can use the Print Preview feature to see how the repeated labels will look before you print your worksheet. For information on using the Print Preview feature, see page 146.

How do I stop repeating labels on printed pages?

Perform steps 1 to 3 below. Then drag the mouse I over the text in the area beside the appropriate option until you highlight the text. Press the Delete key to remove the text from the area and then perform step 7.

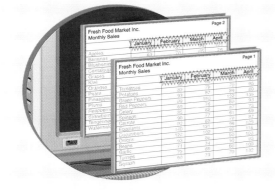

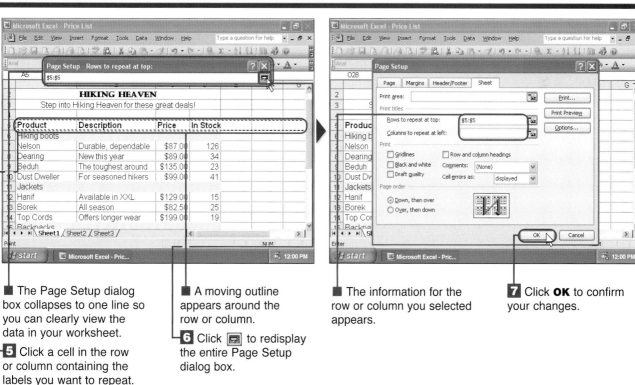

■ The Page Setup dialog box collapses to one line so you can clearly view the data in your worksheet.

5 Click a cell in the row or column containing the labels you want to repeat.

■ A moving outline appears around the row or column.

6 Click 📷 to redisplay the entire Page Setup dialog box.

■ The information for the row or column you selected appears.

7 Click **OK** to confirm your changes.

CHAPTER 9

Work With Multiple Worksheets

Do you want to work with more than one worksheet at a time? This chapter teaches you how to switch between worksheets, move or copy data between worksheets, color worksheet tabs and more.

Switch Between Worksheets..............170

Rename a Worksheet 171

Insert a Worksheet 172

Delete a Worksheet 173

Move a Worksheet 174

Add Color to a Worksheet Tab 175

Move or Copy Data Between
    Worksheets 176

Enter a Formula Across Worksheets ..178

Using the Watch Window Toolbar 180

SWITCH BETWEEN WORKSHEETS

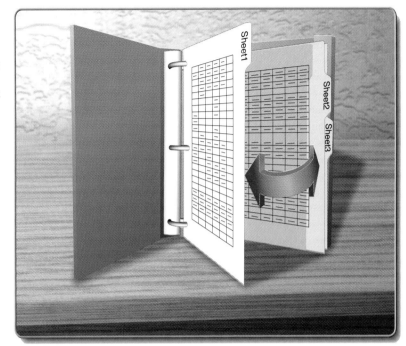

A workbook contains several worksheets. You can easily switch between the worksheets in your workbook to view and compare all the data.

Worksheets can help you organize information in your workbook. For example, you can store information for each division of a company on a separate worksheet.

SWITCH BETWEEN WORKSHEETS

■ This area displays a tab for each worksheet in your workbook. The displayed worksheet has a white tab.

1 Click the tab for the worksheet you want to display.

■ The worksheet you selected appears. The contents of the other worksheets in your workbook are hidden behind the displayed worksheet.

BROWSE THROUGH WORKSHEET TABS

■ If you have many worksheets in your workbook, you may not be able to see all the worksheet tabs.

Note: To insert additional worksheets, see page 172.

1 Click one of the following buttons to browse through the worksheet tabs.

|◄ Display first tab
◄ Display previous tab
► Display next tab
►| Display last tab

You can rename a worksheet in your workbook to better describe the contents of the worksheet.

Each worksheet in a workbook must have a unique name. Short worksheet names are generally better than long names since short names allow you to display more worksheet tabs on your screen at once.

RENAME A WORKSHEET

1 Double-click the tab for the worksheet you want to rename.

■ The name of the worksheet is highlighted.

2 Type a new name for the worksheet and then press the **Enter** key.

Note: A worksheet name can contain up to 31 characters, including spaces.

INSERT A WORKSHEET

You can insert a new worksheet anywhere in your workbook to include additional information.

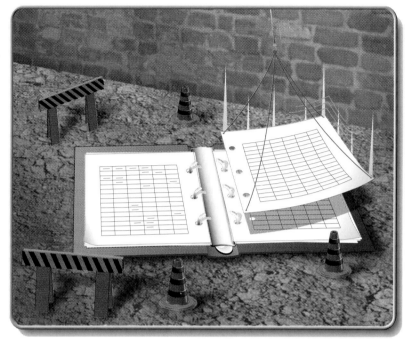

Each workbook you create automatically contains three worksheets. You can insert as many new worksheets as you need.

INSERT A WORKSHEET

1 Click the tab for the worksheet you want to appear after the new worksheet.

2 Click **Insert**.

3 Click **Worksheet**.

■ The new worksheet appears.

■ Excel displays a tab for the new worksheet.

DELETE A WORKSHEET

You can permanently remove a worksheet you no longer need from your workbook.

You cannot restore a worksheet once it has been deleted from your workbook.

DELETE A WORKSHEET

1 Click the tab for the worksheet you want to delete.

2 Click **Edit**.

3 Click **Delete Sheet**.

Note: If Delete Sheet does not appear on the menu, position the mouse ⟍ over the bottom of the menu to display the menu option.

■ A warning dialog box may appear, stating that Excel will permanently delete the data in the worksheet.

4 Click **Delete** to permanently delete the worksheet.

MOVE A WORKSHEET

You can move a worksheet to a new location in your workbook. This allows you to reorganize the data in your workbook.

MOVE A WORKSHEET

1 Position the mouse ⬧ over the tab for the worksheet you want to move.

2 Drag the worksheet to a new location.

■ An arrow (▼) shows where the worksheet will appear.

■ The worksheet appears in the new location.

ADD COLOR TO A WORKSHEET TAB

You can add color to a worksheet tab to make the tab stand out. This allows you to quickly locate a worksheet of interest.

Adding color to worksheet tabs can also help you organize a workbook that contains several worksheets. For example, you can add the same color to the tabs of worksheets that contain similar data.

ADD COLOR TO A WORKSHEET TAB

1 Click the worksheet tab you want to add color to.

2 Click **Format**.

3 Click **Sheet**.

4 Click **Tab Color**.

■ The Format Tab Color dialog box appears.

5 Click the color you want to use.

6 Click **OK**.

■ Excel adds the color you selected to the worksheet tab.

■ To remove color from a worksheet tab, repeat steps **1** to **6**, selecting **No Color** in step **5**.

MOVE OR COPY DATA BETWEEN WORKSHEETS

You can move or copy data from one worksheet to another. This will save you time when you want to use data from another worksheet.

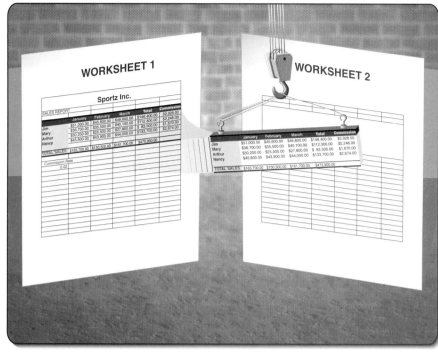

When you move data, the data disappears from its original location.

When you copy data, the data appears in both the original and new locations.

MOVE OR COPY DATA BETWEEN WORKSHEETS

1 Select the cells containing the data you want to move or copy to another worksheet. To select cells, see page 10.

2 Click one of the following buttons.

🔲 Move data

🔲 Copy data

■ The Clipboard task pane may appear, displaying items you have selected to move or copy. To use the Clipboard task pane, see the top of page 177.

How can I use the Clipboard task pane to move or copy data?

The Clipboard task pane displays up to the last 24 items you have selected to move or copy. To place a clipboard item into your worksheet, click the cell where you want to place the item and then click the item in the task pane. For more information on the task pane, see page 16.

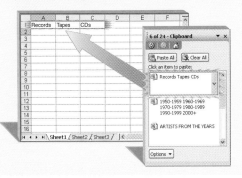

Why does the Paste Options button () appear after I copy data?

You can use the Paste Options button (📋) to change the way Excel copies data. For example, you can specify that you want to use the column width from the original cells in the new location. Click the Paste Options button to display a list of options and then select the option you want to use. The Paste Options button disappears after you perform another task.

3 Click the tab for the worksheet where you want to place the data.

Note: To place the data in another workbook, open the workbook before performing step 3. To open a workbook, see page 32.

4 Click the cell where you want to place the data. This cell will become the top left cell of the new location.

5 Click 📋 to place the data in the new location.

■ The data appears in the new location.

Note: If number signs (#) appear in a cell, the column is too narrow to fit the data. To change the column width, see page 66.

ENTER A FORMULA ACROSS WORKSHEETS

You can enter a formula that uses data from more than one worksheet.

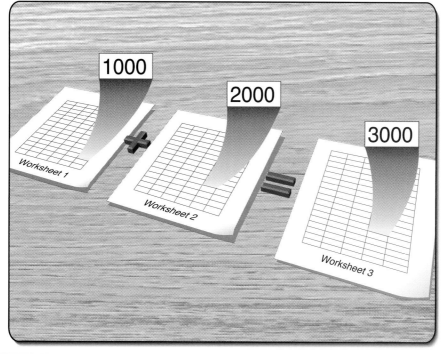

1000

2000

3000

Worksheet 1

Worksheet 2

Worksheet 3

If you change a number used in a formula you entered across worksheets, Excel will automatically redo the calculation for you. This ensures your calculations are always up to date.

ENTER A FORMULA ACROSS WORKSHEETS

1 Click the cell where you want to enter a formula.

2 Type an equal sign (=) to begin the formula.

3 Click the tab for the worksheet containing the data you want to use in the formula.

4 Click a cell containing data you want to use in the formula.

5 Type the operator for the calculation you want to perform. For information on the types of operators you can use, see the top of page 179.

When entering a formula, what types of operators can I use?

Arithmetic operators allow you to perform mathematical calculations.

Arithmetic Operator:	Description:
+	Addition (A1+B1)
-	Subtraction (A1-B1)
*	Multiplication (A1*B1)
/	Division (A1/B1)
%	Percent (A1%)
^	Exponentiation (A1^B1)

Comparison operators allow you to compare two values. A formula that uses only a comparison operator will return a value of TRUE or FALSE.

Comparison Operator:	Description:
=	Equal to (A1=B1)
>	Greater than (A1>B1)
<	Less than (A1<B1)
>=	Greater than or equal to (A1>=B1)
<=	Less than or equal to (A1<=B1)
<>	Not equal to (A1<>B1)

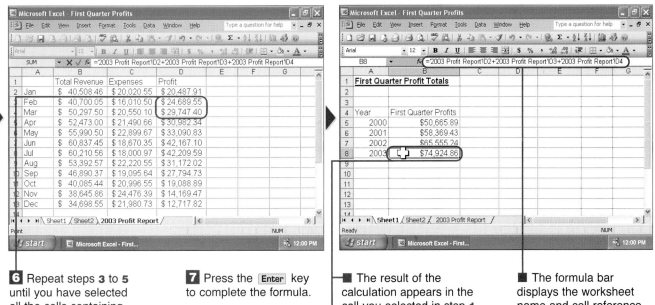

6 Repeat steps **3** to **5** until you have selected all the cells containing the data you want to use in the formula.

Note: In this example, cells **D2** to **D4** are added together.

7 Press the Enter key to complete the formula.

■ The result of the calculation appears in the cell you selected in step **1**.

8 To view the formula you entered, click the cell containing the formula.

■ The formula bar displays the worksheet name and cell reference for each cell used in the formula.

USING THE WATCH WINDOW TOOLBAR

You can use the Watch Window toolbar to see the results of formulas on other worksheets. This saves you from having to switch between worksheets to keep track of formulas of interest.

Using the Watch Window toolbar is useful when you want to watch a formula you entered across worksheets. To enter a formula across worksheets, see page 178.

Watch Window
Add Watch...   Delete Watch

Book	Sheet	Name	Cell	Value	Formula
Sales Report.xls	Sheet3	Profit	B6	3,500.00	=Sheet1!A3+Sheet2!A4

USING THE WATCH WINDOW TOOLBAR

1 Click a cell containing a formula you want to watch.

2 Click **Tools**.

3 Click **Formula Auditing**.

4 Click **Show Watch Window**.

Note: If Show Watch Window does not appear on the menu, position the mouse ⩔ over the bottom of the menu to display the menu option.

■ The Watch Window toolbar appears.

5 Click **Add Watch** to add the formula you selected in step **1** to the Watch Window toolbar.

■ The Add Watch dialog box appears.

■ This area displays the worksheet name and cell reference for the cell containing the formula.

6 Click **Add** to add the formula to the Watch Window toolbar.

How do I change the width of a column in the Watch Window toolbar?

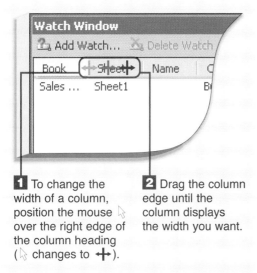

1 To change the width of a column, position the mouse over the right edge of the column heading (changes to).

2 Drag the column edge until the column displays the width you want.

What information appears in the Watch Window toolbar?

■ The name of the workbook containing the formula.

■ The name of the worksheet containing the formula.

■ The name of the cell containing the formula. To name cells, see page 56.

■ The cell reference of the cell containing the formula.

■ The result of the formula.

■ The formula you are watching.

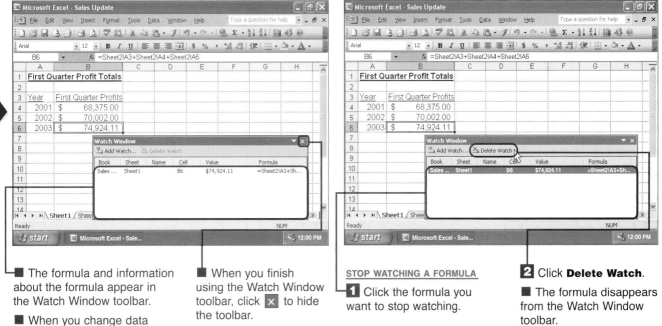

■ The formula and information about the formula appear in the Watch Window toolbar.

■ When you change data used in the formula, the Watch Window toolbar will display the new result of the formula.

■ When you finish using the Watch Window toolbar, click ☒ to hide the toolbar.

STOP WATCHING A FORMULA

1 Click the formula you want to stop watching.

2 Click **Delete Watch**.

■ The formula disappears from the Watch Window toolbar.

CHAPTER 10

Work With Charts

Are you interested in displaying your worksheet data in a chart? In this chapter, you will learn how to create, change and print charts.

Introduction to Charts 184

Create a Chart...............................186

Move or Resize a Chart 190

Print a Chart 192

Change the Chart Type....................193

Change Chart Titles 194

Rotate Chart Text 195

Format Chart Text...........................196

Add Data to a Chart 198

Add a Data Table to a Chart............200

Change the Way Data is Plotted 201

Change the Appearance of a
   Data Series 202

INTRODUCTION TO CHARTS

A chart allows you to visually display your worksheet data and can help you compare data and view trends. Excel offers many different chart types.

PARTS OF A CHART

Data Series

A group of related data representing one row or column from your worksheet. Each data series is represented by a specific color, pattern or symbol.

Chart Title

Identifies the subject of your chart.

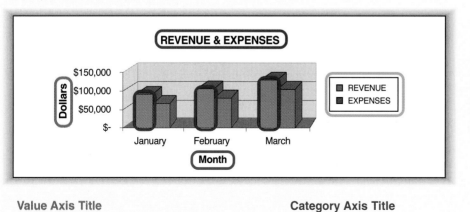

Legend

Identifies the color, pattern or symbol that represents each data series in your chart.

Value Axis Title

Indicates the unit of measure used in your chart.

Category Axis Title

Indicates the categories used in your chart.

COMMON CHART TYPES

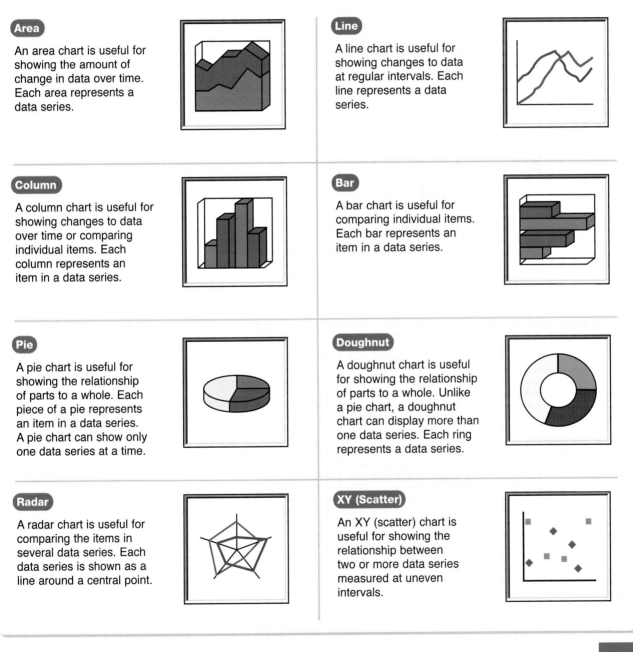

Area

An area chart is useful for showing the amount of change in data over time. Each area represents a data series.

Line

A line chart is useful for showing changes to data at regular intervals. Each line represents a data series.

Column

A column chart is useful for showing changes to data over time or comparing individual items. Each column represents an item in a data series.

Bar

A bar chart is useful for comparing individual items. Each bar represents an item in a data series.

Pie

A pie chart is useful for showing the relationship of parts to a whole. Each piece of a pie represents an item in a data series. A pie chart can show only one data series at a time.

Doughnut

A doughnut chart is useful for showing the relationship of parts to a whole. Unlike a pie chart, a doughnut chart can display more than one data series. Each ring represents a data series.

Radar

A radar chart is useful for comparing the items in several data series. Each data series is shown as a line around a central point.

XY (Scatter)

An XY (scatter) chart is useful for showing the relationship between two or more data series measured at uneven intervals.

CREATE A CHART

You can create a chart to graphically display your worksheet data. Charts allow you to easily compare data and view patterns and trends.

The Chart Wizard takes you step by step through the process of creating a chart.

CREATE A CHART

1 Select the cells containing the data you want to display in a chart, including the row and column labels. To select cells, see page 10.

2 Click 📊 to create a chart.

Note: If 📊 is not displayed, click ⚏ on the Standard toolbar to display the button.

■ The Chart Wizard appears.

3 Click the type of chart you want to create.

■ This area displays the available chart designs for the type of chart you selected.

4 Click the chart design you want to use.

5 Click **Next** to continue.

Can I see a preview of my chart when I'm choosing the chart type and design?

Yes. After performing step **4** below, you can press and hold down the **Press and Hold to View Sample** button to see a preview of how your chart will appear with the chart type and design you selected.

What titles can I add to my chart?

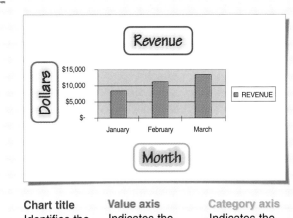

Chart title	**Value axis**	**Category axis**
Identifies the subject of your chart.	Indicates the unit of measure used in your chart.	Indicates the categories used in your chart.

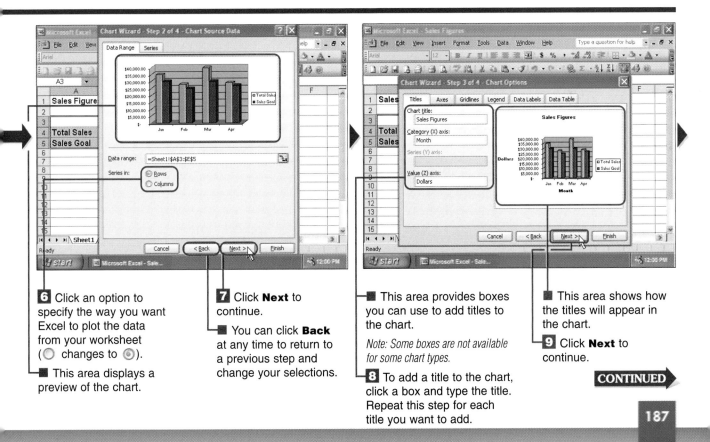

6 Click an option to specify the way you want Excel to plot the data from your worksheet (○ changes to ◉).

■ This area displays a preview of the chart.

7 Click **Next** to continue.

■ You can click **Back** at any time to return to a previous step and change your selections.

■ This area provides boxes you can use to add titles to the chart.

Note: Some boxes are not available for some chart types.

8 To add a title to the chart, click a box and type the title. Repeat this step for each title you want to add.

■ This area shows how the titles will appear in the chart.

9 Click **Next** to continue.

CONTINUED ▶

CREATE A CHART

When creating a chart, you can choose to display the chart on the same worksheet as the data or on its own sheet, called a chart sheet.

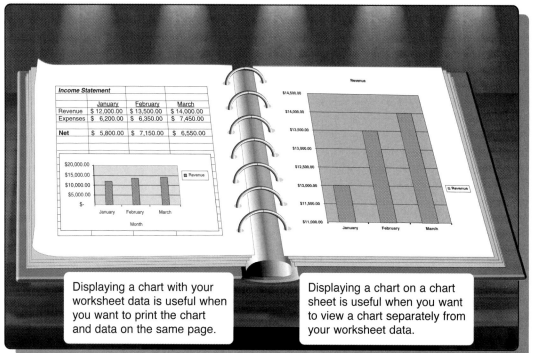

Displaying a chart with your worksheet data is useful when you want to print the chart and data on the same page.

Displaying a chart on a chart sheet is useful when you want to view a chart separately from your worksheet data.

CREATE A CHART (CONTINUED)

10 Click an option to specify where you want to display the chart (○ changes to ◉).

As new sheet - Displays the chart on its own sheet, called a chart sheet.

As object in - Displays the chart on the same worksheet as the data.

■ If you selected **As new sheet** in step **10**, you can type a name for the chart sheet in this area.

11 Click **Finish** to create the chart.

What happens if I change the data I used to create a chart?

If you change the data you used to create a chart, Excel will automatically update the chart to display the changes.

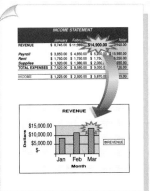

Is there a way to quickly create a chart?

Yes. To quickly create a basic chart, select the cells containing the data you want to display in the chart and then press the F11 key. The chart will appear on its own chart sheet.

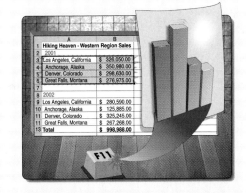

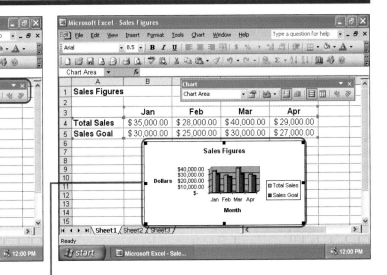

■ In this example, the chart appears on the same worksheet as the data.

■ The Chart toolbar also appears, displaying buttons that allow you to make changes to the chart.

■ Excel outlines the data you selected to create the chart.

■ The handles (■) around a chart let you change the size of the chart. To hide the handles, click outside the chart.

Note: To move or resize a chart, see page 190.

DELETE A CHART

1 Click a blank area in the chart you want to delete. Handles (■) appear around the chart.

2 Press the Delete key to delete the chart.

Note: To delete a chart displayed on a chart sheet, you must delete the sheet. To delete a worksheet, see page 173.

MOVE OR RESIZE A CHART

You can change the location and size of a chart displayed on your worksheet.

– Move –

– Resize –

Moving a chart to another location in your worksheet is useful if the chart covers your data. Increasing the size of a chart is useful if the information in the chart is too small to read.

MOVE A CHART

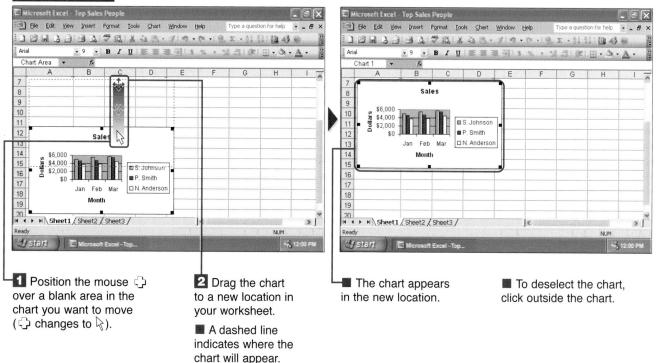

1 Position the mouse ⊕ over a blank area in the chart you want to move (⊕ changes to ⇖).

2 Drag the chart to a new location in your worksheet.

■ A dashed line indicates where the chart will appear.

■ The chart appears in the new location.

■ To deselect the chart, click outside the chart.

What handle (■) should I use to resize a chart?

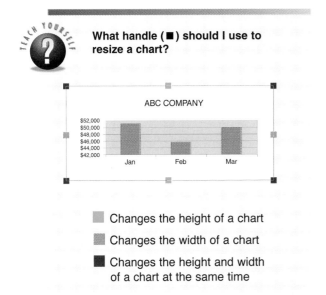

ABC COMPANY

Changes the height of a chart

Changes the width of a chart

Changes the height and width of a chart at the same time

Can I move individual items in a chart?

Yes. To move the chart title, an axis title or the legend to a new location in a chart, position the mouse ↖ over the item. Then drag the item to a new location. You cannot move an item outside of the chart area.

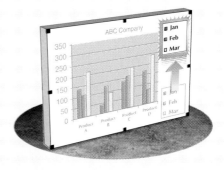

RESIZE A CHART

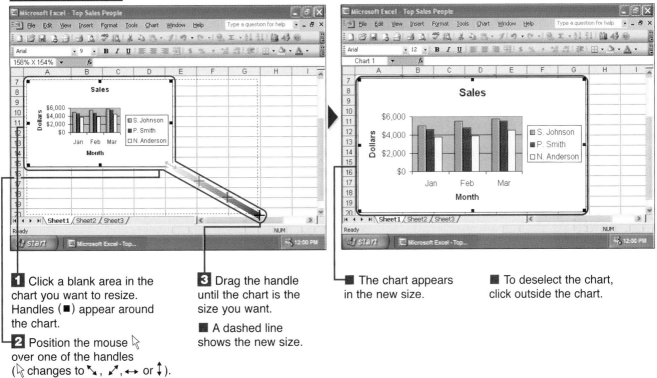

1 Click a blank area in the chart you want to resize. Handles (■) appear around the chart.

2 Position the mouse ↖ over one of the handles (↖ changes to ↘, ↗, ↔ or ↕).

3 Drag the handle until the chart is the size you want.

■ A dashed line shows the new size.

■ The chart appears in the new size.

■ To deselect the chart, click outside the chart.

PRINT A CHART

You can print
your chart with
the worksheet
data or on its
own page.

When you print a
chart on its own
page, the chart
will expand to fill
the page.

Print a chart with
worksheet data

Print a chart on
its own page

PRINT A CHART

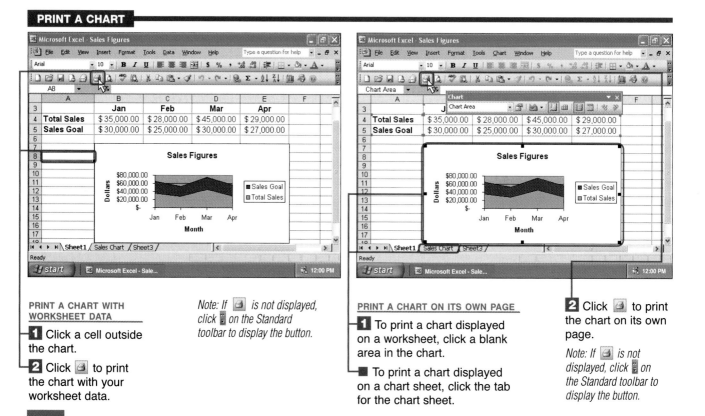

**PRINT A CHART WITH
WORKSHEET DATA**

1 Click a cell outside
the chart.

2 Click 🖨 to print
the chart with your
worksheet data.

*Note: If 🖨 is not displayed,
click ⚘ on the Standard
toolbar to display the button.*

PRINT A CHART ON ITS OWN PAGE

1 To print a chart displayed
on a worksheet, click a blank
area in the chart.

■ To print a chart displayed
on a chart sheet, click the tab
for the chart sheet.

2 Click 🖨 to print
the chart on its own
page.

*Note: If 🖨 is not
displayed, click ⚘ on
the Standard toolbar to
display the button.*

192

CHANGE THE CHART TYPE

After you create a chart, you can change the chart type to present your data more effectively.

The type of chart you should use depends on your data. For example, area, column and line charts are ideal for showing changes to values over time. Pie charts are ideal for showing percentages.

CHANGE THE CHART TYPE

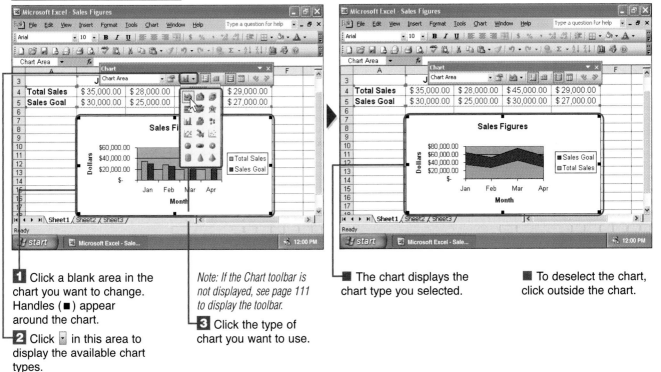

1 Click a blank area in the chart you want to change. Handles (■) appear around the chart.

2 Click ⬚ in this area to display the available chart types.

Note: If the Chart toolbar is not displayed, see page 111 to display the toolbar.

3 Click the type of chart you want to use.

■ The chart displays the chart type you selected.

■ To deselect the chart, click outside the chart.

CHANGE CHART TITLES

You can change the chart and axis titles in a chart to make the titles more meaningful.

CHANGE CHART TITLES

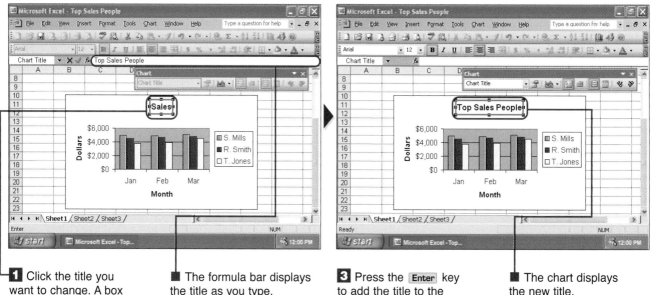

1 Click the title you want to change. A box appears around the title.

2 Type the new title.

■ The formula bar displays the title as you type.

3 Press the Enter key to add the title to the chart.

■ The chart displays the new title.

■ To deselect the title, click outside the chart.

ROTATE CHART TEXT

You can rotate text on a chart axis to improve the appearance of the chart.

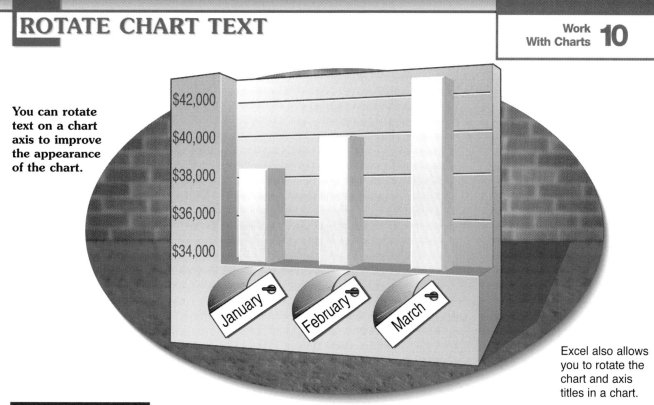

Excel also allows you to rotate the chart and axis titles in a chart.

ROTATE CHART TEXT

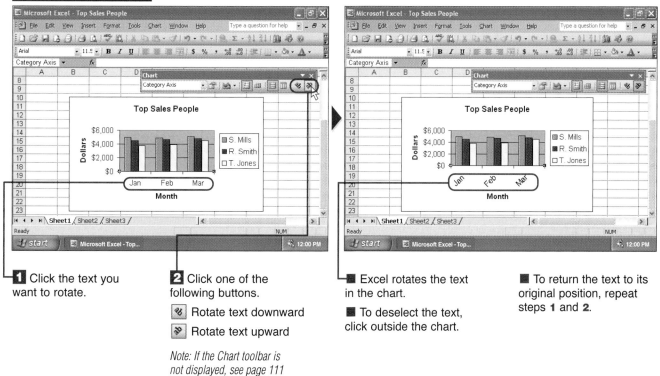

1 Click the text you want to rotate.

2 Click one of the following buttons.

🖉 Rotate text downward

🖉 Rotate text upward

Note: If the Chart toolbar is not displayed, see page 111 to display the toolbar.

■ Excel rotates the text in the chart.

■ To deselect the text, click outside the chart.

■ To return the text to its original position, repeat steps **1** and **2**.

195

FORMAT CHART TEXT

You can enhance the appearance of a chart by changing the font, size or style of text.

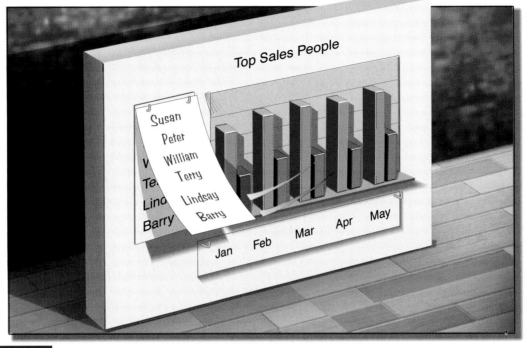

FORMAT CHART TEXT

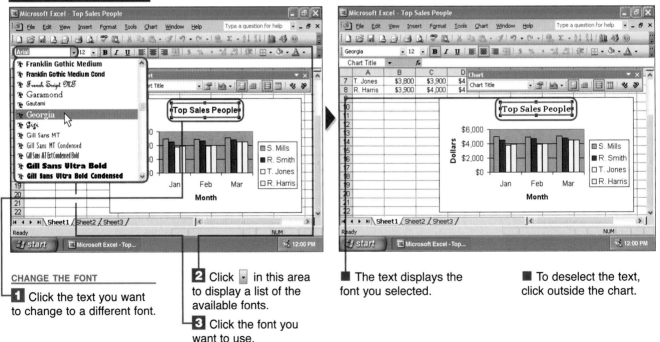

CHANGE THE FONT

1 Click the text you want to change to a different font.

2 Click ▾ in this area to display a list of the available fonts.

3 Click the font you want to use.

■ The text displays the font you selected.

■ To deselect the text, click outside the chart.

196

Can I format numbers in a chart?

Yes. Click the numbers you want to format and then perform the steps below. You can also click one of the following buttons on the Formatting toolbar to change the style of selected numbers in a chart.

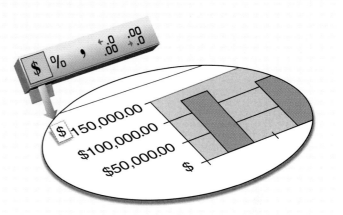

- **$** Currency
- **%** Percent
- **,** Comma
- Add a decimal place
- Remove a decimal place

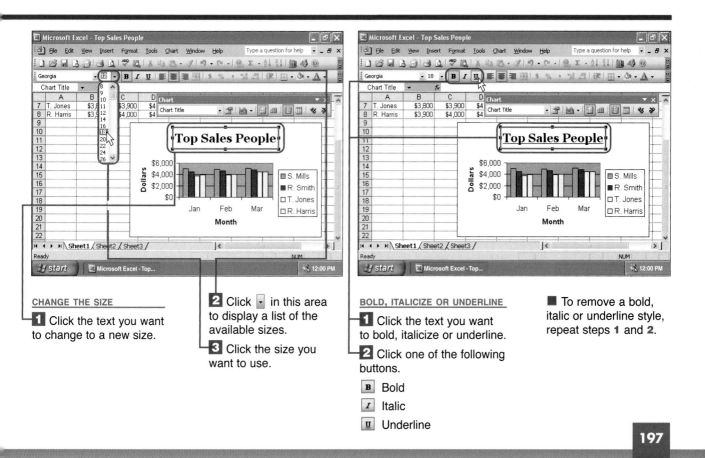

CHANGE THE SIZE

1 Click the text you want to change to a new size.

2 Click ▾ in this area to display a list of the available sizes.

3 Click the size you want to use.

BOLD, ITALICIZE OR UNDERLINE

1 Click the text you want to bold, italicize or underline.

2 Click one of the following buttons.

- **B** Bold
- **I** Italic
- **U** Underline

■ To remove a bold, italic or underline style, repeat steps **1** and **2**.

197

ADD DATA TO A CHART

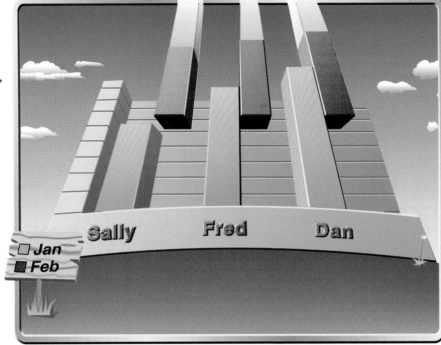

After you create a chart, you can add new data to the chart.

Adding data to a chart is useful when you need to update the chart. For example, you can add the latest sales figures to your chart at the end of each month.

ADD DATA TO A CHART

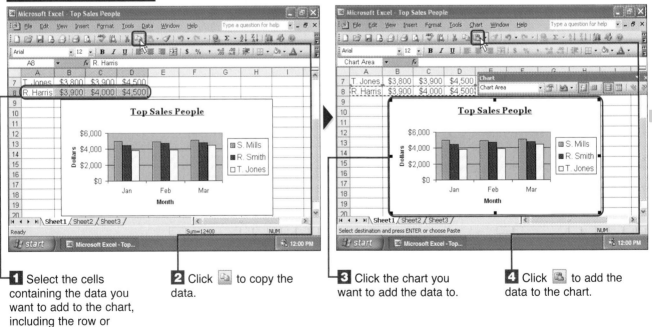

1 Select the cells containing the data you want to add to the chart, including the row or column labels. To select cells, see page 10.

2 Click 📋 to copy the data.

3 Click the chart you want to add the data to.

4 Click 📋 to add the data to the chart.

Can I add a data series to a pie chart?

A pie chart can display only one data series. You cannot add another data series to a pie chart.

 How can I add a data series to a chart displayed on a chart sheet?

To add a data series to a chart displayed on a chart sheet, perform steps **1** and **2** on page 198. Click the tab for the chart sheet containing the chart you want to add the data series to and then perform step **4**.

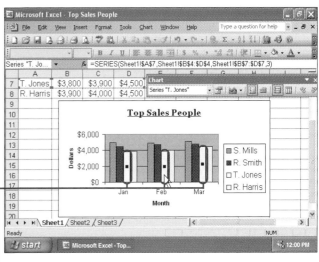

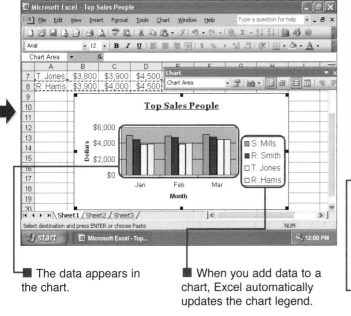

■ The data appears in the chart.

■ When you add data to a chart, Excel automatically updates the chart legend.

DELETE DATA FROM A CHART

1 Click the data you want to remove from the chart. Handles (■) appear on the data series.

2 Press the Delete key to delete the data from the chart.

199

ADD A DATA TABLE TO A CHART

You can add a table to a chart to display the data used to create the chart.

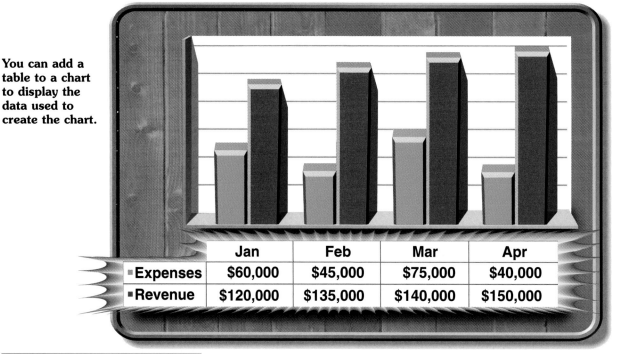

	Jan	Feb	Mar	Apr
■Expenses	$60,000	$45,000	$75,000	$40,000
■Revenue	$120,000	$135,000	$140,000	$150,000

ADD A DATA TABLE TO A CHART

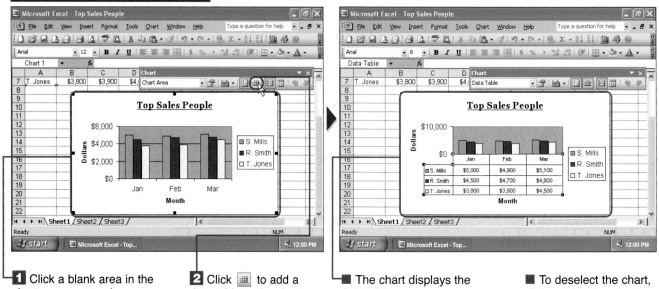

1 Click a blank area in the chart you want to change. Handles (■) appear around the chart.

Note: You cannot add a data table to some types of charts.

2 Click 🔳 to add a data table to the chart.

Note: If the Chart toolbar is not displayed, see page 111 to display the toolbar.

■ The chart displays the data table.

Note: If data in the data table is hidden, you may have to change the width of the chart. To resize a chart, see page 190.

■ To deselect the chart, click outside the chart.

■ To remove the data table from the chart, repeat steps **1** and **2**.

You can change
the way Excel plots
the data in a chart.
This allows you to
emphasize different
information in the
chart.

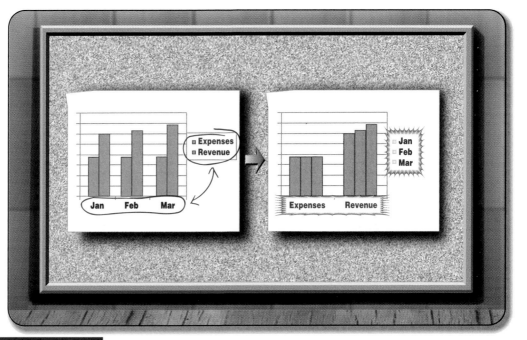

CHANGE THE WAY DATA IS PLOTTED

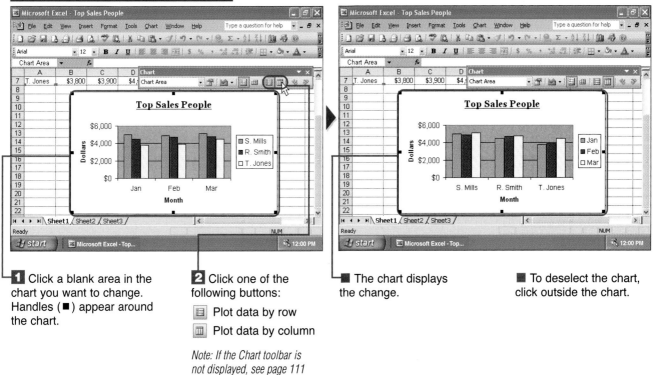

1 Click a blank area in the
chart you want to change.
Handles (■) appear around
the chart.

2 Click one of the
following buttons:

▤ Plot data by row

▥ Plot data by column

Note: If the Chart toolbar is
not displayed, see page 111
to display the toolbar.

■ The chart displays
the change.

■ To deselect the chart,
click outside the chart.

CHANGE THE APPEARANCE OF A DATA SERIES

You can change the color of a data series in a chart. You can also add a pattern to a data series.

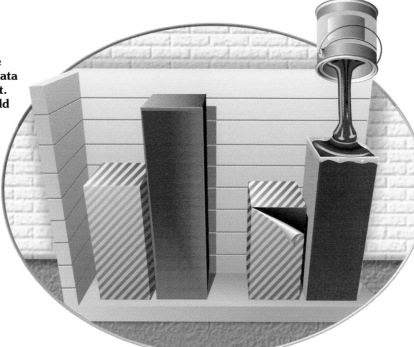

If you will print your chart on a black-and-white printer, adding a pattern to a data series may make it easier to identify the data series in the chart.

When you change the appearance of a data series, Excel automatically updates the chart legend.

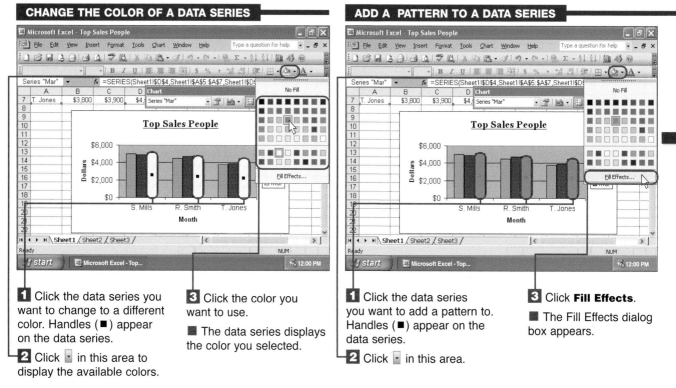

CHANGE THE COLOR OF A DATA SERIES

1 Click the data series you want to change to a different color. Handles (■) appear on the data series.

2 Click ⁚ in this area to display the available colors.

3 Click the color you want to use.

■ The data series displays the color you selected.

ADD A PATTERN TO A DATA SERIES

1 Click the data series you want to add a pattern to. Handles (■) appear on the data series.

2 Click ⁚ in this area.

3 Click **Fill Effects**.

■ The Fill Effects dialog box appears.

Can I change the appearance of other parts of a chart?

You can change the appearance of other parts of a chart, such as the background of the chart or the chart legend.

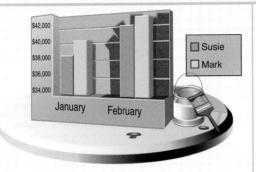

To change the color of part of a chart, click the part you want to change. Then perform steps **2** and **3** on page 202 to select the color you want to use.

To add a pattern to part of a chart, click the part you want to change. Then perform steps **2** to **6** starting on page 202 to select the pattern you want to use.

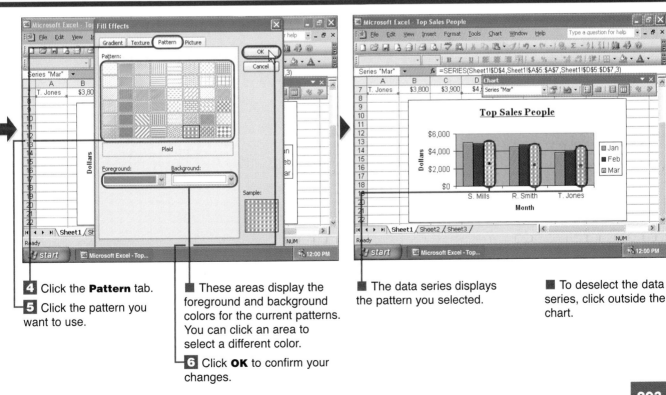

4 Click the **Pattern** tab.

5 Click the pattern you want to use.

■ These areas display the foreground and background colors for the current patterns. You can click an area to select a different color.

6 Click **OK** to confirm your changes.

■ The data series displays the pattern you selected.

■ To deselect the data series, click outside the chart.

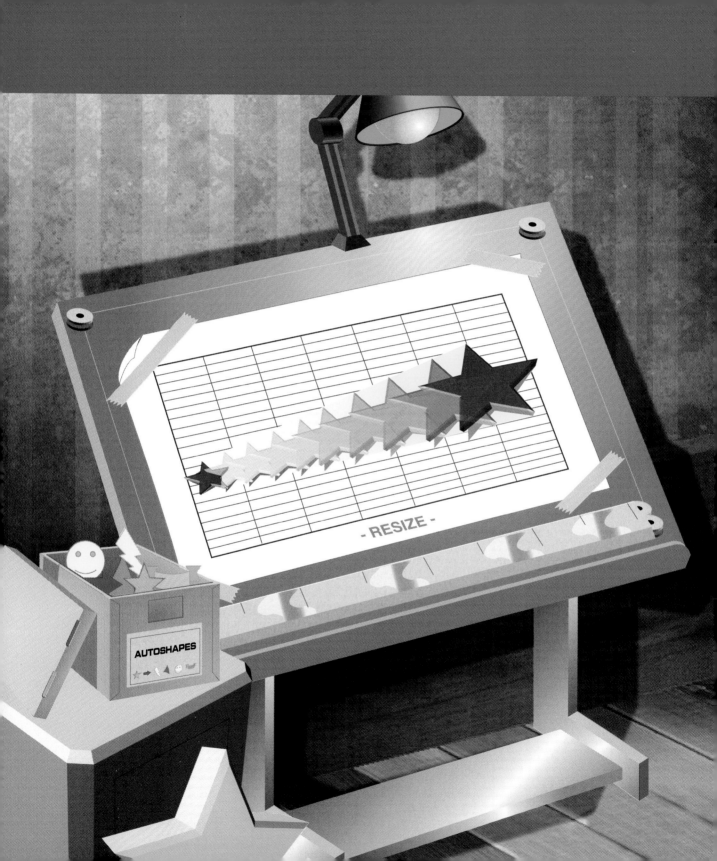

CHAPTER 11

Work With Objects

Are you wondering how to use objects, such as AutoShapes and clip art images, to enhance the appearance of your worksheet? This chapter shows you how.

Add WordArt.................................206

Add an AutoShape.........................208

Add a Text Box 210

Add a Picture................................212

Add a Clip Art Image.....................214

Move or Resize an Object...............218

Change the Color of an Object 220

Rotate an Object 221

Add a Shadow to an Object 222

Make an Object 3-D 223

Add a Diagram 224

Hockey Stats

ADD WORDART

You can add WordArt to your worksheet or chart to create an eye-catching title or draw attention to important information.

WordArt allows you to create decorative text that is skewed, curved, rotated, stretched, three-dimensional or even vertical.

ADD WORDART

1 To add WordArt to your worksheet, click a cell in the worksheet.

■ To add WordArt to a chart, click the chart.

2 Click **Insert**.

3 Click **Picture**.

4 Click **WordArt**.

■ The WordArt Gallery dialog box appears.

5 Click the WordArt style you want to use.

6 Click **OK** to confirm your selection.

How do I edit WordArt text?

To edit WordArt text, double-click the WordArt to display the Edit WordArt Text dialog box. Then perform steps **7** and **8** below to specify the new text you want the WordArt to display.

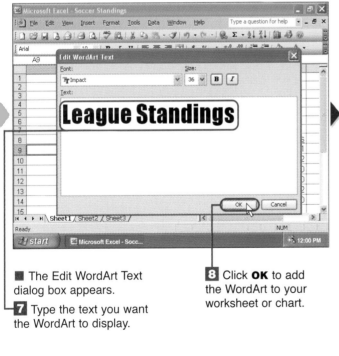

Why does the WordArt toolbar appear when I select WordArt in a worksheet or chart?

The WordArt toolbar contains buttons that allow you to change the appearance of WordArt. For example, you can click one of the following buttons to alter the appearance of WordArt.

Aa Display all the letters in the WordArt at the same height.

Ab Display the WordArt text vertically rather than horizontally.

■ The Edit WordArt Text dialog box appears.

7 Type the text you want the WordArt to display.

8 Click **OK** to add the WordArt to your worksheet or chart.

■ The WordArt appears. The handles (○) around the WordArt allow you to change the size of the WordArt. To move or resize WordArt, see page 218.

■ To deselect WordArt, click outside the WordArt.

DELETE WORDART

1 Click the WordArt you want to delete. Handles (○) appear around the WordArt.

2 Press the Delete key to delete the WordArt.

ADD AN AUTOSHAPE

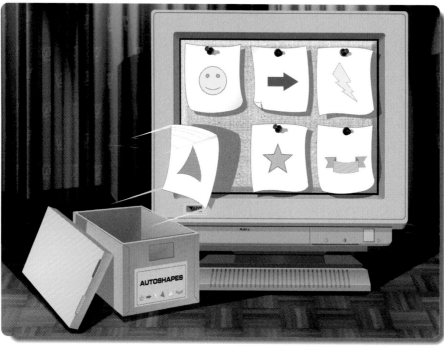

Excel provides ready-made shapes, called AutoShapes, that you can add to your worksheet or chart.

Excel offers several types of AutoShapes such as lines, arrows, stars and banners.

ADD AN AUTOSHAPE

1 To add an AutoShape to your worksheet, click a cell in the worksheet.

■ To add an AutoShape to a chart, click the chart.

2 Click to display the Drawing toolbar.

■ The Drawing toolbar appears.

3 Click **AutoShapes**.

4 Click the type of AutoShape you want to add.

5 Click the AutoShape you want to add.

Can I add text to an AutoShape?

You can add text to most AutoShapes. This is particularly useful for AutoShapes such as banners and callouts. To add text to an AutoShape, click the AutoShape and then type the text you want the AutoShape to display.

 How can I change the shape of an AutoShape?

You can change the shape of any AutoShape that displays a yellow handle (◇). Click the AutoShape and position the mouse ↖ over the yellow handle (↖ changes to ▷). Then drag the mouse until the dashed line displays the way you want the AutoShape to appear.

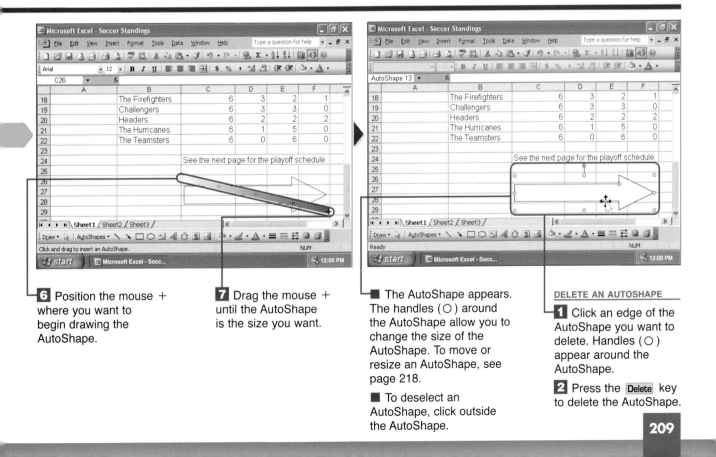

6 Position the mouse + where you want to begin drawing the AutoShape.

7 Drag the mouse + until the AutoShape is the size you want.

■ The AutoShape appears. The handles (○) around the AutoShape allow you to change the size of the AutoShape. To move or resize an AutoShape, see page 218.

■ To deselect an AutoShape, click outside the AutoShape.

DELETE AN AUTOSHAPE

1 Click an edge of the AutoShape you want to delete. Handles (○) appear around the AutoShape.

2 Press the Delete key to delete the AutoShape.

ADD A TEXT BOX

You can add a text box to your worksheet or chart to display additional information.

Text boxes are useful for displaying notes. You can also use text boxes to label or describe items in your worksheet or chart.

---

1 To add a text box to your worksheet, click a cell in the worksheet.

■ To add a text box to a chart, click the chart.

2 Click 🔲 to display the Drawing toolbar.

■ The Drawing toolbar appears.

3 Click 🔲 to add a text box.

4 Position the mouse ↓ where you want to begin drawing the text box.

5 Drag the mouse + until the text box is the size you want.

How do I edit the text in a text box?

To edit the text in a text box, click the text box and then edit the text as you would edit any text in your worksheet. When you finish editing the text, click outside the text box.

Can I format the text in a text box?

Yes. Click the text box and then drag the mouse I over the text you want to format until you highlight the text. You can then format the text as you would format any text in your worksheet. For example, you can change the font and size of text or bold, italicize and underline text. To format text, see pages 116 to 126.

■ The text box appears. The handles (○) around the text box allow you to change the size of the text box. To move or resize a text box, see page 218.

6 Type the text you want the text box to display.

■ To deselect a text box, click outside the text box.

Note: To hide the Drawing toolbar, repeat step 2.

DELETE A TEXT BOX

1 Click an edge of the text box you want to delete. Handles (○) appear around the text box.

2 Press the Delete key to delete the text box.

ADD A PICTURE

You can add a picture stored on your computer to your worksheet or chart.

Adding a picture is useful when you want to display your company logo or a picture of your products.

ADD A PICTURE

1 To add a picture to your worksheet, click a cell in the worksheet.

■ To add a picture to a chart, click the chart.

2 Click **Insert**.

3 Click **Picture**.

4 Click **From File**.

■ The Insert Picture dialog box appears.

■ This area shows the location of the displayed pictures. You can click this area to change the location.

■ This area allows you to access pictures stored in commonly used locations. You can click a location to display the pictures stored in the location.

Note: For information on the commonly used locations, see the top of page 23.

Where can I get pictures that I can add to my worksheet or chart?

You can purchase collections of pictures at stores that sell computer software or obtain pictures on the Internet. You can also use a scanner to scan pictures into your computer or create your own pictures using an image editing program, such as Adobe Photoshop.

Why does the Picture toolbar appear when I select a picture in my worksheet or chart?

The Picture toolbar contains buttons that allow you to change the appearance of a picture. For example, you can click one of the following buttons to alter the appearance of a picture.

Increase the brightness of a picture.

Decrease the brightness of a picture.

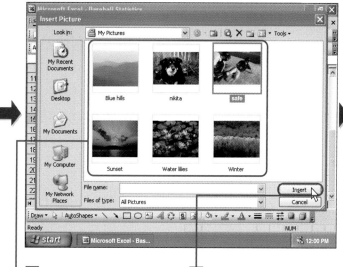

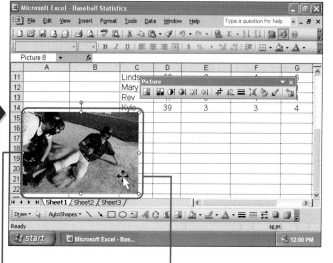

5 Click the picture you want to add to your worksheet or chart.

6 Click **Insert** to add the picture to your worksheet or chart.

■ The picture appears. The handles (○) around the picture allow you to change the size of the picture. To move or resize a picture, see page 218.

■ To deselect a picture, click outside the picture.

DELETE A PICTURE

1 Click the picture you want to delete. Handles (○) appear around the picture.

2 Press the Delete key to delete the picture.

ADD A CLIP ART IMAGE

You can add professionally-designed clip art images to your worksheet or chart. Clip art images can help illustrate concepts and make your worksheet or chart more interesting.

ADD A CLIP ART IMAGE

1 Click **Insert**.

2 Click **Picture**.

3 Click **Clip Art**.

■ The Clip Art task pane appears.

4 Click **Organize clips** to view all the available clip art images in the Microsoft Clip Organizer.

Note: The first time you add a clip art image to a worksheet or chart, the Add Clips to Organizer dialog box appears. To catalog the clip art images and other media files on your computer, click Now in the dialog box.

In the Microsoft Clip Organizer, what type of
clip art images will I find in each collection?

My Collections

Displays images that came with
Microsoft Windows and images
you created or obtained on your
own.

Office Collections

Displays the images that
came with Microsoft Office.

Web Collections

Displays the images that are
available at Microsoft's Web site
and at Web sites in partnership
with Microsoft.

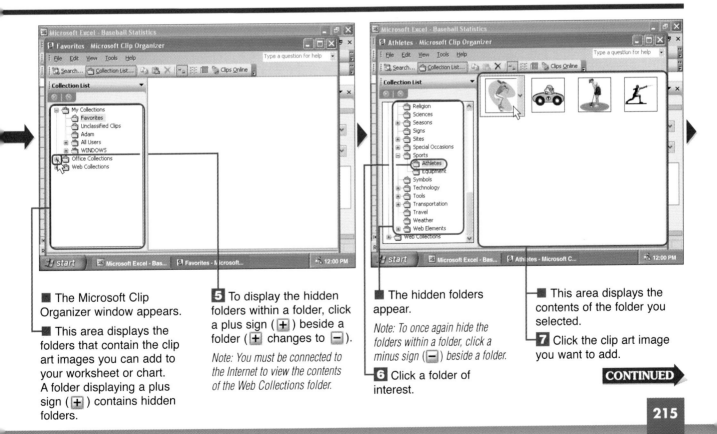

■ The Microsoft Clip
Organizer window appears.

■ This area displays the
folders that contain the clip
art images you can add to
your worksheet or chart.
A folder displaying a plus
sign (⊞) contains hidden
folders.

5 To display the hidden
folders within a folder, click
a plus sign (⊞) beside a
folder (⊞ changes to ⊟).

*Note: You must be connected to
the Internet to view the contents
of the Web Collections folder.*

■ The hidden folders
appear.

*Note: To once again hide the
folders within a folder, click a
minus sign (⊟) beside a folder.*

6 Click a folder of
interest.

■ This area displays the
contents of the folder you
selected.

7 Click the clip art image
you want to add.

CONTINUED

ADD A CLIP ART IMAGE

After you locate an image you want to add to your worksheet or chart, you can copy the image to the clipboard and then place the image in your worksheet or chart.

The clipboard temporarily stores information you have selected to move or copy.

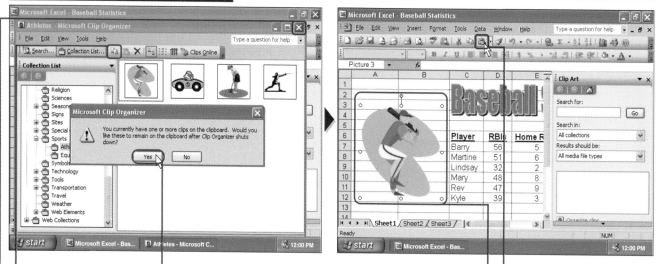

8 Click 🔳 to copy the image you selected to the clipboard.

9 Click ✕ to close the Microsoft Clip Organizer window.

■ A dialog box appears, stating that you have one or more clip art images on the clipboard.

10 Click **Yes** to keep the image on the clipboard.

11 To add the image to your worksheet, click a cell in the worksheet.

■ To add the image to a chart, click the chart.

12 Click 🔳 to place the image in your worksheet or chart.

■ The clip art image appears. The handles (○) around the clip art image allow you to change the size of the image. To move or resize an image, see page 218.

216

Where can I obtain more clip art images?

You can buy collections of clip art images at computer stores. Many Web sites, such as www.noeticart.com, also offer clip art images you can use in your worksheet or chart.

How do I delete a clip art image?

To delete a clip art image, click the clip art image and then press the Delete key.

SEARCH FOR A CLIP ART IMAGE

You can search for clip art images by specifying one or more words of interest in the Clip Art task pane.

1 Click this area and then type one or more words that describe the clip art image you want to find. Then press the Enter key.

Note: To display the Clip Art task pane, perform steps 1 to 3 on page 214.

■ This area displays the images that match the words you specified.

2 To add an image to your worksheet, click a cell in the worksheet.

■ To add an image to a chart, click the chart.

3 Click the image you want to add to your worksheet or chart.

■ The image appears in your worksheet or chart.

217

MOVE OR RESIZE AN OBJECT

You can change the location and size of an object in your worksheet or chart.

For example, you may want to move a picture to a more suitable location or increase the size of a text box to display more text.

MOVE AN OBJECT

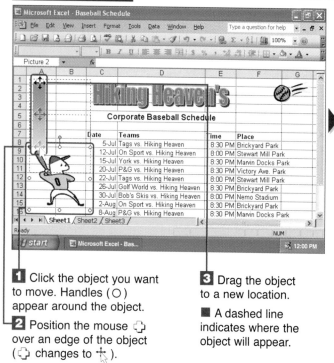

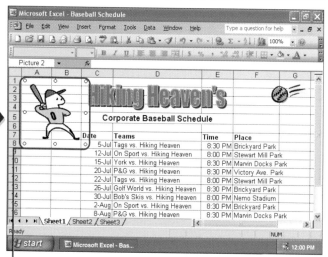

1 Click the object you want to move. Handles (○) appear around the object.

2 Position the mouse ⊹ over an edge of the object (⊹ changes to ✛).

3 Drag the object to a new location.

■ A dashed line indicates where the object will appear.

■ The object appears in the new location.

Note: If the object you are moving is on a chart, you cannot move the object outside the chart area.

■ To deselect the object, click outside the object.

Which handle (○) should I use to resize an object?

The handles that appear at the top and bottom of an object (●) allow you to change the height of the object. The handles at the sides of an object (●) allow you to change the width of the object. The handles at the corners of an object (●) allow you to change the height and width of the object at the same time.

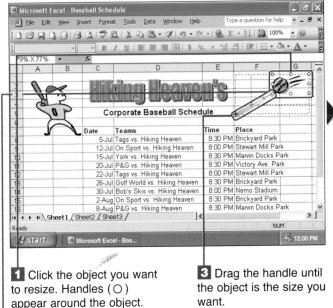

How can I change the way an object is moved or resized?

To move an object only horizontally or vertically, press and hold down the Shift key as you move the object.

To keep the center of an object in the same place while resizing the object, press and hold down the Ctrl key as you resize the object.

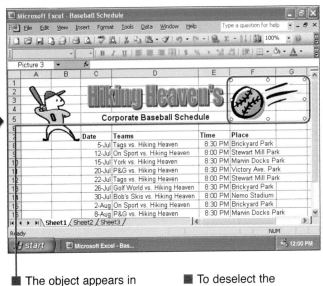

RESIZE AN OBJECT

1 Click the object you want to resize. Handles (○) appear around the object.

2 Position the mouse ⬚ over one of the handles (⬚ changes to ↗, ↘, ↔ or ↕).

3 Drag the handle until the object is the size you want.

■ A dashed line indicates the new size.

■ The object appears in the new size.

■ To deselect the object, click outside the object.

CHANGE THE COLOR OF AN OBJECT

You can change the color of an object in your worksheet or chart.

You cannot change the color of some clip art images and pictures.

CHANGE THE COLOR OF AN OBJECT

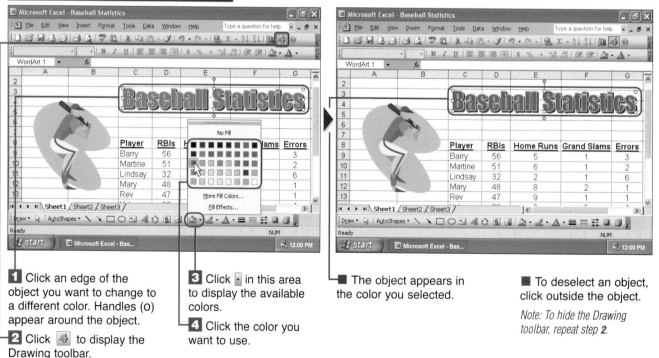

1 Click an edge of the object you want to change to a different color. Handles (○) appear around the object.

2 Click 🖌 to display the Drawing toolbar.

3 Click ▾ in this area to display the available colors.

4 Click the color you want to use.

■ The object appears in the color you selected.

■ To deselect an object, click outside the object.

Note: To hide the Drawing toolbar, repeat step 2.

You can rotate
an object in
your worksheet
or chart.

You cannot
rotate text boxes
and some
AutoShapes.

ROTATE AN OBJECT

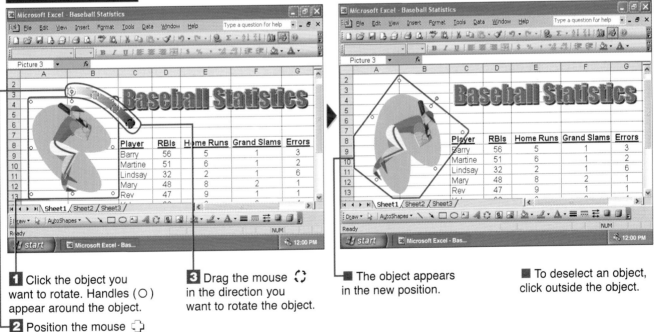

1 Click the object you
want to rotate. Handles (○)
appear around the object.

2 Position the mouse ⟳
over the green dot
(⟳ changes to ⟳).

3 Drag the mouse ⟳
in the direction you
want to rotate the object.

■ The object appears
in the new position.

■ To deselect an object,
click outside the object.

ADD A SHADOW TO AN OBJECT

You can add a shadow to add depth to an object in your worksheet or chart.

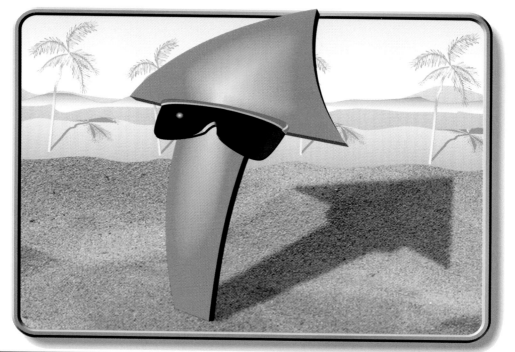

ADD A SHADOW TO AN OBJECT

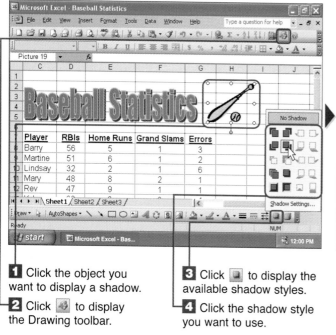

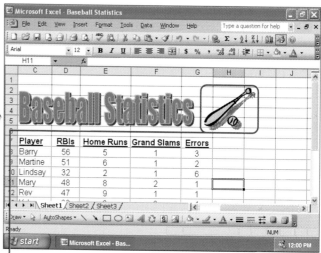

1 Click the object you want to display a shadow.

2 Click ![icon] to display the Drawing toolbar.

3 Click ![icon] to display the available shadow styles.

4 Click the shadow style you want to use.

Note: If a shadow style is dimmed, the style is not available for the object you selected.

■ The object displays the shadow.

Note: To hide the Drawing toolbar, repeat step 2.

■ To remove a shadow from an object, repeat steps **1** to **4**, selecting **No Shadow** in step **4**.

You can make
an object in your
worksheet or
chart appear
three-dimensional.

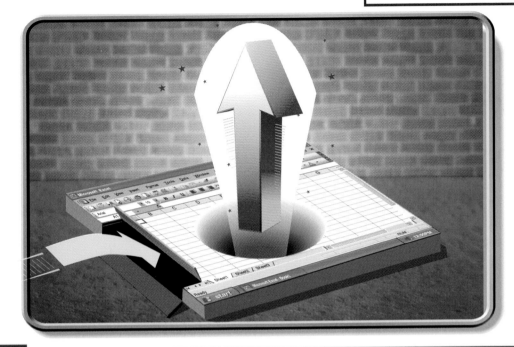

MAKE AN OBJECT 3-D

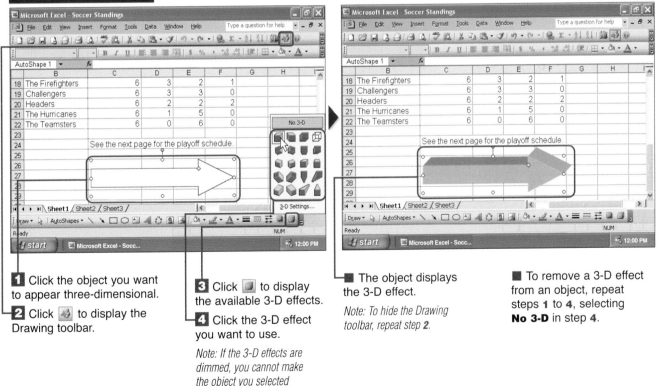

1 Click the object you want
to appear three-dimensional.

2 Click 🔲 to display the
Drawing toolbar.

3 Click 🔲 to display
the available 3-D effects.

4 Click the 3-D effect
you want to use.

Note: If the 3-D effects are
dimmed, you cannot make
the object you selected
three-dimensional.

■ The object displays
the 3-D effect.

Note: To hide the Drawing
toolbar, repeat step 2.

■ To remove a 3-D effect
from an object, repeat
steps 1 to 4, selecting
No 3-D in step 4.

ADD A DIAGRAM

You can add a
diagram to a
worksheet to
illustrate a concept
or idea. Excel
provides several
types of diagrams
for you to choose
from.

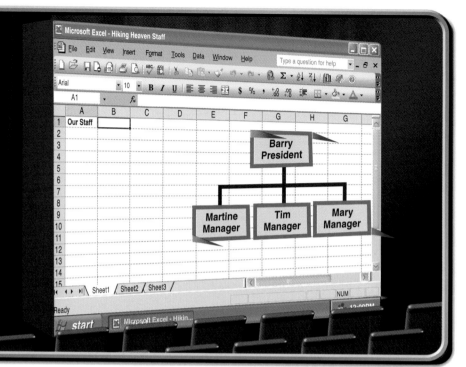

ADD A DIAGRAM

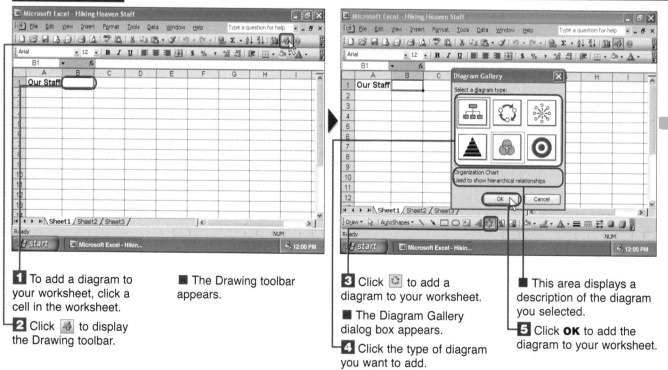

1 To add a diagram to
your worksheet, click a
cell in the worksheet.

2 Click ⬛ to display
the Drawing toolbar.

■ The Drawing toolbar
appears.

3 Click ⬛ to add a
diagram to your worksheet.

■ The Diagram Gallery
dialog box appears.

4 Click the type of diagram
you want to add.

■ This area displays a
description of the diagram
you selected.

5 Click **OK** to add the
diagram to your worksheet.

Where can I position a shape I add to an organization chart?

Subordinate

Adds a shape below the shape you selected.

Coworker

Adds a shape beside the shape you selected.

Assistant

Uses an elbow connector to add a shape below the shape you selected.

How do I delete a diagram?

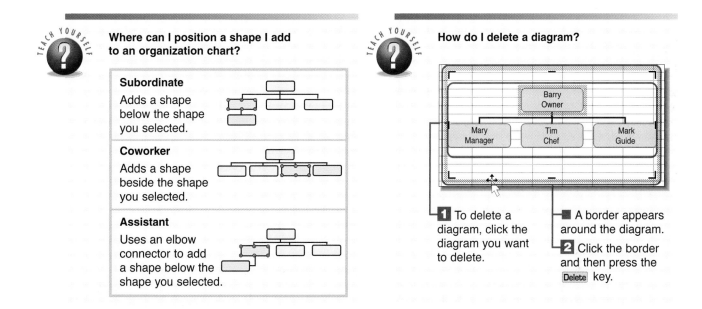

■ **1** To delete a diagram, click the diagram you want to delete.

■ A border appears around the diagram.

■ **2** Click the border and then press the Delete key.

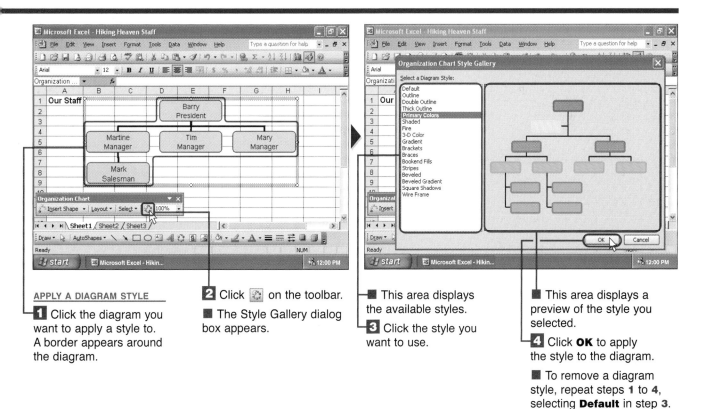

APPLY A DIAGRAM STYLE

1 Click the diagram you want to apply a style to. A border appears around the diagram.

2 Click ⚙ on the toolbar.

■ The Style Gallery dialog box appears.

■ This area displays the available styles.

3 Click the style you want to use.

■ This area displays a preview of the style you selected.

4 Click **OK** to apply the style to the diagram.

■ To remove a diagram style, repeat steps 1 to 4, selecting **Default** in step 3.

Player	RBIs	Home Runs	
		5	1
Barry	56	6	1
Martine	51	2	1
Lindsay	32	8	2
Mary	48	3	3
Kyle	39	3	
*		24	8
Total	226		

Manage Data in a List

Would you like Excel to help you organize a large collection of data? In this chapter, you will learn how to sort data in a list, add totals to a list and more.

Create a List 230

Add a Record 232

Delete a Record 233

Sort Data in a List...........................234

Display a Total Row 238

Filter a List....................................239

CREATE A LIST

You can create a list to organize a large collection of data, such as a mailing list, phone directory, product list or music collection.

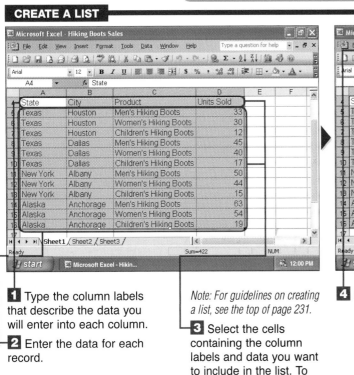

Last Name ▾	First Name ▾	Phone Number ▾	Extension ▾
Petterson	Brenda	555-1234	532
Dean	Chuck	555-2345	722
Robinson	Melanie	555-6971	242
Smith	Michael	555-2451	300
Toppins	Allen	555-3461	225
Marcuson	Jason	555-5249	746
Martin	Jen	555-6842	522
Smith	Linda	555-7914	432
Matthews	Kathleen	555-0001	332
Smith	Jill	555-9421	636

The first row in a list contains the **column labels** for the list. A column label, also called a header, describes the data in a column. Each row in a list contains one record. A record is a group of related data.

CREATE A LIST

1 Type the column labels that describe the data you will enter into each column.

2 Enter the data for each record.

Note: For guidelines on creating a list, see the top of page 231.

3 Select the cells containing the column labels and data you want to include in the list. To select cells, see page 10.

4 Click **Data**.

5 Click **List**.

6 Click **Create List**.

What should I consider when creating a list?

➤ Do not include blank rows or columns in the list.

➤ Keep the list separate from other data or lists on the worksheet. For example, leave a blank row or column between the list and other items.

➤ When entering data into a cell in the list, avoid entering blank spaces at the beginning or end of the data.

Can I quickly print a list I have created?

Yes. You can quickly print only the data in your list, without printing any other data in your worksheet. Click a cell in the list to make the list active. On the List toolbar, click to quickly print your list. If the List toolbar is not displayed, see page 111 to display the toolbar.

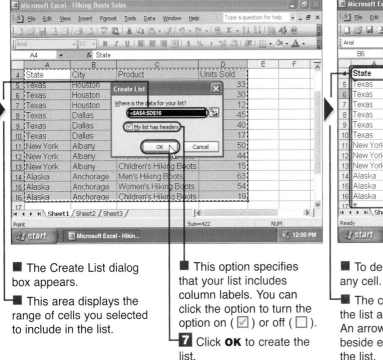

■ The Create List dialog box appears.

■ This area displays the range of cells you selected to include in the list.

■ This option specifies that your list includes column labels. You can click the option to turn the option on (☑) or off (☐).

7 Click **OK** to create the list.

■ To deselect cells, click any cell.

■ The column labels in the list appear in **bold** type. An arrow (▾) also appears beside each column label in the list.

■ A thick blue border appears around the outside of the list.

■ The List toolbar appears on your screen, containing tools you can use to work with the list.

ADD A RECORD

You can add a record to include additional data in your list at any time.

When adding a record to a list, you enter the data for the record at the end of the list. If you later want to change the order of the records in the list, you can sort the records. To sort records, see page 234.

Customers

Customer ID	First Name	Last Name	Phone Number	Fax Number
1064	Carol	Barclay	(201) 555-4591	(201) 555-1264
5469	Mark	Dunn	(201) 555-1278	(201) 555-1287
3570	Peter	Lejcar	(201) 555-1975	(201) 555-1064
2146	Tim	Matthews	(201) 555-1946	(201) 555-1953
7521	Deborah	Peterson	(201) 555-1976	(201) 555-1967
2368	John	Smith	(20..) 55..-194.	(201) 555-1994
3494	Tina	Velu..	(20..	(201) 555-1424
7321	Frank	Dawson	(201) 555-1479	(201) 555-1462

ADD A RECORD

1 Click a cell in the list to make the list active.

Note: An active list displays a thick blue border and arrows (▾) beside the column labels.

2 Click the cell that displays the ✳ symbol.

3 Type the data that corresponds to the first column and then press the [Tab] key. Repeat this step until you have entered all the data for the record.

EDIT DATA

■ You can edit data for a record directly in your list to update or correct the data. To edit data, see page 38.

DELETE A RECORD

You can delete a record to remove data you no longer need from the list. For example, you may want to remove information about a customer who no longer orders your products.

Deleting records keeps your list from becoming cluttered with unnecessary information.

DELETE A RECORD

1 Select the cells that contain the record you want to delete. To select cells, see page 10.

2 Click **Edit**.

3 Click **Delete Row** to delete the row containing the record from the list.

■ The row disappears and all the rows that follow shift upward.

Note: Deleting a row from a list does not affect data in the same row that is not part of the list.

■ To deselect a row, click any cell.

DELETE DATA

■ You can delete data from a record directly in your list. To delete data, see page 40.

SORT DATA IN A LIST

You can change the
order of records in
a list. This can help
you organize and
analyze data.

Last Name	First Name	State	Product
		FL	A
Baldwin	Jerry	CA	B
Coleman	Dan	OR	A
Davis	Scott		

Williams	Cathy		IL	C
Thomas	Jeff	NY		B

SORT BY ONE COLUMN

1 Click a cell in the list
to make the list active.

2 Click ▼ in the column
you want to sort by.

3 Click an option to
sort the data in the list.

Sort Ascending
Sort 0 to 9, A to Z

Sort Descending
Sort 9 to 0, Z to A

■ The records in the list
appear in the new order.

■ In this example, the
records are sorted by
state.

■ To immediately reverse
the results of sorting
records, click ↺ .

*Note: If ↺ is not displayed,
click ⚐ on the Standard toolbar
to display the button.*

Why would I sort my list by more than one column?

Sorting by more than one column allows you to further organize the data in your list. For example, if a last name appears more than once in the Last Name column, you can sort by a second column, such as the First Name column.

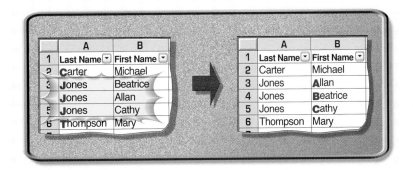

SORT BY TWO COLUMNS

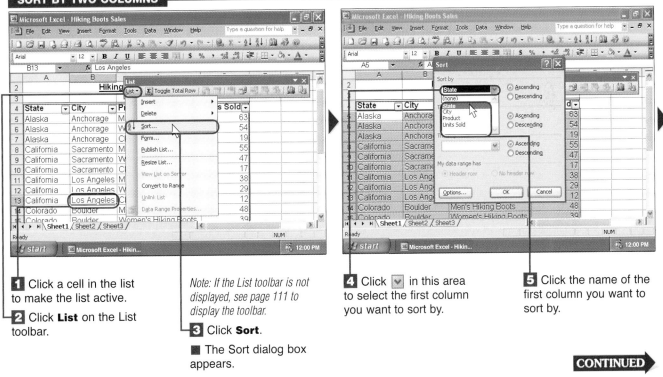

1 Click a cell in the list to make the list active.

2 Click **List** on the List toolbar.

Note: If the List toolbar is not displayed, see page 111 to display the toolbar.

3 Click **Sort**.

■ The Sort dialog box appears.

4 Click ▾ in this area to select the first column you want to sort by.

5 Click the name of the first column you want to sort by.

CONTINUED▶

SORT DATA IN A LIST

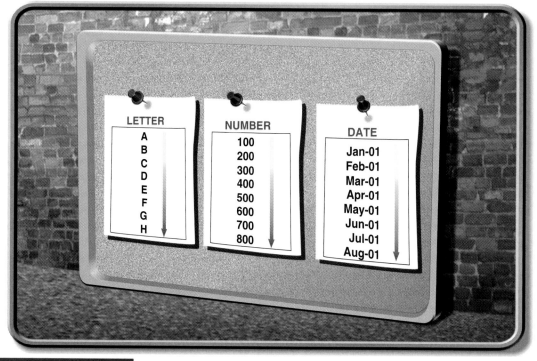

You can sort the records in your list by letter, number or date.

LETTER	NUMBER	DATE
A	100	Jan-01
B	200	Feb-01
C	300	Mar-01
D	400	Apr-01
E	500	May-01
F	600	Jun-01
G	700	Jul-01
H	800	Aug-01

SORT BY TWO COLUMNS (CONTINUED)

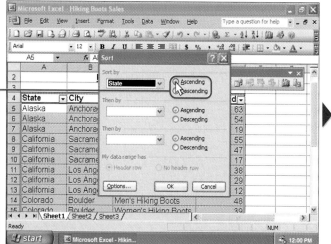

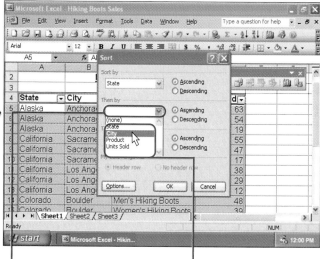

6 Click an option to specify the way you want to sort the first column (○ changes to ◉).

Ascending
Sort 0 to 9, A to Z

Descending
Sort 9 to 0, Z to A

7 Click 🔽 in this area to select the second column you want to sort by.

8 Click the name of the column you want to sort by.

How often can I sort the records in my list?

You can sort the records in your list as often as you like. Sorting is useful if you frequently add new records to your list.

How will Excel sort records if I sort by a column that contains blank cells?

If you sort by a column that contains blank cells, Excel will place the records containing the blank cells at the end of your list.

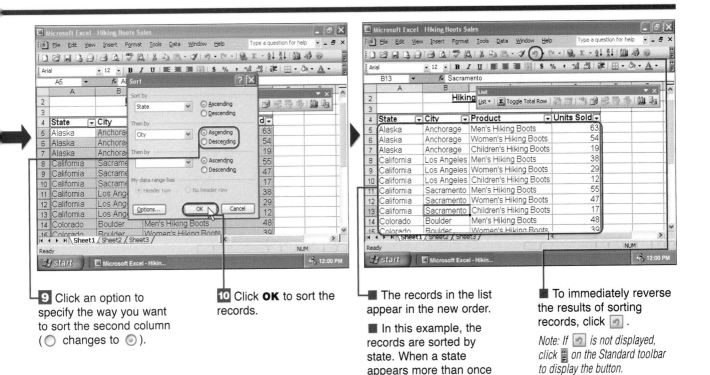

9 Click an option to specify the way you want to sort the second column (○ changes to ◉).

10 Click **OK** to sort the records.

■ The records in the list appear in the new order.

■ In this example, the records are sorted by state. When a state appears more than once in the list, the records are then sorted by city.

■ To immediately reverse the results of sorting records, click ⟳.

Note: If ⟳ is not displayed, click ⯆ on the Standard toolbar to display the button.

DISPLAY A TOTAL ROW

You can display a Total row at the bottom of your list to display the results of common calculations in your list. For example, you can display the sum of a column of numbers or the number of records in the list.

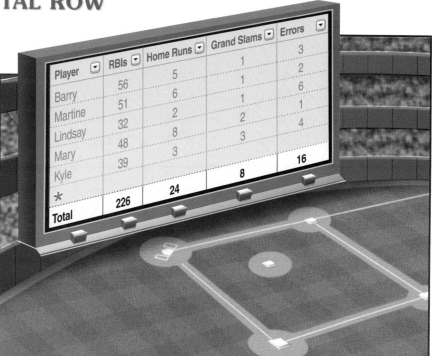

You can display the result of a calculation for any column in your list.

DISPLAY A TOTAL ROW

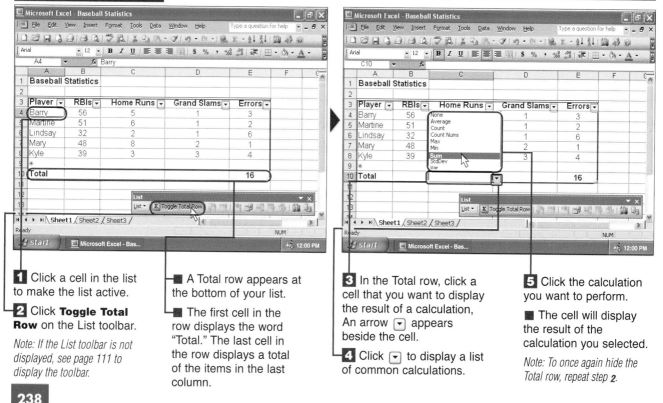

1 Click a cell in the list to make the list active.

2 Click **Toggle Total Row** on the List toolbar.

Note: If the List toolbar is not displayed, see page 111 to display the toolbar.

■ A Total row appears at the bottom of your list.

■ The first cell in the row displays the word "Total." The last cell in the row displays a total of the items in the last column.

3 In the Total row, click a cell that you want to display the result of a calculation, An arrow ⬇ appears beside the cell.

4 Click ⬇ to display a list of common calculations.

5 Click the calculation you want to perform.

■ The cell will display the result of the calculation you selected.

Note: To once again hide the Total row, repeat step 2.

You can filter
your list to
display only
the records
containing the
data you want
to review.

Excel allows you
to analyze your
data by placing
related records
together and
hiding the records
you do not want
to review.

FILTER A LIST

1 Click a cell in the list to make the list active.

2 Click ⏷ in the column containing the data you want to use to filter the list.

3 Click the data you want to use to filter the list.

■ The list displays only the records containing the data you specified. The other records are temporarily hidden.

■ In this example, the list displays only the records for products that sold 50 units.

REDISPLAY ALL RECORDS

■ To redisplay all the records, perform steps **2** and **3** in the column you used to filter the list, except click **(All)** in step **3**.

CONTINUED ▶

FILTER A LIST

You can filter your list to display only records containing data within a specific range.

For example, you can display records for employees whose sales are greater than or equal to $500.

FILTER A LIST BY COMPARING DATA

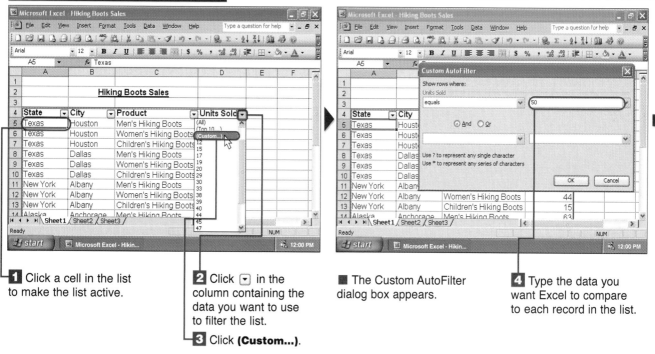

1 Click a cell in the list to make the list active.

2 Click ▼ in the column containing the data you want to use to filter the list.

3 Click **(Custom...)**.

■ The Custom AutoFilter dialog box appears.

4 Type the data you want Excel to compare to each record in the list.

How can I compare data in my list?

Excel offers many ways you can compare data to help you analyze the data in your list.

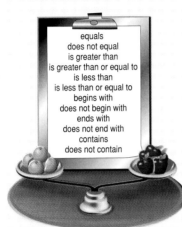

equals
does not equal
is greater than
is greater than or equal to
is less than
is less than or equal to
begins with
does not begin with
ends with
does not end with
contains
does not contain

How can I use the (Blanks) and (NonBlanks) options to filter my list?

The (Blanks) and (NonBlanks) options are available when you filter a list using a column that contains blank cells. You can select the (Blanks) option to display only the records containing blank cells. You can select the (NonBlanks) option to display only the records without blank cells.

Filter by: (Blanks)

HIKING BOOT SALES

State	Product	Units Sold
	Men's Hiking Boots	50
New York	Women's Hiking Boots	
	Children's Hiking Boots	109
	Men's Hiking Boots	64
Florida	Women's Hiking Boots	
	Children's Hiking Boots	77
	Men's Hiking Boots	
Texas	Women's Hiking Boots	13
	Children's Hiking Boots	4

5 Click this area to select how you want Excel to compare the data.

6 Click the way you want Excel to compare the data.

7 Click **OK** to filter the list.

■ The list displays only the records containing the data you specified. The other records are temporarily hidden.

■ In this example, the list displays only the records for products that sold 50 units or more.

REDISPLAY ALL RECORDS

■ To redisplay all the records, perform steps **2** and **3** in the column you used to filter the list, except click **(All)** in step **3**.

241

CHAPTER 13

Protect Your Data

Do you want to prevent other people from making changes to your workbooks or worksheets? Learn how in this chapter.

Protect a Workbook 244

Protect Workbook Elements 248

Protect a Worksheet 250

PROTECT A WORKBOOK

You can prevent other people from opening or making changes to a workbook by protecting it with a password.

PLEASE ENTER YOUR PASSWORD

★★★★★

You should save a workbook before protecting it with a password. To save a workbook, see page 22.

To save a workbook, see page 22.

PROTECT A WORKBOOK

1 Click **File**.

2 Click **Save As**.

■ The Save As dialog box appears.

3 Click **Tools**.

4 Click **General Options**.

■ The Save Options dialog box appears.

What password should I use to protect my workbook?

When choosing a password, you should not use words that people can easily associate with you, such as your name or favorite sport. The most effective passwords connect two words or numbers with a special character (example: **car#123**). A password can contain up to 15 characters and be any combination of letters, numbers and symbols.

Should I take any special precautions with my password?

You should write down your password and keep it in a safe place. If you forget the password, you may not be able to open the workbook.

5 Click the box for the type of password you want to enter.

Password to open

Prevents people from opening the workbook without entering the correct password.

Password to modify

Prevents people from making changes to the workbook without entering the correct password.

6 Type the password you want to use.

7 Click **OK** to continue.

CONTINUED

PROTECT A WORKBOOK

After you protect a workbook with a password, Excel will ask you to enter the password each time you open the workbook.

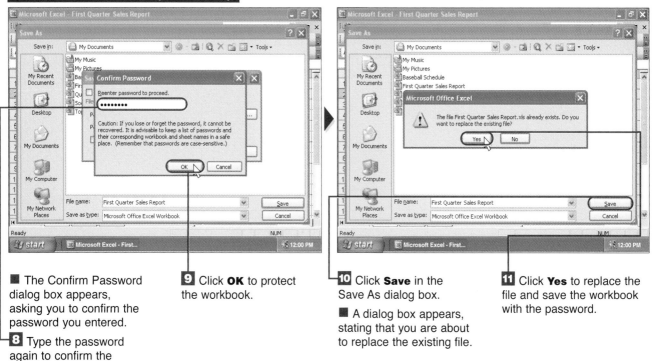

■ The Confirm Password dialog box appears, asking you to confirm the password you entered.

8 Type the password again to confirm the password.

9 Click **OK** to protect the workbook.

10 Click **Save** in the Save As dialog box.

■ A dialog box appears, stating that you are about to replace the existing file.

11 Click **Yes** to replace the file and save the workbook with the password.

I typed the correct password, but Excel will not open my workbook. What is wrong?

Passwords in Excel are case sensitive. If you do not enter the correct uppercase and lowercase letters, Excel will not accept the password. For example, if your password is **car#123**, you cannot enter **Car#123** or **CAR#123** to open the workbook.

How do I unprotect a workbook?

To unprotect a workbook, perform steps **1** to **7** starting on page 244, except in step **6**, drag the mouse I over the existing password until you highlight the password and then press the Delete key. Then perform steps **10** and **11**.

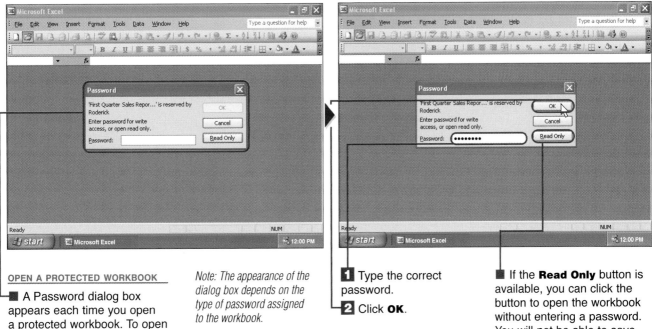

OPEN A PROTECTED WORKBOOK

■ A Password dialog box appears each time you open a protected workbook. To open a workbook, see page 32.

Note: The appearance of the dialog box depends on the type of password assigned to the workbook.

1 Type the correct password.

2 Click **OK**.

■ If the **Read Only** button is available, you can click the button to open the workbook without entering a password. You will not be able to save changes you make to the workbook.

PROTECT WORKBOOK ELEMENTS

You can prevent people from changing the structure of a workbook and the way the workbook window is displayed. For example, you can prevent people from inserting a new worksheet into a workbook and resizing the workbook window.

PROTECT WORKBOOK ELEMENTS

1 Click **Tools**.

2 Click **Protection**.

3 Click **Protect Workbook**.

■ The Protect Workbook dialog box appears.

■ This area displays the workbook elements Excel can protect.

■ A check mark (✔) beside an element indicates that Excel will prevent people from changing the element.

4 You can click the box beside an element to add (☑) or remove (☐) a check mark.

What workbook elements can Excel protect?

Structure

Prevents people from renaming, inserting, deleting, moving or copying worksheets in a workbook.

Windows

Prevents people from moving, resizing or closing the window for a workbook.

How do I unprotect workbook elements?

1 Perform steps **1** to **3** below, selecting **Unprotect Workbook** in step **3**.

■ The Unprotect Workbook dialog box appears.

2 Type the password for the workbook.

3 Click **OK** to unprotect the workbook.

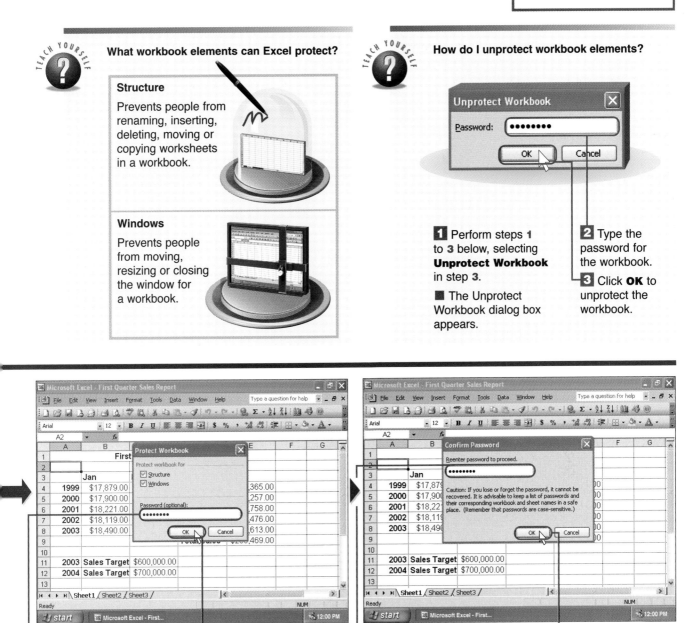

5 Click this area and type the password you want people to enter to unprotect workbook elements.

Note: A password can be any combination of letters, numbers and symbols.

6 Click **OK** to continue.

■ The Confirm Password dialog box appears, asking you to confirm the password you entered.

7 Type the password again to confirm the password.

8 Click **OK** to protect the workbook.

PROTECT A WORKSHEET

You can prevent other people from making changes to your worksheet. This helps to prevent other users from accidentally making changes to your data while reviewing your worksheet.

PROTECT A WORKSHEET

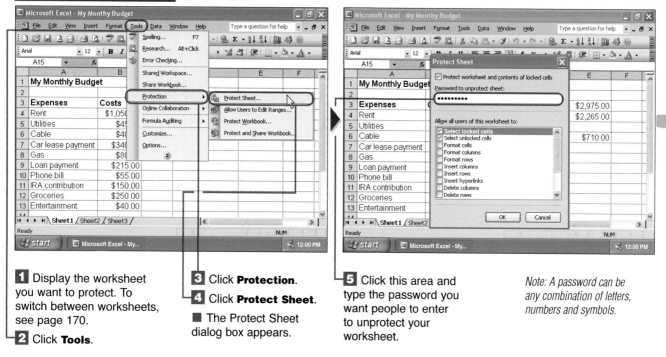

1 Display the worksheet you want to protect. To switch between worksheets, see page 170.

2 Click **Tools**.

3 Click **Protection**.

4 Click **Protect Sheet**.

■ The Protect Sheet dialog box appears.

5 Click this area and type the password you want people to enter to unprotect your worksheet.

Note: A password can be any combination of letters, numbers and symbols.

What are some of the tasks I can allow people to perform in my protected worksheet?

Format Cells	Allow people to change the formatting of data in cells, such as the font or style.
Format Columns	Allow people to change the width of columns and hide columns.
Insert Columns	Allow people to insert columns.
Delete Columns	Allow people to delete columns.
Sort	Allow people to sort data.
Edit Objects	Allow people to change objects such as charts, AutoShapes and text boxes.

How do I unprotect a worksheet?

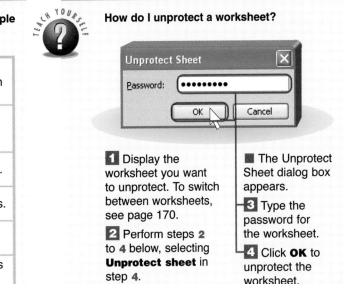

1 Display the worksheet you want to unprotect. To switch between worksheets, see page 170.

2 Perform steps **2** to **4** below, selecting **Unprotect sheet** in step **4**.

■ The Unprotect Sheet dialog box appears.

3 Type the password for the worksheet.

4 Click **OK** to unprotect the worksheet.

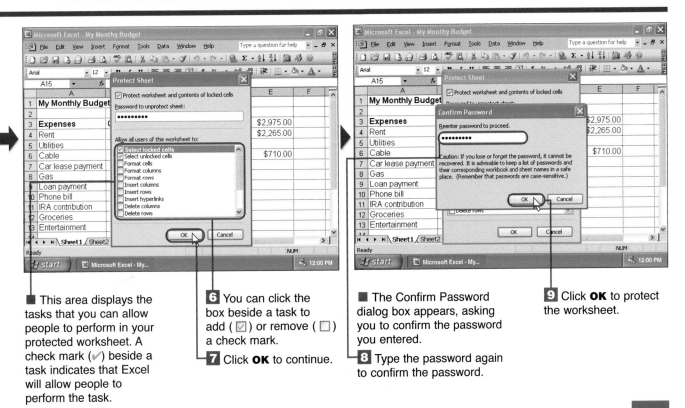

■ This area displays the tasks that you can allow people to perform in your protected worksheet. A check mark (✔) beside a task indicates that Excel will allow people to perform the task.

6 You can click the box beside a task to add (☑) or remove (☐) a check mark.

7 Click **OK** to continue.

■ The Confirm Password dialog box appears, asking you to confirm the password you entered.

8 Type the password again to confirm the password.

9 Click **OK** to protect the worksheet.

CHAPTER 14

Time-Saving Features

Would you like to learn how to customize Excel to help you save time? In this chapter, you will learn how to create your own toolbar, use smart tags to perform tasks and much more.

Create a Custom Series....................254

Customize a Toolbar........................256

Create a New Toolbar 260

Turn on Smart Tags.........................262

Using Smart Tags 264

Create a Macro 266

Run a Macro 270

Calculate First Quarter

Ctrl J

CREATE A CUSTOM SERIES

You can create a custom series that you can quickly enter into your worksheets. Creating a custom series is useful if you frequently enter the same data, such as a list of employee names.

CREATE A CUSTOM SERIES

1 Enter the text you want to save as a series.

■ To include numbers in a series, you must first format the cells that will contain the numbers as text. To format cells as text, see page 134.

2 Select the cells containing the text you entered. To select cells, see page 10.

3 Click **Tools**.

4 Click **Options**.

■ The Options dialog box appears.

5 Click the **Custom Lists** tab.

6 Click **Import** to create the custom series.

■ This area displays the text in the series.

7 Click **OK** to confirm your change.

How do I complete a custom series that begins with a number?

If the first item in a custom series is a number, you must format the cell that will contain the number as text before performing steps 1 to 4 on page 255. To format cells as text, see page 134.

When creating a custom series that contains numbers, why do green triangles appear in the cells I formatted as text?

Excel displays green triangles in the top left corner of cells that may contain errors, such as cells formatted as text that contain numbers.

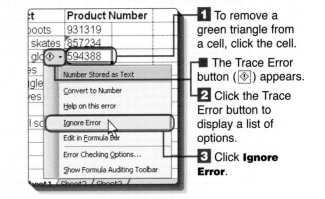

1 To remove a green triangle from a cell, click the cell.

■ The Trace Error button (◈) appears.

2 Click the Trace Error button to display a list of options.

3 Click **Ignore Error**.

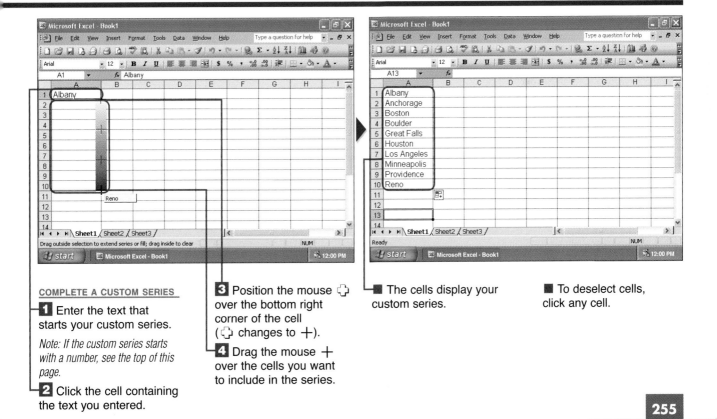

COMPLETE A CUSTOM SERIES

1 Enter the text that starts your custom series.

Note: If the custom series starts with a number, see the top of this page.

2 Click the cell containing the text you entered.

3 Position the mouse ⊕ over the bottom right corner of the cell (⊕ changes to +).

4 Drag the mouse + over the cells you want to include in the series.

■ The cells display your custom series.

■ To deselect cells, click any cell.

255

CUSTOMIZE A TOOLBAR

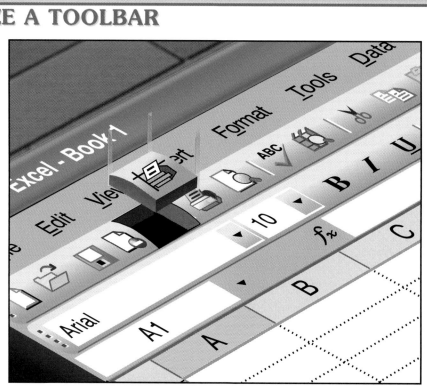

You can add buttons to a toolbar to provide quick access to the commands you use most often. This can help you work more efficiently.

Excel offers hundreds of buttons for you to choose from.

ADD A BUTTON

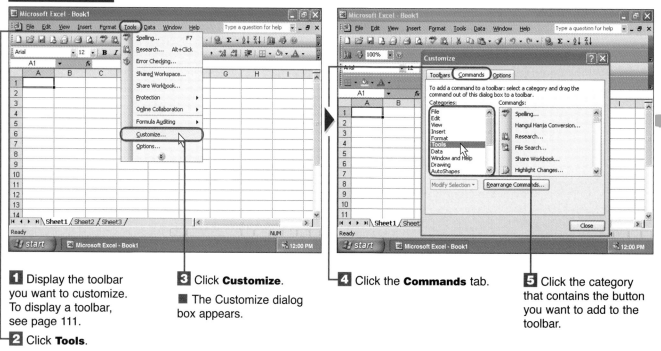

1 Display the toolbar you want to customize. To display a toolbar, see page 111.

2 Click **Tools**.

3 Click **Customize**.

■ The Customize dialog box appears.

4 Click the **Commands** tab.

5 Click the category that contains the button you want to add to the toolbar.

I don't like my customized toolbar. How can I return the toolbar to its original appearance?

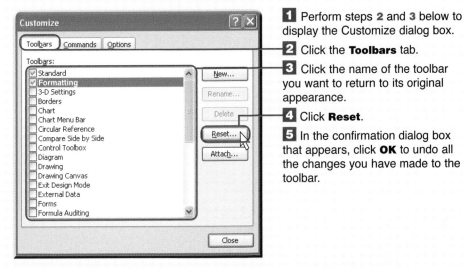

1 Perform steps **2** and **3** below to display the Customize dialog box.

2 Click the **Toolbars** tab.

3 Click the name of the toolbar you want to return to its original appearance.

4 Click **Reset**.

5 In the confirmation dialog box that appears, click **OK** to undo all the changes you have made to the toolbar.

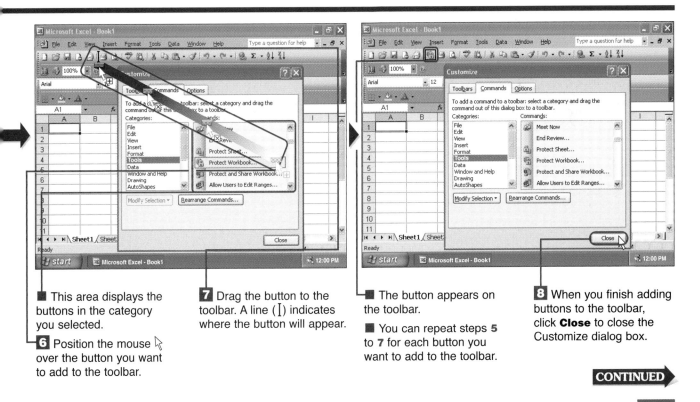

■ This area displays the buttons in the category you selected.

6 Position the mouse ⬚ over the button you want to add to the toolbar.

7 Drag the button to the toolbar. A line (I) indicates where the button will appear.

■ The button appears on the toolbar.

■ You can repeat steps **5** to **7** for each button you want to add to the toolbar.

8 When you finish adding buttons to the toolbar, click **Close** to close the Customize dialog box.

CONTINUED

CUSTOMIZE A TOOLBAR

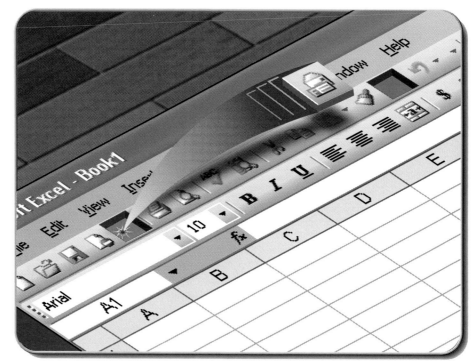

You can move buttons on a toolbar to place buttons for related tasks together. This can make it easier to find the buttons you need.

MOVE A BUTTON

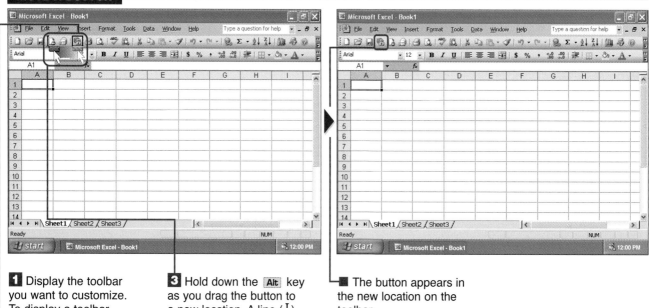

1 Display the toolbar you want to customize. To display a toolbar, see page 111.

2 Position the mouse ⍉ over the button you want to move to a new location.

3 Hold down the **Alt** key as you drag the button to a new location. A line (I) indicates where the button will appear.

■ The button appears in the new location on the toolbar.

You can remove
buttons you do
not use from a
toolbar.

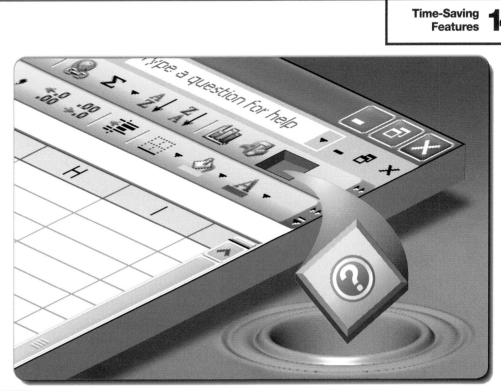

REMOVE A BUTTON

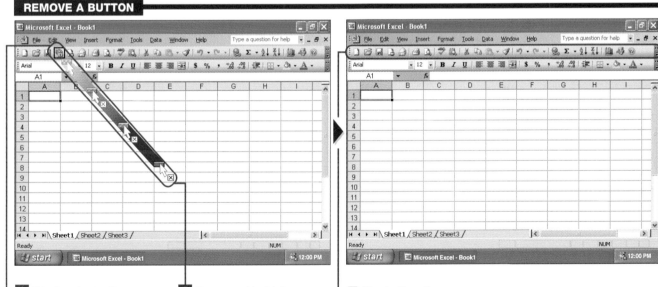

1 Display the toolbar
you want to customize.
To display a toolbar,
see page 111.

2 Position the mouse ▷
over the button you want
to remove from the toolbar.

3 Press and hold down
the **Alt** key as you drag
the button downward off
the toolbar.

■ The button disappears
from the toolbar.

CREATE A NEW TOOLBAR

You can create a new toolbar containing buttons you frequently use.

Creating a toolbar allows you to have a specific toolbar for a task you regularly perform, such as printing workbooks or adding AutoShapes.

CREATE A NEW TOOLBAR

1 Click **Tools**.

2 Click **Customize**.

■ The Customize dialog box appears.

3 Click the **Toolbars** tab.

4 Click **New** to create a new toolbar.

■ The New Toolbar dialog box appears.

How can I move a toolbar I created?

After you create a new toolbar, you can move the toolbar to a new location on your screen. To move a toolbar, position the mouse ⟍ over the title bar and then drag the toolbar to a new location (⟍ changes to ✛).

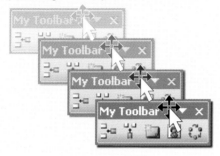

How can I hide a toolbar I created?

You can hide or display a toolbar you created as you would any toolbar. To hide or display a toolbar, see page 111.

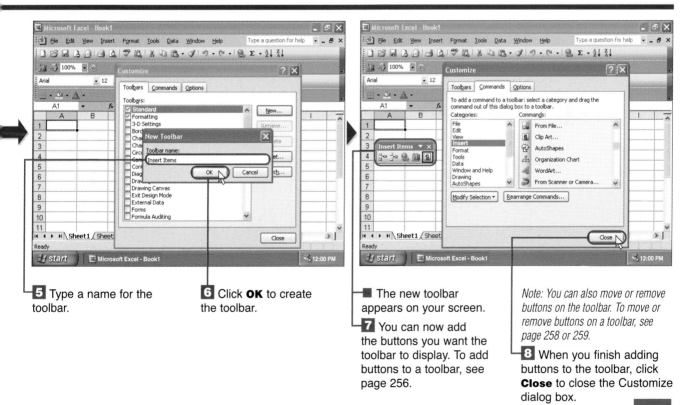

5 Type a name for the toolbar.

6 Click **OK** to create the toolbar.

■ The new toolbar appears on your screen.

7 You can now add the buttons you want the toolbar to display. To add buttons to a toolbar, see page 256.

Note: You can also move or remove buttons on the toolbar. To move or remove buttons on a toolbar, see page 258 or 259.

8 When you finish adding buttons to the toolbar, click **Close** to close the Customize dialog box.

TURN ON SMART TAGS

You can use smart tags to perform actions in Excel that you would normally have to open another program to perform, such as scheduling a meeting or displaying stock information. Before you can use smart tags in Excel, you must turn on smart tags.

After you turn on smart tags, smart tags will be available in all your workbooks.

TURN ON SMART TAGS

1 Click **Tools**.

2 Click **AutoCorrect Options**.

Note: If AutoCorrect Options does not appear on the menu, position the mouse ⏳ over the bottom of the menu to display the menu option.

■ The AutoCorrect dialog box appears.

3 Click the **Smart Tags** tab.

4 Click **Label data with smart tags** (☐ changes to ☑).

What types of data can Excel label with a smart tag?

Date

Excel can label dates you type, such as 12/23/2003 or 4/21/2004.

Financial Symbol

Excel can label financial symbols you type in capital letters. For example:

To obtain information about:	Type:
Microsoft Corporation	MSFT
Intel Corporation	INTC
Coca-Cola Bottling Co.	COKE
Hershey Foods Corporation	HSY

Person Name

Excel can label e-mail addresses of people you sent messages to using Microsoft Outlook.

Note: After sending an e-mail message to a person using Microsoft Outlook, you may have to restart Outlook and Excel to have Excel label the address with a smart tag.

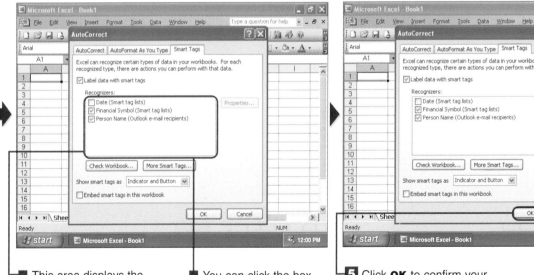

■ This area displays the types of data Excel can label with a smart tag. A check mark (✔) beside a type of data indicates Excel will label the data with a smart tag.

■ You can click the box beside a type of data to add (☑) or remove (☐) a check mark.

5 Click **OK** to confirm your changes.

■ You can now use smart tags in your workbooks.

■ To turn off smart tags for your workbooks, repeat steps **1** to **5** (☑ changes to ☐ in step **4**).

Note: You must close and reopen your open workbooks for the change to take effect in the workbooks. To close a workbook, see page 29. To open a workbook, see page 32.

USING SMART TAGS

Excel labels certain types of data, such as financial symbols, with smart tags. You can use a smart tag to perform an action, such as getting a stock price or displaying information about a company.

Before you can use smart tags, you must turn on smart tags. For more information, see page 262.

USING SMART TAGS

■ A purple triangle appears in the bottom right corner of a cell containing data Excel labels with a smart tag.

1 To perform an action using a smart tag, click a cell containing a purple triangle.

■ The Smart Tag Actions button appears.

2 Click the Smart Tag Actions button to display a list of actions you can perform using the smart tag.

3 Click the action you want to perform.

■ In this example, we insert a refreshable stock price.

■ To remove a smart tag from a cell, click **Remove this Smart Tag**.

What actions can I perform for a date labeled with a smart tag?

You can display your calendar or schedule a meeting in Microsoft Outlook for a date in your worksheet labeled with a smart tag.

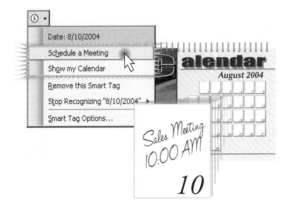

What actions can I perform for an e-mail address labeled with a smart tag?

You can perform one of several actions such as sending the person an e-mail message, scheduling a meeting with the person or adding the person to your list of contacts in Microsoft Outlook.

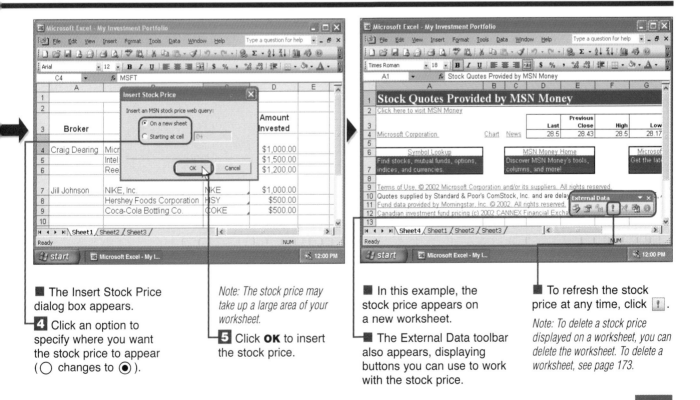

■ The Insert Stock Price dialog box appears.

4 Click an option to specify where you want the stock price to appear (○ changes to ◉).

Note: The stock price may take up a large area of your worksheet.

5 Click **OK** to insert the stock price.

■ In this example, the stock price appears on a new worksheet.

■ The External Data toolbar also appears, displaying buttons you can use to work with the stock price.

■ To refresh the stock price at any time, click 🔳.

Note: To delete a stock price displayed on a worksheet, you can delete the worksheet. To delete a worksheet, see page 173.

CREATE A MACRO

A macro saves you time by combining a series of actions into a single command. Macros are ideal for tasks you frequently perform.

For example, you can create a macro to enter a formula or insert your company logo into your worksheet.

Before creating a macro, you should plan and practice all the actions you want the macro to include.

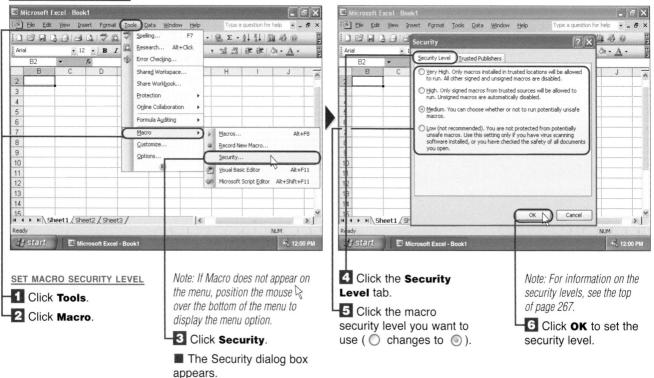

SET MACRO SECURITY LEVEL

1 Click **Tools**.

2 Click **Macro**.

Note: If Macro does not appear on the menu, position the mouse over the bottom of the menu to display the menu option.

3 Click **Security**.

■ The Security dialog box appears.

4 Click the **Security Level** tab.

5 Click the macro security level you want to use (○ changes to ◉).

Note: For information on the security levels, see the top of page 267.

6 Click **OK** to set the security level.

Why should I set the macro security level?

Some macros may contain viruses that could damage your computer. Setting the macro security level can help protect your computer from viruses.

Very High

Excel enables only macros from trusted sources and disables all other macros in the workbooks you open.

High

Excel enables only macros that are digitally signed in the workbooks you open.

Medium

You can disable or enable the macros in the workbooks you open.

Low

Excel automatically enables the macros in the workbooks you open.

RECORD A MACRO

1 Click **Tools**.

2 Click **Macro**.

Note: If Macro does not appear on the menu, position the mouse over the bottom of the menu to display the menu option.

3 Click **Record New Macro**.

■ The Record Macro dialog box appears.

4 Type a name for the macro.

Note: A macro name must begin with a letter and cannot contain spaces. A macro name cannot be a cell reference.

CONTINUED

CREATE A MACRO

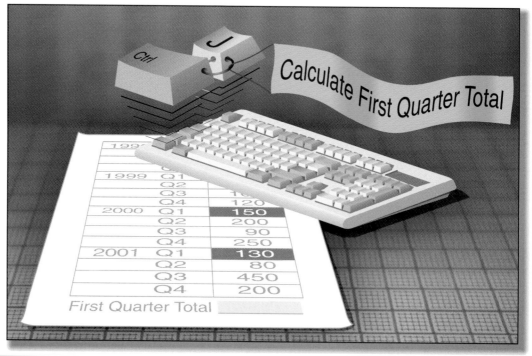

You can assign a keyboard shortcut, such as Ctrl+j, to a macro you create. A keyboard shortcut allows you to quickly run the macro.

Calculate First Quarter Total

CREATE A MACRO (CONTINUED)

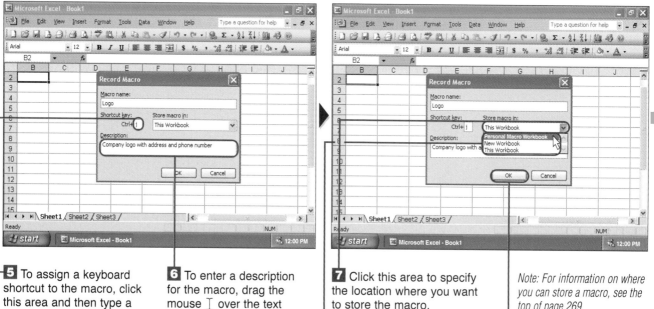

5 To assign a keyboard shortcut to the macro, click this area and then type a lowercase letter you want to use with the **Ctrl** key as the shortcut.

6 To enter a description for the macro, drag the mouse I over the text in this area until you highlight the text. Then type a description.

7 Click this area to specify the location where you want to store the macro.

8 Click the location where you want to store the macro.

Note: For information on where you can store a macro, see the top of page 269.

9 Click **OK** to continue.

Where can I store a macro?

Personal Macro Workbook

If you want to use a macro with all your workbooks, you can store the macro in the Personal Macro Workbook.

New Workbook

You can have Excel create a new workbook to store the macro. You will only be able to use the macro when the new workbook is open.

This Workbook

You can store the macro in the current workbook. You will only be able to use the macro when this workbook is open.

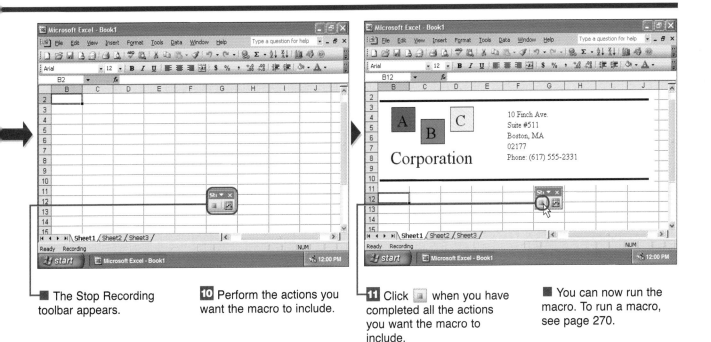

■ The Stop Recording toolbar appears.

10 Perform the actions you want the macro to include.

11 Click ▣ when you have completed all the actions you want the macro to include.

■ You can now run the macro. To run a macro, see page 270.

RUN A MACRO

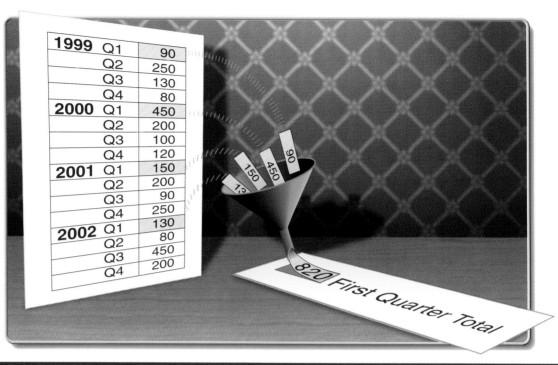

When you run a macro, Excel automatically performs the actions you recorded.

You should save your workbook before running a macro. After the macro runs, you will not be able to use the Undo feature to reverse the results of the macro or any changes you made before running the macro.

RUN A MACRO

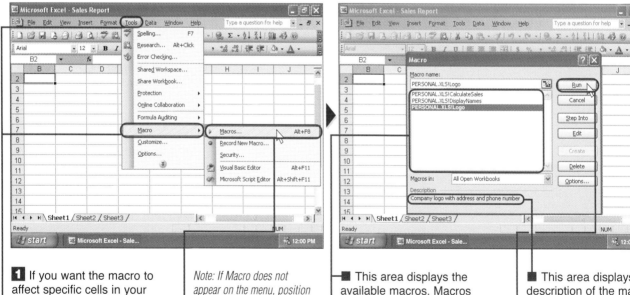

1 If you want the macro to affect specific cells in your worksheet, select the cells you want to change. To select cells, see page 10.

2 Click **Tools**.

3 Click **Macro**.

Note: If Macro does not appear on the menu, position the mouse over the bottom of the menu to display the menu option.

4 Click **Macros**.

■ The Macro dialog box appears.

■ This area displays the available macros. Macros you stored in the Personal Macro Workbook begin with PERSONAL.XLS!.

5 Click the name of the macro you want to run.

■ This area displays a description of the macro you selected.

6 Click **Run** to run the macro.

Why does this dialog box appear when I open a workbook containing a macro?

This dialog box may appear when you set your macro security level to Medium. To open the workbook, click one of the following options.

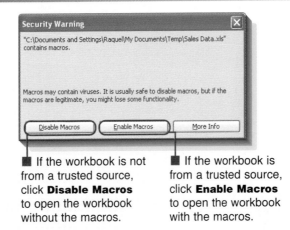

■ If the workbook is not from a trusted source, click **Disable Macros** to open the workbook without the macros.

■ If the workbook is from a trusted source, click **Enable Macros** to open the workbook with the macros.

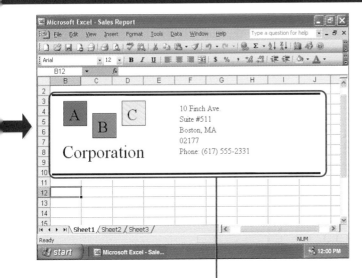

■ The macro performs the actions you recorded.

■ In this example, the macro entered company information into the worksheet.

RUN A MACRO USING THE KEYBOARD SHORTCUT

1 If you want the macro to affect specific cells in your worksheet, select the cells you want to change. To select cells, see page 10.

2 Press the keyboard shortcut you assigned to the macro.

■ The macro performs the actions you recorded.

CHAPTER 15

Using Speech Recognition

Would you like to use your voice to enter data into a worksheet? Read this chapter to learn how to enter data and select commands using your voice.

Set Up Speech Recognition 274

Using Dictation Mode 280

Using Voice Command Mode 282

Using Text to Speech 284

SET UP SPEECH RECOGNITION

Speech recognition allows you to use your voice to enter data into a worksheet and select commands from menus and toolbars. Before you can use speech recognition, you must set up the feature on your computer.

I am using Office Speech Recognition.

You can set up speech recognition in Microsoft Word, a word processing program included in the Microsoft Office 2003 suite. Once speech recognition is set up, the feature will be available in Excel.

Before setting up speech recognition, make sure your microphone and speakers are connected to your computer.

SET UP SPEECH RECOGNITION

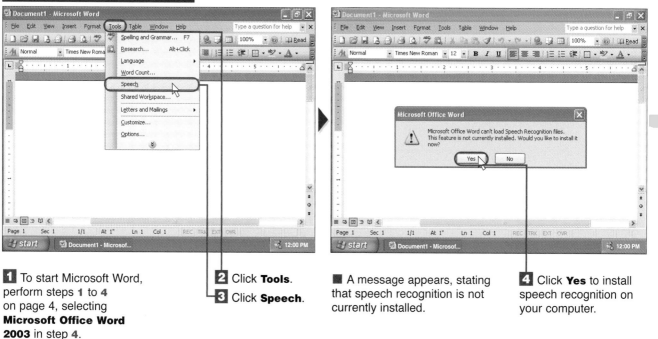

1 To start Microsoft Word, perform steps **1** to **4** on page 4, selecting **Microsoft Office Word 2003** in step **4**.

2 Click **Tools**.

3 Click **Speech**.

■ A message appears, stating that speech recognition is not currently installed.

4 Click **Yes** to install speech recognition on your computer.

What are the minimum hardware requirements for using speech recognition?

Speech recognition requires a 400 MHz computer with at least 128 MB of memory to run. You cannot set up speech recognition if your computer does not meet the minimum hardware requirements.

What type of microphone should I use with speech recognition?

You should use a high quality headset microphone that supports gain adjustment. Gain adjustment allows your computer to automatically make your speech louder. For best results, you should position the microphone approximately one inch from the side of your mouth so that you are not breathing directly into the microphone.

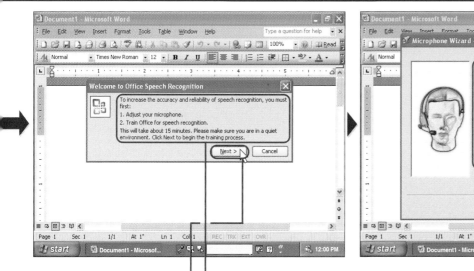

■ When the installation is complete, the Welcome to Office Speech Recognition dialog box appears.

■ This area describes the process of setting up speech recognition on your computer.

5 To begin setting up speech recognition, click **Next**.

■ The Microphone Wizard appears. The wizard will help you adjust your microphone for use with speech recognition.

■ This area describes the wizard and provides instructions for positioning your microphone.

6 To begin adjusting your microphone, click **Next**.

CONTINUED

SET UP SPEECH RECOGNITION

The Microphone Wizard helps you adjust the volume and position of your microphone for best results with speech recognition.

Once your microphone is properly set up, you can follow the step-by-step instructions in the Microsoft Speech Recognition Training Wizard to train speech recognition to recognize how you speak.

SET UP SPEECH RECOGNITION (CONTINUED)

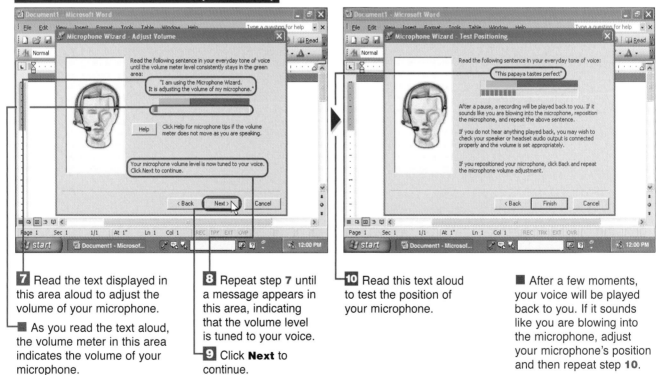

7 Read the text displayed in this area aloud to adjust the volume of your microphone.

■ As you read the text aloud, the volume meter in this area indicates the volume of your microphone.

8 Repeat step **7** until a message appears in this area, indicating that the volume level is tuned to your voice.

9 Click **Next** to continue.

10 Read this text aloud to test the position of your microphone.

■ After a few moments, your voice will be played back to you. If it sounds like you are blowing into the microphone, adjust your microphone's position and then repeat step **10**.

Do I have to train speech recognition?

If you do not train speech recognition, the feature may not work properly. During the training, the Microsoft Speech Recognition Training Wizard gathers information about your voice. The speech recognition feature uses this information to recognize the words you say when entering data or selecting commands.

How should I speak during the training process?

You should speak in your everyday tone of voice, pronouncing words clearly and not pausing between words. You should also speak at a consistent speed.

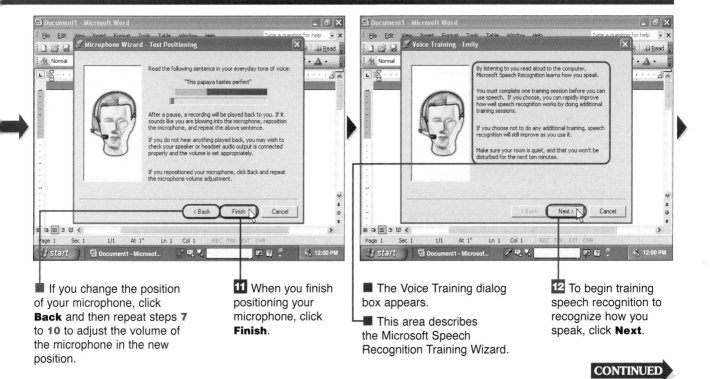

■ If you change the position of your microphone, click **Back** and then repeat steps **7** to **10** to adjust the volume of the microphone in the new position.

11 When you finish positioning your microphone, click **Finish**.

■ The Voice Training dialog box appears.

■ This area describes the Microsoft Speech Recognition Training Wizard.

12 To begin training speech recognition to recognize how you speak, click **Next**.

CONTINUED

SET UP SPEECH RECOGNITION

The Microsoft Speech Recognition Training Wizard provides text you can read aloud to train speech recognition.

You should train speech recognition in a quiet area so that background noise does not interfere with the sound of your voice.

SET UP SPEECH RECOGNITION (CONTINUED)

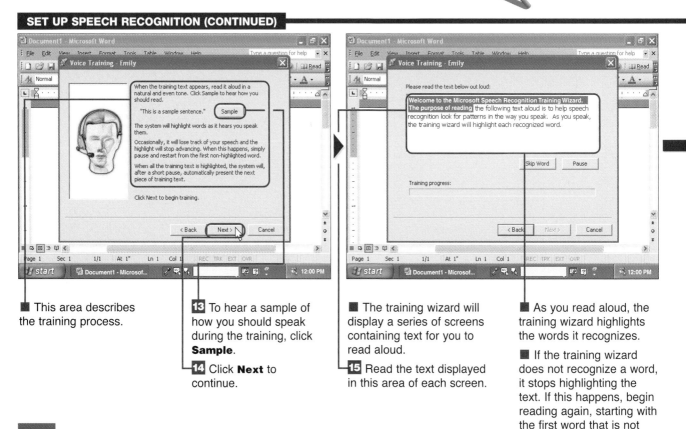

■ This area describes the training process.

13 To hear a sample of how you should speak during the training, click **Sample**.

14 Click **Next** to continue.

■ The training wizard will display a series of screens containing text for you to read aloud.

15 Read the text displayed in this area of each screen.

■ As you read aloud, the training wizard highlights the words it recognizes.

■ If the training wizard does not recognize a word, it stops highlighting the text. If this happens, begin reading again, starting with the first word that is not highlighted.

I have repeated a word several times, but the wizard still does not recognize the word. What should I do?

If the wizard cannot recognize a word you say, you can click the **Skip Word** button to move on to the next word.

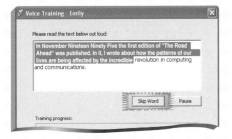

Can I perform more training?

Microsoft Speech Recognition provides additional training sessions you can perform to improve the accuracy of speech recognition.

1 To perform additional training, click **Tools** on the Language bar.

2 Click **Training**.

■ The Voice Training dialog box will appear, displaying the available training sessions. Select a training session and then perform steps **14** to **17** below.

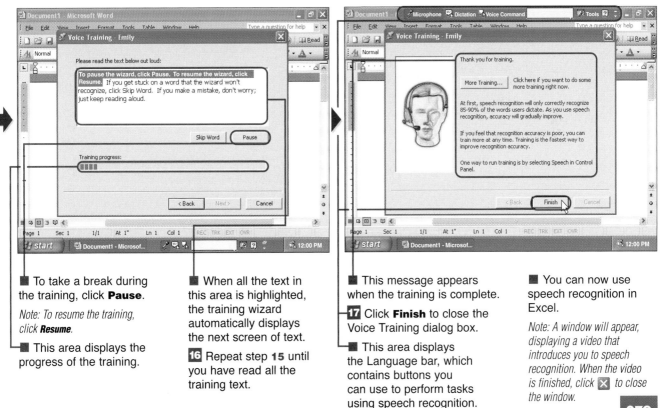

■ To take a break during the training, click **Pause**.

Note: To resume the training, click Resume.

■ This area displays the progress of the training.

■ When all the text in this area is highlighted, the training wizard automatically displays the next screen of text.

16 Repeat step **15** until you have read all the training text.

■ This message appears when the training is complete.

17 Click **Finish** to close the Voice Training dialog box.

■ This area displays the Language bar, which contains buttons you can use to perform tasks using speech recognition.

■ You can now use speech recognition in Excel.

Note: A window will appear, displaying a video that introduces you to speech recognition. When the video is finished, click ☒ to close the window.

279

USING DICTATION MODE

Once you have set up speech recognition, you can use Dictation mode to enter data into a worksheet using your voice.

Speech recognition is designed to be used along with your mouse and keyboard. You can use your voice to enter data into a worksheet and then use your mouse and keyboard to edit the data you entered.

USING DICTATION MODE

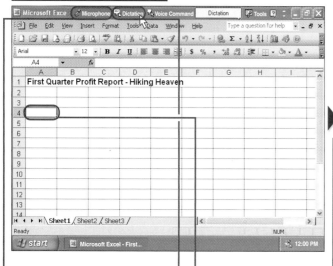

1 If your microphone is turned off, click **Microphone** on the Language bar to turn on the microphone.

Note: When your microphone is turned on, the Dictation and Voice Command buttons appear on the Language bar.

2 Click a cell where you want to enter data using your voice.

3 Click **Dictation** to turn on Dictation mode.

4 Speak into your microphone to enter data into the cell.

■ As you speak, a gray bar appears on the screen to indicate that the computer is processing your voice. You can continue to speak while the gray bar is displayed on the screen.

■ You should not use your mouse or keyboard while the gray bar is displayed on the screen.

What are some of the symbols I can enter using my voice?

To enter:	Say:
=	"Equals"
+	"Plus sign"
%	"Percent sign"
$	"Dollar sign"
>	"Greater than"
<	"Less than"
(	"Open parenthesis"
)	"Close parenthesis"

How should I speak when using speech recognition?

You should speak to your computer in your everyday tone of voice, pronouncing words clearly and not pausing between words. You should also speak at a consistent speed. If you speak too quickly or too slowly, the computer may not be able to recognize what you say.

■ As the computer processes your voice, words appear on the screen.

5 To enter data into another cell using your voice, click the cell.

6 To enter a symbol, say the name of the symbol.

Note: For a list of symbols you can enter, see the top of this page.

7 To enter a number, say the number you want to enter.

Note: Numbers less than 20 are entered as words. Numbers greater than 20 are entered as digits.

8 When you finish entering data using your voice, click **Microphone** to turn off your microphone.

■ You can now edit the data you entered using your voice as you would edit any data. To edit data, see page 38.

USING VOICE COMMAND MODE

You can use Voice Command mode to select commands from menus and toolbars using your voice.

You can also use Voice Command mode to select options in dialog boxes.

USING VOICE COMMAND MODE

1 If your microphone is turned off, click **Microphone** on the Language bar to turn on the microphone.

Note: When your microphone is turned on, the Dictation and Voice Command buttons appear on the Language bar.

2 Click **Voice Command** to turn on Voice Command mode.

SELECT MENU COMMANDS

1 To select a command from a menu, say the name of the menu.

■ A short version of the menu appears, displaying the most commonly used commands.

Note: To expand the menu and display all the commands, say "expand."

2 To select a command from the menu, say the name of the command.

■ To close a menu without selecting a command, say "escape."

Can I use Voice Command mode to select an option in a task pane?

Yes. Task panes display links that allow you to perform common tasks. To select a link in a task pane using your voice, say the full name of the link. For more information on task panes, see page 16.

Can I use Voice Command mode to perform other tasks?

In addition to selecting commands, you can use Voice Command mode to change the active cell.

To:	Say:
Move down one cell	"Down" or "Enter"
Move up one cell	"Up"
Move left one cell	"Left"
Move right one cell	"Right"

SELECT TOOLBAR COMMANDS

1 To select a command from a toolbar, say the name of the toolbar button.

■ To determine the name of a toolbar button, position the mouse ⟨ over the button. After a few seconds, the name of the button appears in a yellow box.

SPELLING...

SELECT DIALOG BOX OPTIONS

■ A dialog box may appear when you select a menu or toolbar command.

1 To select an option in a dialog box, say the name of the option.

■ If the dialog box contains tabs, you can say the name of a tab to display the tab.

2 When you finish selecting commands using your voice, click **Microphone** to turn off your microphone.

LANDSCAPE...

USING TEXT TO SPEECH

You can have your computer read the data in your worksheet back to you. This can help you confirm that you entered the data correctly.

Before using the text to speech feature, make sure your speakers are connected to your computer.

USING TEXT TO SPEECH

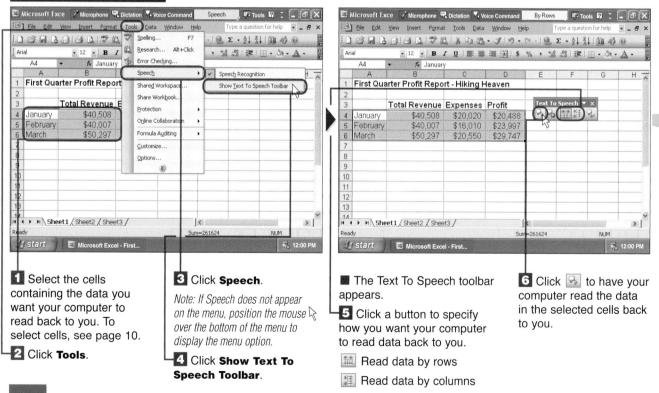

1 Select the cells containing the data you want your computer to read back to you. To select cells, see page 10.

2 Click **Tools**.

3 Click **Speech**.

Note: If Speech does not appear on the menu, position the mouse over the bottom of the menu to display the menu option.

4 Click **Show Text To Speech Toolbar**.

■ The Text To Speech toolbar appears.

5 Click a button to specify how you want your computer to read data back to you.

▦ Read data by rows

▦ Read data by columns

6 Click ▦ to have your computer read the data in the selected cells back to you.

How can I have my computer read data back to me as I enter data into cells?

1 Perform steps **2** to **4** below to display the Text To Speech toolbar.

2 Click 🖳 to have your computer read data back to you as you enter data into cells.

■ You can click 🖳 again to stop your computer from reading data you enter into cells.

Will my computer read data in hidden rows or columns?

No. Your computer will not read data in hidden rows or columns. For information on hiding rows and columns, see page 74.

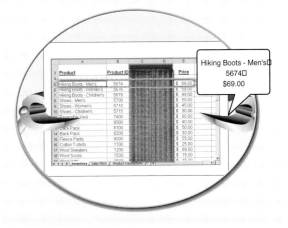

Hiking Boots - Men's
5674
$69.00

■ Your computer reads the data in the selected cells.

■ The cell your computer is currently reading is highlighted.

■ To stop your computer from reading data back to you, click 🖳.

Note: You can click 🖳 to once again have your computer read data back to you.

7 When your computer finishes reading data back to you, click ✕ to hide the Text To Speech toolbar.

CHAPTER 16

Excel and the Internet

Are you wondering how you can use Excel to share data with other people on the Internet? In this chapter, you will learn how to e-mail a worksheet, save a workbook as a Web page and more.

E-mail a Worksheet...........................288

Create a Hyperlink...........................290

Preview a Workbook as a
  Web Page....................................292

Save a Workbook as a Web Page....294

E-MAIL A WORKSHEET

You can e-mail the worksheet displayed on your screen to exchange data with a friend, family member or colleague.

When you e-mail a worksheet, the worksheet appears in the body of the e-mail message.

Before you can e-mail a worksheet, Microsoft Office Outlook 2003 must be set up on your computer.

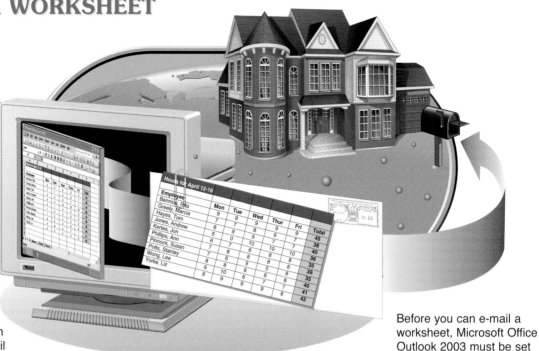

E-MAIL A WORKSHEET

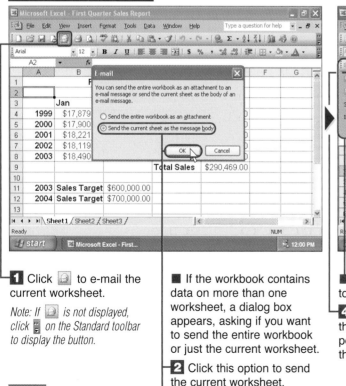

1 Click 🖃 to e-mail the current worksheet.

Note: If 🖃 is not displayed, click ▪ on the Standard toolbar to display the button.

■ If the workbook contains data on more than one worksheet, a dialog box appears, asking if you want to send the entire workbook or just the current worksheet.

2 Click this option to send the current worksheet.

3 Click **OK**.

■ An area appears for you to address the message.

4 Click this area and type the e-mail address of the person you want to receive the message.

5 To send a copy of the message to a person who is not directly involved but would be interested in the message, click this area and type the e-mail address.

Note: To enter more than one e-mail address in step 4 or 5, separate each e-mail address with a semicolon (;).

Why would I include an introduction for a worksheet I am e-mailing?

Including an introduction allows you to provide the recipient of the message with additional information about the worksheet. For example, the recipient may require instructions or an explanation of the content of the worksheet.

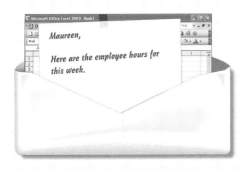

How do I e-mail an entire workbook?

To e-mail an entire workbook, perform steps **1** to **6** below, selecting **Send the entire workbook as an attachment** in step **2**. Then click **Send** to send the message. When you e-mail an entire workbook, the workbook is sent as an attached file.

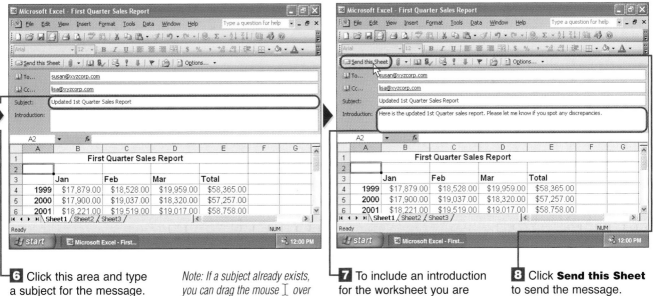

6 Click this area and type a subject for the message.

Note: If a subject already exists, you can drag the mouse ⊥ over the existing subject and then type a new subject.

7 To include an introduction for the worksheet you are e-mailing, click this area and type the introduction.

8 Click **Send this Sheet** to send the message.

Note: If you are not currently connected to the Internet, a dialog box will appear allowing you to connect.

CREATE A HYPERLINK

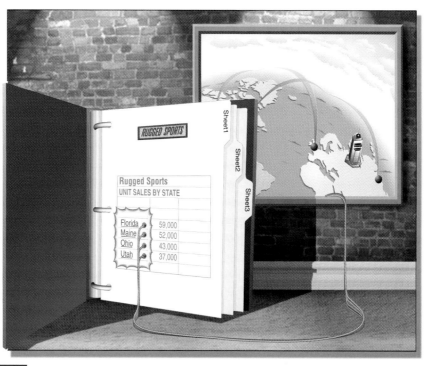

You can create a hyperlink to connect data in your workbook to another document on your computer, network, corporate intranet or the Internet.

Hyperlinks are also known as links.

You can easily identify hyperlinks in your workbook. Hyperlinks appear underlined and in color.

An intranet is a small version of the Internet within a company or organization.

CREATE A HYPERLINK

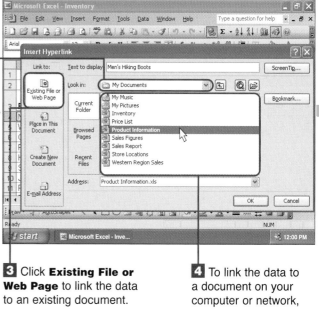

1 Select the cells containing the data you want to make a hyperlink. To select cells, see page 10.

2 Click 🔗 to create a hyperlink.

Note: If 🔗 is not displayed, click ▾ on the Standard toolbar to display the button.

■ The Insert Hyperlink dialog box appears.

3 Click **Existing File or Web Page** to link the data to an existing document.

■ This area shows the location of the displayed documents. You can click this area to change the location.

4 To link the data to a document on your computer or network, click the document in this area.

290

Can I select a cell that contains a hyperlink?

Yes. Excel allows you to select a cell that contains a hyperlink without displaying the document or Web page connected to the hyperlink. This is useful when you want to change the format of a hyperlink. To select a cell that contains a hyperlink, position the mouse 🖑 over the cell and then hold down the left mouse button until the mouse 🖑 changes to ⬩.

Can Excel automatically create a hyperlink for me?

When you type a Web page address in an Excel worksheet, Excel will automatically change the address to a hyperlink for you.

■ To link the data to a page on the Web, click this area and then type the address of the Web page (example: www.maran.com).

5 Click **OK** to create the hyperlink.

■ Excel creates the hyperlink. Hyperlinks appear underlined and in color.

■ When you position the mouse 🖑 over a hyperlink, a yellow box appears, indicating where the hyperlink will take you.

■ You can click the hyperlink to display the document or Web page connected to the hyperlink.

Note: If the hyperlink connects to a Web page, your Web browser will open and display the page.

PREVIEW A WORKBOOK AS A WEB PAGE

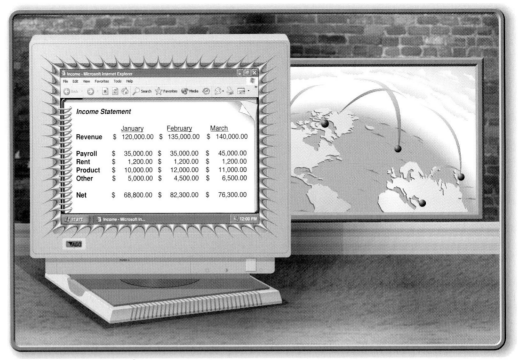

You can preview how your workbook will look as a Web page. This allows you to see how the workbook will appear on the Internet or your company's intranet.

An intranet is a small version of the Internet within a company or organization.

PREVIEW A WORKBOOK AS A WEB PAGE

1 Open the workbook you want to preview as a Web page. To open a workbook, see page 32.

2 Click **File**.

3 Click **Web Page Preview** to preview your workbook as a Web page.

Will my Web page look the same when displayed in different Web browsers?

No. Different Web browsers may display your Web page differently. There are many Web browsers used on the Web.

Can I make changes to a workbook I am previewing as a Web page?

You cannot make changes to a workbook displayed in a Web browser window. If you want to change the way the data appears on the Web page, you must make the changes to the workbook in the Microsoft Excel window and then repeat steps **2** and **3** below to preview the changes in the Web browser window.

Inventory

Product	Product ID	Supplier	Units in Stock	Sizes	Colors
Men's Hiking Boots	5674	Nelson	65	9 to 14	Black
Women's Hiking Boots	5675	Dearing	60	4 to 10	Brown, Black
Children's Hiking Boots	5676	Dearing	45	3 to 6	Brown, Black
Fleece Pullover	6770	Harris	100	S, M, L, XL	Gray, Yellow
Hooded Sweatshirt	6774	Harris	100	S, M, L, XL	Red, Blue, Yellow
Sweatshirt	6775	Northward	40	S, M, L, XL	Red, Blue, Yellow
Jersey	6776	Northward	35	S, M, L	Red, Blue, Yellow
Raincoat	7000	Borek	50	M, L	Yellow only
Fleece Jacket	7100	Borek	52	S, M, L, XL	Gray, Yellow

■ Your Web browser window opens, displaying your workbook as a Web page.

4 To maximize the Web browser window to fill your screen, click 🗖.

■ The gridlines that separate each cell do not appear in the Web browser window.

■ If your workbook contains data on more than one worksheet, this area displays a tab for each worksheet.

5 To display the contents of a different worksheet, click a tab.

6 When you finish previewing your workbook as a Web page, click ✕ to close the Web browser window.

SAVE A WORKBOOK AS A WEB PAGE

You can save a workbook as a Web page. This allows you to place the workbook on the Internet or your company's intranet.

An intranet is a small version of the Internet within a company or organization.

SAVE A WORKBOOK AS A WEB PAGE

1 Open the workbook you want to save as a Web page. To open a workbook, see page 32.

2 Click **File**.

3 Click **Save as Web Page**.

■ The Save As dialog box appears.

4 Type a file name for the Web page.

■ This area shows the location where Excel will store the Web page. You can click this area to change the location.

■ This area allows you to access commonly used locations. You can click a location to save the Web page in the location.

Note: For information on the commonly used locations, see the top of page 23.

What is the difference between the file name and the title of a Web page?

The file name is the name you use to store the Web page on your computer. The title is the text that will appear at the top of the Web browser window when a person views your Web page.

How do I make my Web page available for other people to view?

After you save your workbook as a Web page, you can transfer the page to a computer that stores Web pages, called a Web server. Once the Web page is stored on a Web server, the page will be available for other people to view. For information on transferring a Web page to a Web server, contact your network administrator or Internet service provider.

5 Click **Change Title** to specify a title for the Web page.

■ The Set Page Title dialog box appears.

6 Type a title for the Web page.

7 Click **OK** to confirm the title.

■ This area displays the title you specified for the Web page.

8 Click an option to specify whether you want to save the entire workbook or just the current worksheet as a Web page (○ changes to ◉).

9 Click **Save** to save the Web page.

INDEX

Numbers & Symbols

(error message), 99
#DIV/0! (error message), 99
#NAME? (error message), 99
#REF! (error message), 71, 99
#VALUE! (error message), 99
$ (dollar sign) in absolute references, 95
- (minus sign) beside items, 35, 105
() (parentheses)
    in formulas, 83
    in functions, 83, 89
: (colon), in functions, 83, 89
, (comma), in functions, 83, 89
* (asterisk), wildcard character, 53
? (question mark), wildcard character, 53
+ (plus sign) beside items, 35, 105
= (equal sign)
    in formulas, 82, 84
    in functions, 83, 89
3-D effects, add to objects, 223

A

absolute references, in formulas, 95
Accounting, data format, 135
active cell
    change, 6
        using Voice Command mode, 283
    overview, 5
active sheets, print, 148-149
align data
    horizontally, 121
    vertically, 122-123
area, chart type, 185
arithmetic operators, in formulas, 82, 179
arrange open workbooks on screen, 26-27
asterisk (*), wildcard character, 53
Auto Fill Options button, 13, 93, 95
AutoComplete, use, 9
AutoCorrect entries
    create, 46-47
    delete, 47
    insert, 47
autoformats
    apply, 138-139
    remove, 139
AutoShapes. See also objects
    add, 208-209
        text to, 209
    delete, 209
    shape of, change, 209

Average, calculation, 91
axis titles on charts, 184
    move, 191

B

bar, chart type, 185
black and white, print worksheets in, 156-157
Blanks option, filter lists using, 241
bold
    data, 120, 124-125
    text, on charts, 197
borders of cells
    add, 132-133
    remove, 133
buttons on toolbars
    add, 256-257
    move, 258
    remove, 259

C

calculations
    order of, in formulas, 83
    perform common, 90-91
cancel changes, 41
category axis titles, on charts, 184, 187
cell references, for formulas
    absolute, 95
    enter quickly, 85
    overview, 6, 83
    relative, 93
cells
    active
        change, 6
            using Voice Command mode, 283
        overview, 5
    borders
        add, 132-133
        remove, 133
    color, change, 127
    delete, 73
    errors
        print, 156-157
        when creating custom series, 255
    formatting
        copy, 136-137
        remove, 137
    insert, 72
    name, 56-57
    named
        select, 56-57
        use in formulas and functions, 57
    overview, 5

repeat data in, 13
replace data in, 39
select, 10-11
    all, 11
    when containing hyperlinks, 291
text
    shrink to fit, 131
    wrap in, 130-131
center data, 121
    across columns, 129
    on printed pages, 152
    vertically in cells, 122-123
chart sheets, 188
charts
    background, add color or pattern to, 203
    create, 186-189
    data
        add to, 198-199
        delete, 199
    data series
        color, change, 202
        patterns, add to, 202-203
    data tables
        add, 200
        remove, 200
    delete, 189
    legend, add color or pattern to, 203
    move, 190
    overview, 184-185
    parts of, 184
    plot style of data, change, 201
    preview, 187
    print, 192
    resize, 191
    text
        bold, 197
        font, change, 196
        italicize, 197
        rotate, 195
        size, change, 197
        underline, 197
    titles
        change, 194
        move, 191
        overview, 184, 187
    types, 184
        change, 193
circular reference, error in formulas, 99
clear print area, 151
clip art images. See also objects
    add, 214-217
    delete, 217
    search for, 217

Clip Art task pane, 17
Clipboard task pane, 17
    use, 43, 177
close workbooks, 29
colons (:), in functions, 83, 89
color
    of cells, change, 127
    of chart background, change, 203
    of data, change, 124-125, 126
    of data series on charts, change, 202
    of legends, on charts, change, 203
    of objects, change, 220
    of worksheet tabs, change, 175
column, chart type, 185
columns
    center data across, 129
    delete, 70, 71
    display hidden, 75
    freeze, 76-77
    headings, print, 156-157
    hide, 74, 75
    insert, 69
    labels
        in lists, 230
            sort records using, 234-237
            repeat on all printed pages, 166-167
    overview, 5
    plot data by, on charts, 201
    scroll through, 7
    select, 11
    width, change, 66
        in Watch Window toolbar, 181
comma (,), in functions, 83, 89
commands, select, 14-15
    using Voice Command mode, 282-283
comments
    add, 58
    delete, 59
    display, 59
    print, 156-157
compare workbooks, 28
comparison operators, in formulas, 82, 179
conditional formatting
    apply, 140-143
    copy, 143
    remove, 143
copy
    conditional formatting, 143
    data, 42-43
        between worksheets, 176-177
    formatting, 136-137
    formulas
        using absolute references, 94-95
        using relative references, 92-93

Count, calculation, 91
Currency, data format, 135
Custom, data format, 135
custom series
    complete, 255
    create, 254
Cycle diagrams, 225

D

data. *See also* records
    add to charts, 198-199
    align
        horizontally, 121
        vertically in cells, 122-123
    autoformats, apply to, 138-139
    bold, 120, 124-125
    center, 121
        across columns, 129
        on printed pages, 152
    on charts, change plot style, 201
    color, change, 124-125, 126
    compare, in lists, 240-241
    copy, 42-43
        between worksheets, 176-177
    delete, 40
        from charts, 199
    edit, 38-39
    effects, add to, 124-125
    enter, 8-9
        using Dictation mode, 280-281
    find, in worksheets, 50-51
    font, change, 116, 124-125
        for all new workbooks, 118-119
    formatting, copy, 136-137
    indent, 128
    italicize, 120, 124-125
    label with smart tags, 262-263
    left align, 121
    link, 54-55
        between worksheets, 55
        to Web pages, 290-291
    make computer read aloud, 284-285
    move, 42-43
        between worksheets, 176-177
    print, 148-149
    printed, size, change, 164-165
    repeat in cells, 13
    replace
        in cells, 39
        in worksheets, 52-53
    right align, 121

rotate, 123
select, 11
series
    complete, 12-13
        custom, 255
    create, 254
size, change, 117, 124-125
    for all new workbooks, 118-119
sort, in lists, 234-237
underline, 120, 124-125
undo changes to, 41
data series, on charts
    color, change, 202
    overview, 184
    patterns, add to, 202-203
data tables, on charts
    add, 200
    remove, 200
Date, data format, 135
dates
    current, insert in custom header or footer, 163
    label with smart tags, 263
    perform actions for, using smart tags, 264-265
decimal places, add or remove, 135
delete. *See also* remove
    AutoCorrect entries, 47
    AutoShapes, 209
    cells, 73
    charts, 189
    clip art images, 217
    columns, 70, 71
    comments, 59
    data, 40
        from charts, 199
    diagrams, 227
    page breaks, 159
    pictures, 213
    records, 233
    rows, 70, 71
    scenarios, 103
    shapes, from diagrams, 226
    text boxes, 211
    WordArt, 207
    worksheets, 173
desktop, 23
diagrams
    add, 224-225
    delete, 227
    shapes, add to, 226
    style, change, 227
    text, add to, 225
    types, 225

dialog boxes
get help information when using, 19
select options in, using Voice Command mode, 282-283
Dictation mode. *See also* speech recognition
enter data using, 280-281
display
columns, 75
comments, 59
formulas, 96-97
full screen, 109
page breaks, 159
rows, 75
scenarios, 103
status bar, 110
task panes, 16, 17
toolbars, 111
Total row, 238
dollar sign ($) in absolute references, 95
doughnut, chart type, 185
draft quality, print in, 156-157

E

edit
data, 38-39
formulas, 85
text, in text boxes, 211
WordArt, 207
effects, add to data, 124-125
e-mail
addresses
label with smart tags, 263
perform actions for, using smart tags, 264-265
workbooks, 289
worksheets, 288-289
enter
cell references for formulas, quickly, 85
data, 8-9
using Dictation mode, 280-281
formulas, 84, 85
using data from multiple worksheets, 178
functions, 86-89
equal signs (=)
in formulas, 82, 84
in functions, 83, 89
Error Checking button, 98
errors
in cells
print, 156-157
when creating custom series, 255
in formulas, check, 98-99
spelling, check, 44-45

Excel. *See also specific subject or feature*
exit, 4
get help information on, 18-19
overview, 2-3
parts of window, 5
start, 4
exit Excel, 4

F

File menu, open workbooks using, 33
file names of Web pages, 295
files. *See* workbooks; worksheets
filter lists, 239
by comparing data, 240-241
financial symbols
find for companies, 63
label with smart tags, 263
perform actions, for using smart tags, 264-265
find
clip art images, 217
data in worksheets, 50-51
workbooks, 34-35
font
of data, change, 116, 124-125
for all new workbooks, 118-119
of text on charts, change, 196
footers
add, 160-161
custom, 162-163
remove, 161
format
custom header or footer text, 163
of numbers, change, 134-135
on charts, 197
text
on charts, 196-197
in text boxes, 211
formatting
conditional
apply, 140-143
copy, 143
remove, 143
copy, 136-137
remove, 137
Formatting toolbar, 5
Formula Auditing toolbar, 97
formula bar, 5
edit data in, 39
formulas
check errors, 98-99
copy
using absolute references, 94-95
using relative references, 92-93
display all, 96-97

INDEX

edit, 85
enter, 84, 85
    using data from multiple worksheets, 178
named cells, use in, 57
overview, 82-83
track, using Watch Window toolbar, 180-181
Fraction, data format, 135
freeze
    columns, 76-77
    rows, 76-77
full screen, display worksheet using, 109
functions
    enter, 86-89
    named cells, use in, 57
    overview, 83

G

gain adjustment, of microphones, 275
Gale Company Profiles, use, 63
General, data format, 135
gridlines, print, 156-157

H

handles on objects, 219
headers
    add, 160-161
        custom, 162-163
    remove, 161
height of rows, change, 67
help information, obtain, 18-19
hide
    columns, 74, 75
    parts of screen, 109
    rows, 75
    status bar, 110
    task panes, 16, 17
    toolbars, 111
    Total row, 238
hyperlinks, create, 290-291

I

icons beside help topics, 19
images, clip art, add, 214-217
indent data, 128
intranets, 290
introductions, include when e-mailing worksheets, 289
italicize
    data, 120, 124-125
    text on charts, 197

K

keyboard
    display formulas using, 97
    edit data using, 39
    shortcuts
        assign to macros, 268
        run macros using, 271

L

left align data, 121
legends, on charts
    add color or pattern to, 203
    overview, 184
line, chart type, 185
link data, 54-55
    between worksheets, 55
    to Web pages, 290-291
links. See also hyperlinks
    in task panes, select, using Voice Command mode, 283
lists
    create, 230-231
    filter, 239
        by comparing data, 240-241
    print, 231
    records
        add, 232
        delete, 233
        redisplay hidden, 239, 241
    sort data in, 234-237
    Total row, display or hide, 238

M

macros
    record, 267-269
    run, 270-271
    security level, set, 266, 267
magnify pages in Print Preview window, 147
margins of worksheets, change, 154-155
Max, calculation, 91
menu bar, 5
    commands, select, using Voice Command mode, 282
menus, select commands using, 14, 15
microphone, set up for speech recognition, 274-277
Microsoft Clip Organizer, use, 215-216
Microsoft Word, set up speech recognition using, 274-279
Min, calculation, 91
minus signs (-) beside items, 35, 105

move
    buttons on toolbars, 258
    chart titles, 191
    charts, 190
    data, 42-43
        between worksheets, 176-177
    objects, 218, 219
    Scenario Manager dialog box, 103
    toolbars, 112, 261
    worksheets, 174
My Collections, 215
My Computer, 23
My Documents, 23
My Network Places, 23
My Recent Documents, 23

N

name cells, 56-57
named cells
    select, 56-57
    use in formulas and functions, 57
names
    of workbooks, insert in custom header or footer, 163
    of worksheets, change, 171
New Workbook task pane, 17
NonBlanks option, filter lists using, 241
Number, data format, 135
number
    of pages, insert in custom header or footer, 163
    series
        complete, 13
            custom, 255
        create, custom, 254
numbers. *See also* data
    add, quickly, 91
    format, change, 134-135
        on charts, 197
    formatting, copy, 136-137
    perform common calculations on, 90-91

O

objects. *See also specific object*
    3-D effects
        add, 223
        remove, 223
    color, change, 220
    handles, 219
    move, 218, 219
    resize, 219
    rotate, 221
    shadow
        add, 222
        remove, 222

Office Collections, in Microsoft Clip Organizer, 215
open workbooks, 32-33
    arrange on screen, 26-27
    when password protected, 247
operators, in formulas, 82, 141
    arithmetic, 179
    comparison, 179
order of calculations in formulas, 83
organization chart diagram, 225
orientation of pages, change, 153

P

page
    breaks
        delete, 159
        insert, 158, 159
        view, 159
    numbers, insert in custom header or footer, 163
pages. *See also* worksheets
    magnify in Print Preview window, 147
    orientation, change, 153
    printed
        center data on, 152
        repeat labels on, 166-167
parentheses ()
    in formulas, 83
    in functions, 83, 89
passwords, protect workbooks using, 244-247
Paste Options button, 43, 177
patterns, add to charts
    background, 203
    data series, 202-203
    legends, 203
Percentage, data format, 135
Picture toolbar, 213
pictures. *See also* objects
    add, 212-213
    delete, 213
    format, in custom header or footer, 163
    insert, in custom header or footer, 163
pie, chart type, 185
plot style of data on charts, change, 201
plus signs (+) beside items, 35, 105
points, data size, 117
preview
    charts, 187
    workbooks, as Web pages, 292-293
    worksheets, 146-147
print
    black and white, 156-157
    cell errors, 156-157
    charts, 192

INDEX

column headings, 156-157
comments, 156-157
draft quality, 156-157
gridlines, 156-157
lists, 231
print area, 150
row headings, 156-157
workbooks, 148-149
worksheets, 148-149
    on specific number of pages, 164-165
print area
    clear, 151
    override, 151
    print, 150
    set, 150
Print Preview feature, use, 146-147
    to change worksheet margins, 155
printed pages
    center data on, 152
    repeat labels on, 166-167
protect
    workbook elements, 248-249
    workbooks, with password, 244-247
    worksheets, 250-251
pyramid diagrams, 225

Q

question mark (?), wildcard character, 53

R

radar, chart type, 185
radial diagrams, 225
record macros, 267-269
records, in lists. *See also* data
    add, 232
    delete, 233
    hide, 239, 240-241
    order, change, 234-237
    overview, 230
    redisplay, 239, 241
relative references, in formulas, 92-93
remove. *See also* delete
    3-D effects from objects, 223
    autoformats, 139
    bolding from data, 120
    borders from cells, 133
    buttons from toolbars, 259
    color
        from cells, 127
        from worksheet tabs, 175
    conditional formatting, 143
    data tables from charts, 200

footers, 161
formatting from cells, 137
headers, 161
italics from data, 120
page breaks, 159
shadow, from objects, 222
split in worksheets, 79
symbols, 61
underlines from data, 120
worksheets, 173
replace data
    in cells, 39
    in worksheets, 52-53
Research task pane, use, 48-49
reset toolbars, 257
resize. *See also* size
    charts, 191
    objects, 219
    toolbars, 113
right align data, 121
rotate
    data, 123
    objects, 221
    text on charts, 195
rows
    delete, 70, 71
    freeze, 76-77
    headings, print, 156-157
    height, change, 67
    insert, 68, 69
    labels, repeat on all printed pages, 166-167
    overview, 5
    plot data by, on charts, 201
    scroll through, 7
    select, 11
run macros, 270-271

S

save workbooks, 22-23
    as Web pages, 294-295
    with new name, 31
    in workspace file, 30
Scenario Manager dialog box, move, 103
scenarios
    create, 100-102
    delete, 103
    display, 103
    summary report, create, 104-105
Scientific, data format, 135
scroll
    bars, 5
    through worksheets, 7
search
    for clip art images, 217
    for data in worksheets, 50-51
    for workbooks, 34-35

Search Results task pane, 17
security level for macros, set, 266, 267
select
 cells, 10-11
  named, 56-57
 columns, 11
 commands, 14-15
  using Voice Command mode, 282-283
 data, 11
 rows, 11
selections in worksheets, print, 148-149
series
 complete, 12-13
  custom, 255
 create, 254
shadow, add to objects, 222
shape of AutoShapes, change, 209
shapes
 add to diagrams, 226
 delete from diagrams, 226
shrink text to fit in cells, 131
size, change
 of charts, 191
 of data, 117, 124-125
  for all new workbooks, 118-119
 of objects, 219
 of printed data, 164-165
 of text on charts, 197
 of toolbars, 113
smart tags
 turn on, 262-263
 use, 264-265
sort data in lists, 234-237
Special, data format, 135
speech recognition
 Dictation mode, use, 280-281
 set up, 274-279
 text to speech, use, 284-285
 train, 277-279
 Voice Command mode, use, 282-283
spelling, check, 44-45
split worksheets, 78-79
Standard toolbar, 5
start Excel, 4
status bar, display or hide, 110
stock quotes, insert, 62-63
strikethrough effect, 125
style
 of diagrams, change, 227
 of text, on charts, change, 197
subscript effect, 125
Sum, calculation, 91
summary report for scenarios, create, 104-105

superscript effect, 125
switch between
 workbooks, 25
 worksheets, 170
symbols
 enter, using Dictation mode, 281
 financial
  find for companies, 63
  label with smart tags, 263
  perform actions for using smart tags, 264-265
 insert, 60-61
 remove, 61

T

tables, data. *See* data tables
tabs, worksheets. *See* worksheets, tabs
target diagrams, 225
task panes
 open workbooks using, 33
 overview, 5
 select links in, using Voice Command mode, 283
 use, 16-17
text. *See also* data
 add
  to AutoShapes, 209
  to diagrams, 225
 on charts
  bold, 197
  font, change, 196
  italicize, 197
  rotate, 195
  size, change, 197
  underline, 197
 format, in custom header or footer, 163
 series
  complete, 12, 13
   custom, 255
  create, 254
 shrink to fit in cells, 131
 in text boxes
  edit, 211
  format, 211
 wrap in cells, 130-131
text boxes. *See also* objects
 add, 210-211
 delete, 211
 edit text in, 211
Text, data format, 135
text to speech. *See also* speech recognition
 use to read data aloud in worksheets, 284-285
Time, data format, 135
times, current, insert in custom header or footer, 163
title bar, 5

INDEX

titles
    of charts
        change, 194
        move, 191
    of Web pages, 295
toolbars
    buttons
        add, 256-257
        move, 258
        remove, 259
    commands, select, 15
        using Voice Command mode, 282-283
    create, 260-261
    display or hide, 111
    move, 112, 261
    reset, 257
    resize, 113
Total row, display or hide, 238
Trace Error button, 255
turn on smart tags, 262-263
types of charts, change, 193

U

underline
    data, 120, 124-125
    text on charts, 197
undo changes, 41
unfreeze
    columns, 77
    rows, 77
unprotect
    workbook elements, 249
    workbooks, 247
    worksheets, 251

V

value axis titles, on charts, 184, 187
Venn diagrams, 225
Voice Command mode. *See also* speech recognition
    change active cell using, 282-283
    select commands using, 282-283

W

Watch Window toolbar, use, 180-181
Web Collections, in Microsoft Clip Organizer, 215
Web pages
    file name vs. title, 295
    link data to, 290-291
    preview workbooks as, 292-293
    save workbooks as, 294-295

width of columns, change, 66
    in Watch Window toolbar, change, 181
wildcard characters, find data in worksheets using, 53
WordArt. *See also* objects
    add, 206-207
    delete, 207
    edit, 207
WordArt toolbar, 207
workbooks. *See also* Excel; worksheets
    arrange open, 26-27
    close, 29
    compare, 28
    create, 24
    elements
        protect, 248-249
        unprotect, 249
    e-mail, 289
    font of data, change default, 118-119
    open, 32-33
        when password protected, 247
    overview, 2
    path and name, insert in custom header or footer, 163
    preview as Web pages, 292-293
    print, 148-149
    protect by assigning password to, 244-247
    save, 22-23
        as Web pages, 294-295
        with new name, 31
        in workspace file, 30
    search for, 34-35
    size of data, change default, 118-119
    switch between, 25
    unprotect, 247
    worksheets
        add to, 172
        delete from, 173
worksheets. *See also* cells; columns; data; Excel; pages; rows
    cells
        delete, 73
        insert, 72
    columns
        delete, 71
        display hidden, 75
        freeze, 76-77
        hide, 74, 75
        insert, 69
        width, change, 66
    comments
        add, 58
        delete, 59
        display, 59
    copy data between, 176-177

delete, 173
display
    formulas in, 96-97
    full screen, 109
e-mail, 288-289
enter
    data in, 8-9
    formulas using data from multiple, 178
fit to specific number of printed pages, 164-165
footers
    add, 160-161
        custom, 162-163
    remove, 161
headers
    add, 160-161
        custom, 162-163
    remove, 161
insert, 172
link data between, 55
make computer read data aloud in, 284-285
margins, change, 154-155
move, 174
    data between, 176-177
page breaks
    delete, 159
    insert, 158, 159
    view, 159
preview, 146-147
print, 148-149
print area
    clear, 151
    override, 151
    print, 150
    set, 150
print options, change, 156-157
printed pages
    center data on, 152
    orientation, change, 153
    repeat labels on, 166-167
protect, 250-251
rename, 171
rows
    delete, 70, 71
    freeze, 76-77
    height, change, 67
    hide or display, 75
    insert, 68, 69
scroll through, 7
select all cells in, 11
spelling, check, 44-45

split, 78-79
    remove, 79
switch between, 170
symbols
    insert, 60-61
    remove, 61
tabs
    browse through, 170
    color
        add, 175
        remove, 175
    overview, 5
undo changes, 41
unprotect, 251
zoom in or out, 108
workspace file, save workbooks in, 30
wrap text in cells, 130-131

X

XY (scatter), chart type, 185

Z

zoom in or out of worksheets, 108

Introducing Our New Consumer Books...

Our new Teach Yourself VISUALLY Consumer books are an excellent resource for people who want to learn more about general interest topics. We have launched this new groundbreaking series with three exciting titles: *Teach Yourself VISUALLY Weight Training*, *Teach Yourself VISUALLY Yoga* and *Teach Yourself VISUALLY Guitar*. These books maintain the same design and structure of our computer books—graphical, two-page lessons that are jam-packed with useful, easy-to-understand information.

Each full-color book includes over **500** photographs, accompanied by step-by-step instructions to guide you through the fundamentals of each topic. "Teach Yourself" sidebars also provide practical tips and tricks to further fine tune your skills and introduce more advanced techniques.

By using top experts in their respective fields to consult on our books, we offer our readers an extraordinary opportunity to access first-class, superior knowledge in conjunction with our award winning communication process. Teach Yourself VISUALLY Consumer is simply the best way to learn!

Teach Yourself VISUALLY **WEIGHT TRAINING**

ISBN: 0-7645-2582-4
Price: $24.99 US; $36.99 CDN; £14.99 UK
Page count: 320

Teach Yourself VISUALLY **YOGA**

ISBN: 0-7645-2580-8
Price: $24.99 US; $36.99 CDN; £14.99 UK
Page count: 320

Teach Yourself VISUALLY **GUITAR**

ISBN: 0-7645-2581-6
Price: $24.99 US; $36.99 CDN; £14.99 UK
Page count: 320

Read Less – Learn More™

Visual

Simplified®

Simply the Easiest Way to Learn

For visual learners who are brand-new to a topic and want to be shown, not told, how to solve a problem in a friendly, approachable way.

All *Simplified*® books feature friendly Disk characters who demonstrate and explain the purpose of each task.

Title	ISBN	U.S. Price
America Online Simplified, 3rd Ed. (Version 7.0)	0-7645-3673-7	$24.99
Computers Simplified, 5th Ed.	0-7645-3524-2	$27.99
Creating Web Pages with HTML Simplified, 2nd Ed.	0-7645-6067-0	$27.99
Excel 97 Simplified	0-7645-6022-0	$27.99
Excel 2002 Simplified	0-7645-3589-7	$27.99
FrontPage 2000 Simplified	0-7645-3450-5	$27.99
FrontPage 2002 Simplified	0-7645-3612-5	$27.99
Internet and World Wide Web Simplified, 3rd Ed.	0-7645-3409-2	$27.99
Microsoft Excel 2000 Simplified	0-7645-6053-0	$27.99
Microsoft Office 2000 Simplified	0-7645-6052-2	$29.99
Microsoft Word 2000 Simplified	0-7645-6054-9	$27.99
More Windows 98 Simplified	0-7645-6037-9	$27.99
Office 97 Simplified	0-7645-6009-3	$29.99
Office XP Simplified	0-7645-0850-4	$29.99
PC Upgrade and Repair Simplified, 2nd Ed.	0-7645-3560-9	$27.99
Windows 98 Simplified	0-7645-6030-1	$27.99
Windows Me Millennium Edition Simplified	0-7645-3494-7	$27.99
Windows XP Simplified	0-7645-3618-4	$27.99
Word 2002 Simplified	0-7645-3588-9	$27.99

Over 10 million *Visual* books in print!

with these full-color Visual™ guides

The Fast and Easy Way to Learn

Title	ISBN	U.S. Price
Teach Yourself FrontPage 2000 VISUALLY	0-7645-3451-3	$29.99
Teach Yourself HTML VISUALLY	0-7645-3423-8	$29.99
Teach Yourself the Internet and World Wide Web VISUALLY, 2nd Ed.	0-7645-3410-6	$29.99
Teach Yourself Microsoft Access 2000 VISUALLY	0-7645-6059-X	$29.99
Teach Yourself Microsoft Excel 2000 VISUALLY	0-7645-6056-5	$29.99
Teach Yourself Microsoft Office 2000 VISUALLY	0-7645-6051-4	$29.99
Teach Yourself Microsoft Word 2000 VISUALLY	0-7645-6055-7	$29.99
Teach Yourself VISUALLY Access 2002	0-7645-3591-9	$29.99
Teach Yourself VISUALLY Adobe Acrobat 5 PDF	0-7645-3667-2	$29.99
Teach Yourself VISUALLY Adobe Premiere 6	0-7645-3664-8	$29.99
Teach Yourself VISUALLY Computers, 3rd Ed.	0-7645-3525-0	$29.99
Teach Yourself VISUALLY Digital Photography	0-7645-3565-X	$29.99
Teach Yourself VISUALLY Digital Video	0-7645-3688-5	$29.99
Teach Yourself VISUALLY Dreamweaver 3	0-7645-3470-X	$29.99
Teach Yourself VISUALLY Dreamweaver MX	0-7645-3697-4	$29.99
Teach Yourself VISUALLY E-commerce with FrontPage	0-7645-3579-X	$29.99
Teach Yourself VISUALLY Excel 2002	0-7645-3594-3	$29.99
Teach Yourself VISUALLY Fireworks 4	0-7645-3566-8	$29.99
Teach Yourself VISUALLY Flash 5	0-7645-3540-4	$29.99
Teach Yourself VISUALLY Flash MX	0-7645-3661-3	$29.99
Teach Yourself VISUALLY FrontPage 2002	0-7645-3590-0	$29.99
Teach Yourself VISUALLY Illustrator 10	0-7645-3654-0	$29.99
Teach Yourself VISUALLY iMac	0-7645-3453-X	$29.99
Teach Yourself VISUALLY Investing Online	0-7645-3459-9	$29.99
Teach Yourself VISUALLY Mac OS X	0-7645-1802-X	$29.99
Teach Yourself VISUALLY Macromedia Web Collection	0-7645-3648-6	$29.99
Teach Yourself VISUALLY Networking, 2nd Ed.	0-7645-3534-X	$29.99
Teach Yourself VISUALLY Office XP	0-7645-0854-7	$29.99
Teach Yourself VISUALLY Photoshop 6	0-7645-3513-7	$29.99
Teach Yourself VISUALLY Photoshop 7	0-7645-3682-6	$29.99
Teach Yourself VISUALLY PowerPoint 2002	0-7645-3660-5	$29.99
Teach Yourself VISUALLY Quicken 2001	0-7645-3526-9	$29.99
Teach Yourself VISUALLY Windows 2000 Server	0-7645-3428-9	$29.99
Teach Yourself VISUALLY Windows Me Millennium Edition	0-7645-3495-5	$29.99
Teach Yourself VISUALLY Windows XP	0-7645-3619-2	$29.99
Teach Yourself VISUALLY MORE Windows XP	0-7645-3698-2	$29.99
Teach Yourself VISUALLY Word 2002	0-7645-3587-0	$29.99
Teach Yourself Windows 95 VISUALLY	0-7645-6001-8	$29.99
Teach Yourself Windows 98 VISUALLY	0-7645-6025-5	$29.99
Teach Yourself Windows 2000 Professional VISUALLY	0-7645-6040-9	$29.99

For visual learners who want to guide themselves through the basics of any technology topic. *Teach Yourself VISUALLY* offers more expanded coverage than our best-selling *Simplified* series.

The **Visual**™ series is available wherever books are sold, or call 1-800-762-2974.

Outside the US, call 317-572-3993.

Other Visual Series That Help You Read Less - Learn More™

Teach Yourself VISUALLY™

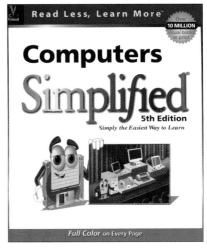

Simplified®

Master VISUALLY™

Visual Blueprint™

In an Instant

Available wherever books are sold

To view a complete listing of our publications,
please visit **www.maran.com**

Wiley Publishing, Inc.